Music
On The Move
Out West

Matthew Gonder

Music On The Move Out West

Matthew Gonder

ISBN: 0985200237

ISBN-13: 978-0-9852002-3-7

For Donna —
Hoping my story takes
you back to your own
story —
Matthew Gazda

"If one should desire to know whether a kingdom is well governed, if its morals are good or bad, the quality of its music will furnish the answer."
- Confucius

GRATITUDE

Soon after I completed my first memoir, "Christmas On The Move Out West", I received many requests to write another. Initially, I didn't think it was possible, because as far as I'm concerned, life stories are interesting only if they really tell a story, and I wasn't sure I had another one in me. I was mistaken. After allowing myself time to ponder, I realized that every life tells many stories; so now I want to thank those who inspired me to write a second book that has given me an even longer stroll down memory lane. I wish to honor and thank my two big brothers, Mark and John, never further than an email or a phone call away and ready at a moment's notice to answer questions or jump in the car to revisit the places we lived. From the bottom of my heart, I am grateful to everyone who played a part in these true stories: my parents James and Catherine, my sisters Monica and Marguerite, my brothers and family members including my Gonder and Kraft relatives, foster family members, friends and teachers. You have certainly marked my adventure on this planet and made it memorable for me.

My sincere gratitude to Carroll Saint Paul, an amazingly analytical proofreader and dear friend who questions every comma. Heaps of grateful kudos to my graphic artist pals, Dan Benesch in LA and Lou Benesch in Bruxelles, for together capturing the essence of my story in what I find to be an amazing book cover. Finally and forever, I wish to honor my wife, Pamela Gonder, the patient beauty who calmly allows me to spend so many hours writing out these stories and forgives my mental absences whenever I'm lost in my bubble, tenderly waiting to welcome me back to earth in her loving arms.

CONTENTS
or "Songs of Life" (you guess the melodies)

FOREWARD

(Lost in the Ether)

Memories are tattooed in indelible ink onto our cerebral hard drives, inciting us to smile joyfully or cringe in remorse whenever they resurface and claim space in fleeting thoughts; some through snapshot or moving visions, others in entire conversations or situations. In my case, they are almost always attached to music, be it song or symphonic. Whenever I hear a particular melody, I travel back in time, returning to the "scene of the crime" where that music entered my life, and instantly the dormant emotional and visual details of the moment - good or bad - wash over me in living colors.

The stories I tell in "Christmas On The Move Out West" and the following recollections in this second book of the series are as clear in my mind today as if they happened yesterday. In my family, we entertain ourselves by recounting the many adventures we lived to keep the laughs - and/or humiliation - alive. I'm sure my siblings could recite other moments of our lives that I've missed, because it's true that we're often marked by different facets of the same events. Thanks to the meager selection of but three television channels we had back in the '60s and '70s, family reunions invariably entail

i

competitive "Remember when..." rerun sessions that carry on for hours. Yes, when we were kids (I never thought I'd crank out that cliché, but somehow I can't remember to never say never), outdoor activities and conversing with other humans were the norm as opposed to endless hours spent alone keyboarding to silent computer screens in chat rooms, playing video games or "texting" on a "smart" phone. That thought leaves me wondering what young people of today will recall (aside from Carpal Tunnel syndrome) when years from now they take a moment to reflect on their own days gone by. When that day dawns, and it shall, someone will undoubtedly have invented an "App" that automatically records what everyone deems worthy of remembering. So instead of worrying, let's just pray they'll never (there's that damn word again) encounter a bug in the software.

Honestly, I can't and won't pretend to remember every detail of my past. There are gaps that are simply lost in the ether, but what follows are moments that are branded in my conscious mind forever, thanks to the musical underscore. Hopefully, I'll fill in the missing blanks of my ledger when I travel through the tunnel of light and watch my entire life story flash by in Technicolor HD images on my way to the other side (accompanied by an amazing celestial orchestra while munching popcorn, if wishes really do come true).

Matthew Gonder

In honor of my father, James Joseph Gonder, and dedicated to all single parents like him, who strive to raise and keep their families together.

1. ONE

"Yeah, it got a little cool."

The unforgettable blizzard that appeared like an early gift from Santa Claus in December 1968 continued to intermittently blanket Portland in layers of fresh white powder throughout the month of January 1969. Yet to our dismay, the snow was now accompanied by hacking icy winds that peppered winter insults with injuries. Long frosty weeks passed by in succession, and although my siblings and I happily spent many hours engaged in snowball fights, cardboard sledding, and hooky bobbing, the flaky white novelty slowly but surely wore out its welcome. As the thermometer's mercury danced up and down, the snowmen that survived the temperature abuse slowly mutated into grey blobs with blackheads while all but a few Portlanders grew sick and tired of wet clothes, frostbitten fingers or toes, dirty slush and the nagging obligation of shoveling sidewalks. In our rickety beige Craftsman home on

North Emerson Street, mornings dawned with moans as Mark, John and I bellyached while stuffing our paperboy ponchos with the Oregonians I helped them deliver before school. Fortunately, the last snow fell on February 1st, and by the end of that month, winter had become nothing but a collection of distant snowy recollections to laugh about in detail as we marched hopeful into spring.

One evening, I was sitting on the floor of the living room re-reading my book report on Joan of Arc for Sister Raphael's Religion class, trying unsuccessfully to concentrate. I couldn't hear myself think over the noise level of Dad and Aunt Mary's hysterical cackles while they enjoyed the weekly antics of Hogan's Heroes on our black and white television. During the first commercial break, as their laughter explosion quieted down to a rumble, I sang along with the advertisement melody claiming how "Winston tastes good like a cigarette should" while Dad and Aunt Mary pumped away in their parallel rocking chairs, gulping down cups of instant coffee; Dad, toking on a Chesterfield non-filter as Aunt Mary puffed away on a filtered Pall Mall.

"So tell me, how is it going at work, Seamus?" Aunt Mary inquired.

Throughout his life, Dad held a variety of jobs. He'd earned a Bachelor's degree, but gave up his studies and all dreams of earning his Master's degree and becoming a college psychology professor when Mom died suddenly of a cerebral hemorrhage in May 1962. After winning an unprecedented custody battle in court to keep his five children, a legal right not granted to single fathers at the time in the State of Washington, he willingly accepted whatever job came his way. He drove fork lifts for grocery stores, taught English and Math as an elementary schoolteacher and would rush after class to work the swing-shift as a plastics technician, spinning huge rolls of commercial plastic until midnight, to then hurry home for a few hours of sleep before waking up for school the next morning. At another time, he worked the graveyard shift assembling food rations for the military, but one day noticed that something was wrong with the packages being sealed up on the conveyor belt, so he abruptly stopped the entire production line. His boss fired him on the spot, telling him he had no authority to make that decision, while Dad, having served as a Petty Officer First Class-Radioman in the US Navy throughout the Second World War and the Korean War, was acting out of compassion and respect for the devoted soldiers who would discover that the chocolate bar was missing from their meal. Whatever job he took, no matter how menial, he swallowed his pride and never missed a day, giving total devotion to the task he was being paid for to make ends meet in our lives. Currently, he was working for a small automotive company called Sporty Tops, where he and a crew of men installed custom vinyl roofs and various designer accessories by hand onto cars of the late '60s to give them more style.

Dad turned his head to answer Aunt Mary's

question as he rocked on.

"Well, Mary, since you asked, the owners are trying to talk me into starting up a little shop in Seattle, doing the same thing I've been doing here."

She stopped rocking in her tracks and turned to face Dad.

"Jesus, Mary and Joseph! Seattle, is it now?"

"Well, business is goin' real good here in Portland, and they want me to manage and run the new expansion up north."

Aunt Mary was as quick as a whip when it came to paring down to the essential, or as Dad would have said "cutting through the happy horseshit". She thought silently for a moment then regained her rocking rhythm, pumping up the pace as her mind seared.

"Do they now? Well, that's what THEY want. What do YOU want, Seamus?"

Dad truly loved his sister in all her colorful facets and knew precisely which buttons to push. He suppressed a grin as he toyed on with her, choosing his words carefully for maximum effect.

"Well, they think I'm the man for the job," he answered coyly. Aunt Mary blared on.

"That's what THEY think! What do YOU think, Seamus?"

He knew she'd reach her boiling point if he remained vague.

"Well, the more I think about it the more I admit I kinda like the idea, and they're tryin' real hard to convince me," he offered meekly.

She blew.

"Well, I DON'T GIVE A DAMN what THEY think, what THEY like or what THEY'RE trying to do, but if YOU like it, Seamus, then you must DO IT!" erupted Aunt Mary's loud, high-pitched, Irish-accented volcano. Dad burst into laughter. As soon as I joined his raspy chuckles, she looked at the two of us and realized she'd been had. She rubbed her face and moaned for once again being so gullible as to lay herself at the mercy of her brother's teasing.

And that was that. Aunt Mary's statement is the last one I distinctly remember hearing in Portland, until I woke up at the Anderson house on 45th and Asotin Street in Tacoma, Washington. We knew the Andersons very well. The judge who handled our custody case had placed us with the Andersons as foster children in June 1962 shortly after Mom died, and we lived with them until June 1965, when Richard Anderson, a Technical Sergeant-Supply in the US Air Force, moved his entire family to Korea. Before they flew overseas, we packed up kit and caboodle and moved to Spokane to live with Dad's brother Arthur (known affectionately as Uncle Porky throughout the entire Gonder family) and his wife Aunt Val, pregnant with their second child, in their 16th Street house on the South Hill, where we lived for a year. Then Dad bought a huge Expando trailer that he set up on his brother Leo and Aunt Delphine's land on Fruit Hill Road further east out in the Spokane Valley, where we camped for another year. We enjoyed many joyful adventures with our slew of cousins on both the Gonder and Kraft sides of the family while our uncles and aunts teased, tickled and treated us as their own. Our circus trailer then pulled into Chehalis for yet another year, where Dad's sister, Aunt Mary, living in a small apartment of her own in town, joined us for another year before we were off to Portland, where for two more years we finally began to sprout roots in our lives through the floorboards of that rotting, yet cozy Craftsman house on Emerson Street. Finally, through some strange twist of fate, here we were again, Dad and the five of us without Aunt Mary (who chose to remain in Portland), full circle back to square one in Tacoma with the foster family we had left behind years ago, in a different house and neighborhood from the one we had known back in 1965. Dad must have thought that the transition up north would be easier for us to make by returning to familiar faces, not to mention that his daily commute to Seattle for work would be much easier from Tacoma than from Portland.

It was the summer of '69, and I felt as if I was on

an extended vacation, reconnecting with the same big family we lived with during our early childhood years. Naturally, everyone had grown, and we had a blast running over to Wapato Park with the Anderson kids to swim, suntan, chase crows, play Truth-or-Dare or Hide 'n Seek. At the Anderson house, rock-'n-roll music blared out from the radio all day long, and I danced often with my foster sister Cindy in the living room, singing along to *One* by Three Dog Night, the soundtrack from *Hair*, *Time of the Season* by the Zombies, *Crystal Blue Persuasion* and *Crimson and Clover* by Tommy James & The Shondells, *Honkey Tonk Woman* by the Rolling Stones, *Sugar Sugar* by the Archies, *Baby I'm Yours* by Barbara Lewis, *Galveston* by Glen Campbell, *More Today Than Yesterday* by The Spiral Starecase, *I'm Gonna Make You Love Me* by Diana Ross and the Supremes. Musically, it was quite a change from the classical, folklore and powerful symphonic music Aunt Mary weaned me on in Portland and I loved it all. A few of the Anderson kids were a little older than we were and their hormones had already started kicking in, so they shared their knowledge and insight on "everything we always wanted to know about sex but were afraid to ask". Apparently, our Catholic education was lacking on certain subjects. We also learned how to smoke and do other things considered sinfully wrong but were exciting and dangerously "grown-up", thanks to a few colorful yet slightly shady characters who also funneled through the house.

One day, I returned from chasing garter snakes in a

vacant field not far away with my foster siblings Little Mark, Marvin, and Cindy, to find a U-Haul truck parked in front of the house. I watched numbly as Dad and a few others stacked and piled our Portland furniture and the remnants of our worldly possessions on the oil-stained concrete floor of the garage. I sadly realized at that very moment that I'd never see our house on Emerson Street again and that what I thought to be nothing more than a summer vacation was, in fact, another major move with no time for goodbyes from the friendly faces I had grown to love in Portland. I silently wondered where Aunt Mary was living and hoped I'd see her again someday. Maybe the reality of the move was made easier that way, allowing no time for regret. Moving so often forced us to adapt and fit into new surroundings, but I don't know if that was good or bad in the long run. That's just the way it was for us. Some say a rolling stone gathers no moss. If that's so, then we were Gonder skimmer stones, shiny from many bounces across the waters of change. We were vagabonds without the luxury of choice. That afternoon, John's and my bunk beds were installed in the basement against a wall in the same big room with our foster brothers, dormitory style, next to another room that Mark (known as Big Mark because there were two Marks in the house) shared with Mike. Monica and Marguerite were installed in Jeannie's room. When you finally master going with the flow without asking questions, you learn how to adapt easily to whatever the wind brings your way.

The sun blazed hot through days that blended one

into the next. We frolicked outdoors, sleeping under the stars, jumping in the pool, having a grand old time with our foster playmates in a summer of discoveries. All eyes were glued to television sets on July 20th to watch the Apollo 11 Moon Landing as Neil Armstrong and Buzz Aldrin walked on the lunar surface, justifiably touted as one of the biggest events of the century. The excitement continued throughout the next day when I celebrated my eleventh birthday that I remember so fondly because not only was I given my first pair of bell-bottomed plaid pants, but Linda Brevik, a little blond girl who lived across the street, also gave me my first real kiss on the mouth that sent rockets of electricity through my body.

Pocket money was scarce for those like us who did not receive an allowance, so some of us picked strawberries on a farm nearby, but the job only lasted a few days because the long hours in the heat were too much for us to endure at our tender ages. John, however, had an enterprising business mowing neighborhood lawns with Marvin. They would drag the lawn mower door to door, knock and ask, "You want your lawn mowed? Only two bucks." One day they came home with eleven dollars in their pockets, a fortune at that time. Meanwhile, Mark, not aware of what he had gotten himself into, made a deal with Dad to work the entire summer in the Seattle Sporty Tops shop on 128th and Aurora Avenue North in exchange for a new 3-speed bike. Dad's boss gladly accepted the cheap child labor deal so we didn't see much of Mark during the weekdays.

The Anderson house was full of mementos from the three years they had lived in Korea. There were bright kimonos and Asian mother-of-pearl inlaid tables and collector pieces all throughout the rooms. On the countertop in the kitchen sat a large clay jar of spicy Kim-Chee marinated cabbage, a recipe Mae "Mom" Anderson discovered overseas, and we rapidly acquired a taste for the hot condiment with our meals. The Andersons had adopted Johnnie Lee and Okhi, two Korean children they brought back with them to offer a better life in Tacoma. The Anderson family now totaled nine children: Patty, Mike, Linda, Cindy, "Little" Mark, Marvin, Jeannie, Johnnie Lee and Okhi. So with the five of us: "Big" Mark, John, Matthew, Monica, Marguerite and our Dad plus Mae and Rich Anderson, the house all but burst at the seams. But somehow we squeezed in. Rapidly, we fell into a whole new regimen with the Andersons and their circle of friends. Dad was introduced to Dolores Tan, a very nice divorced lady-friend of the Andersons who had two grown children and a younger son who lived with his father. Dad and Dolores soon began dating, and it was strange at first but nice to see Dad laughing and enjoying female company while we were busy with our own activities. One day at Wapato Park, little Okhi, sitting in the sun on a towel with the rest of us, began to sing a Korean lullaby about a mountain rabbit. I loved hearing the sounds from her far-away homeland, and I asked her to sing it again and again until I had the song memorized.

Santoki toki yah

Uhdeereul gahneunyah?

Kang-choong kang-choong ddee-myun-suh

Uhdeereul gahneunyah?

A wide variety of parties, barbecues, picnics and typical summer activities kept us all busily entertained as time flew by. The house was like Grand Central Station, full of people and an array of animals, so no one ever felt alone. Cats, dogs, snakes and even a spider monkey: there seemed to be room for all God's creatures in the Anderson's humble dwelling. Little Mark caught a crow at Wapato Park and brought it home, naming it Tammy. Linda's dog Babe had puppies that were quickly up and running about, so it appeared as if we lived in a zoo. Summer's end finally arrived and Mark proudly rode his hard-earned, gold Schwinn 3-speed bike around while the topic on everyone's lips became school. Reality sank in as summer vacation came to an end.

I walked the dry Tacoma streets to Seward Elementary School in a state of silent despair. I couldn't believe I wasn't strolling my well-worn path in Portland to Blessed Sacrament to find dear Sister Raphael speedwriting on the chalkboard. My green plaid Catholic school uniform was history and I hated my bell-bottomed trousers that morning for the first time. I stood silently in the school office as Mom Anderson registered Monica, Marguerite and me, handing over our birth certificates and filling out the necessary forms. I was shuffled off to a classroom where I felt miserable every day I attended. I longed for Blessed Sacrament's red brick solidity and Sister Raphael's stimulating, rapid-fire lessons in Portland. Coming from a Catholic to a public elementary school, I found myself way ahead of the class in terms of my education level. My thoughts drifted constantly as I watched the clock on the wall or gazed out the window.

After a short period of time at Seward Elementary, perhaps only a month or two, the Andersons decided to move into a bigger house on the corner of 51st and Park. Our Portland furniture that Dad had stored in the garage on Asotin simply disappeared into thin air. Once we had settled in the new house, Dad and Delores stopped dating for some unknown reason. She would come by from time to time, and although she remained good friends with Dad, I was glad their romance was over, because I did not like the thought of Delores becoming our new stepmother. I don't really know why. She was nice enough, but somehow she and Dad just didn't seem to fit, or maybe it was more due to the fact that I had idealized my deceased mother into a saintly goddess, while poor Dolores, no matter what she did, could never hope to live up to Mom's angelic image in my mind.

The Andersons chose to paint the dining and living rooms of the new house oriental red and black to accentuate their collection of Korean artifacts, and Dad willingly joined in, lending his expert painter's hand to ensure that the red paint lines didn't bleed onto the ceiling. In the new house, the boys' dormitory was moved to a large airy room upstairs filled with daylight from a big window, which was a nice change from the dark basement we slept in on Asotin.

The move across town put us into a new district, which meant we would have to change schools. Fine with me. Horace Mann Elementary was the closest school to the new house, about five blocks away. I was registered into Mr. Lewellyn's class. He was a nice man, but I was tired of all the upheaval in my life and again, concentrated little on my studies, which I found to be simplistic and dull. One day, one of my classmates heard me singing to myself at recess and mentioned that the school had a choir, with rehearsals that took place before school began. I thought of all the fun I had singing at Blessed Sacrament, and felt this might be something for me to get involved with that would resemble what I had left behind in Portland, or at least fill the empty gap in my life. After school let out for the day, I went to the music room and introduced myself to Mrs. Brown, a lady with short auburn hair and a "matter-of-fact" demeanor.

"Hi, Mrs. Brown, I'm Matt Gonder. I heard you got a choir?"

"Hello, Matt Gonder, and yes, we *have* a choir. Have you sung in choir before?"

"Oh, yeah, sure. Last year in Portland, at Blessed Sacrament School with Sister Amelia."

She studied me quietly for a beat.

"Hmm, Catholic. Tell me Matt, what did you sing?"

"Oh, we sang lots. We sang 'Alleluia' and stuff like that all the time at Mass, and we also sang 'Oh No, Don't Let the Rain Come Down', and 'Born Free' and...

She cut me off, sitting at the piano.

"Sing something for me now."

"Okay. Whaddya' want me to sing? I even know a song in Korean."

"Do you? No thanks. Sing 'My Country 'tis of Thee', starting on this note."

She tapped one white key on the piano and I took it from there, singing out the patriotic song, holding my pitch. She listened attentively until I finished then responded by raising one eyebrow at me.

"That's fine. Now listen closely to what I play first and then sing the groups of notes you hear back to me, like this...la la la."

She played weird clusters of three or four dissonant notes that I sang back to her "la la la", which I found oddly lacking in melody but easy enough to do. After

14

four or five groups of notes, she stood up abruptly.

"Choir begins one half hour before school on Tuesdays and Thursdays. Here's a schedule to show your parents."

She handed me a mimeographed calendar full of information, which I folded and put into my pocket.

"We'll see you tomorrow morning, then. Good bye, Matt."

The next morning I got out of bed early enough to get to choir practice, but in doing so, I woke up my foster brothers as I tried unsuccessfully to sneak out of the house quietly. I somehow managed to arrive a few minutes late for practice, which had already begun, but Mrs. Brown nodded her head and quietly directed me to sit in a chair. She handed me some music as the other singers chimed onward. Never having received any formal music theory training, I just followed the words while I listened to and repeated the melody the other members were singing near me. It was a nice enough distraction while it lasted. Afterwards I returned to Mr. Lewellyn's class and continued my normal dull day.

The following Thursday I didn't return to Mrs. Brown's choir. Although I often sang to myself, this choir wasn't as fun as Sister Amelia's at Blessed Sacrament, and I didn't want to wake up the whole Anderson house, so I didn't give it another thought. However, a week later, I ran into Mrs. Brown in the hallway at school. She cornered me, blocking any thoughts of escape.

"Hello Matt, can I ask you a question?"

"Hi, sure, Mrs. Brown."

"Why aren't you coming to choir? Didn't you have a good time with us?"

"It was okay."

"Don't you want to sing?"

"I dunno. I guess, maybe. It's kinda early though."

She sliced through that one in a heartbeat.

"A half hour before school isn't what I'd call impossibly early."

"I- it's- hard for me to get up that early."

"Really? Well, it's up to you. We'd love to have you if you want to come back."

"Okay."

She didn't press the issue, thank God, but I could tell she was disappointed with me. I felt bad but didn't know what else to say. Her choir just didn't seem worth the trouble. Besides, nothing really mattered to me at that point. When you don't feel like you belong where you are, daydreaming and gliding through the motions without conviction become routine activities.

At home, Mom and Dad Anderson laughed with or yelled at my siblings and me as much as they did their own kids when necessary, but as a foster child, I always felt somewhat like a guest in someone else's home, living on borrowed time. We were all fed, our clothes were washed, and we went to school and played games along with the others. We celebrated our birthdays, did our share of chores and goofed off like everyone else, but if ever there was an argument, your word meant nothing against theirs. I didn't feel entitled to be totally myself, in fear of not being accepted. As a result, there were times when I found myself holding back my true feelings or I rendered favors for people I wouldn't normally have done in the hope of being loved, which once accomplished, left me with an even deeper loss of self. We enjoyed innumerable good times with the Andersons, where we all co-existed under their roof, but we were also coming of age where frictions occurred or angers flared when our natural reactions to situations were not considered. I'm not pointing a finger at anyone and have no bones to pick because we weren't abused. The Andersons simply had their way of seeing and doing things and we had our own, which best describes the situation. But despite our differences, the bottom line is that the Andersons opened their home to us twice in our lives, which gave us the opportunity to remain a family united throughout our difficult transitional periods, and for that I am and will always remain truly thankful to them.

Throughout autumn whenever Dad was home, he'd embarrass Monica, Marguerite and me by dancing with us in the living room to whatever current music was blaring out from the stereo, then he'd make us laugh by reading the newspaper aloud in Morse code. Both families harmoniously celebrated Thanksgiving together with a huge turkey dinner and all the trimmings, and on December 25th, 1969, Dad gave us each two presents for Christmas, a rarity as we usually only received one gift. He bought me the Johnny Lightning 500 Track Set I coveted, Mark and John each got a BB Gun, Monica opened a huge oil and pastel paint set while Marguerite spun her battery-powered Dancerina doll. In addition to the toys, Dad bought us all new winter parkas. Mark, John and I were given matching lime green coats with silver snaps while Monica and Marguerite's were cream-colored. It's easy to remember all the new clothes we received; it wasn't often we were given garments that weren't hand-me-downs from some other family. We didn't have the laundry basket cornucopia of goodies that year sitting under the tree like Dad had prepared for us in Portland, Chehalis or Spokane, but we knew that some traditions had to be tucked away in our hearts whenever we weren't under our own roof.

Once the Christmas excitement was over, the Andersons readied the house for a big New Year's party to which many of their friends had been invited. We all were given chores to execute, so we cleaned, dusted and vacuumed the rooms, made food in assembly-line formation in the kitchen, filled bowls with potato chips and snacks, laid out glasses and welcomed the guests we all knew as they arrived, bottles in hand. A few hours into the celebration, Cindy, Little Mark and I laughed at all the adults in varying stages of sloppy inebriation as we munched goodies from the table. Dad was there too, lounging on the couch and nursing his fifth of Canadian Lord Calvert along with everyone else while the rest of the adults made love to their own beverages of choice. All of a sudden, Mom Anderson, sitting at the table, called me to her side and slurred out a sloshy request.

"Matthew James, do me a favor, will ya?"

I figured she wanted me to run to the kitchen for something.

"Sure, whaddya want?"

"Sing a song for me, please?

"Sing? Now? You crazy? No way!"

"Oh, but you got such a beautiful voice, I want everyone to hear. C'mon, will ya?"

"I don't wanna."

"Please," she begged, "sing that song I heard you singin' the other day about the hills are alive or something. That was so pretty. Please. For me?"

I knew right away she meant the theme song from The Sound of Music, the musical film I'd seen in Portland with Sister Raphael and fellow classmates from school. I'd sing the song around the house from time to time to myself, but Mom Anderson's public request was quickly tarnishing my fond musical memory.

"I don't wanna sing in front of everybody," I protested, shaking my head.

"I'll give you twenty five cents if you do."

"Fifty," I answered, certain she'd never bite.

"Alright."

"Fifty cents?" I reiterated for confirmation, peering hard through clenched eyes.

"I guess."

"Really?"

"Yeesss," she burped.

"You pay me now?"

"I'll give it to you tomorrow."

"Ya promise?"

"Yeessss! Now sing it before I change my mind."

"Deal."

I offered my hand to shake, but she didn't notice it as she stood up and hushed everyone, announcing that I was going to sing. Suddenly my stomach tightened up and I felt real terror for the first time in my life. I was nauseous and shaky. I'd never sung a solo in public before nor been put on the spot like that and I did not like it at all. Mom Anderson turned off the stereo as I stood by the dining room table, gathering my gumption to perform one of Julie Andrews' biggest hits. There I stood in front of a room full of drunks, their bloodshot eyes were glued to me and the room went silent, except for a few percussive ice cubes clinking in glasses. I saw Dad smile proudly and nod his head. All I could think about was that fifty-cent fee I was going to receive and hoped I'd survive the torture of my first real attack of stage fright. I grabbed onto the edge of the table to calm my shaking body, closed my eyes, took a deep breath and sang out "The hills are alive with the sound of music", and the rest of the words poured out until I got to the last phrase, which promised that "I'll sing once more"; I sure as hell hoped not. I opened my eyes and everyone started to clap. It was all too much energy for me to handle. I looked out and felt self-conscious, exposed and frightened, not understanding why. The emotion boiled up inside me to the point where I could tell I was going to cry, so I ran through the living room and into Mom and Dad Anderson's bedroom and hid inside the deep closet and let it pour out of me. I cried for a couple of minutes, and then the door opened. I looked up and there was Dad, reaching his hand inside to grab hold of my arm.

"Matt-sue from Kalamazoo, c'mon out here."

"No! Leave me alone."

"Matt, c'mon, I want to talk to you."

He pulled me onto his lap and hugged me. I kept on crying as he slurred inebriated words of wisdom to me.

"There's no reason to cry, and you sure as h...ell got no reason to hide, Matt."

"It was ssscary, Dad. Everyone was lookin' at me."

"They were just listening, Matt, and you sang real nice."

"I was embarrassed."

Then he looked hard at me, straight into my eyes as his voice became more and more animated through his killer whisky breath.

"Embarrassed? What the hell for? What've YOU got to be embarrassed about, Matt? You should be proud of yourself, goddammit! You got somethin' not one o' those sonsobitches has, a voice, a talent that only you got and you just DO it, use it! That's your job. Your job is to sing if that's what you want to do and those goddamn sonsobitches' job is to LISTEN to you when you do, if and when YOU decide you want to do it."

"But I don't wanna do it."

"Well then, by God, don't do it! But later on if you decide you DO wanna do it, and you might, don't you ever, EVER be embarrassed to do it! No matter what you do, you just do it and don't be embarrassed to do it. You do what you gotta do, what you wanna do, when you choose to do it and never, I mean NEVER be embarrassed to do what you wanna do. 'To thine own self be true'. Every man's gotta do what he's gotta do. You too. Okay?"

"Okay."

As usual when Dad hit the bottle, he repeated himself over and over to make his point. I had completely calmed down. Dad looked at me, his eyes blinking wildly.

"Let's get back to the party now. You walk back into that room and be proud of yourself."

"Okay, Dad."

We joined the others and partied the rest of the night, welcoming in the New Year 1970.

The next day while Mom Anderson leaned against the kitchen counter for support as she made coffee, I hit her up to get the money she had pledged the night before.

"You gonna give me my fifty cents now for the song I sang last night?"

She turned and peered at me through her hangover daze.

"Fifty? What fifty? I'm not giving you fifty. Twenty-five is plenty."

"But you promised me fifty."

"Well, I was drunk. Twenty-five is all you're gonna get."

She reached into her purse that was sitting on the counter, pulled out a quarter and handed it to me. I took it begrudgingly, fully aware that I was not destined for a lucrative singing career, as I had just gotten screwed on my first paid gig.

2. SPINNING WHEEL

While predictable Pacific Northwest winter rains washed the streets outside the house on South Park Avenue in late February, some unforeseen event or maybe a combination of things occurred and we had to move away from the Anderson home. I know that Joe Caro, along with his three brothers and sister came to live with them after we left, but whether or not that was the catalyst for our move, no one recalls. It was just time to move on. Period. In a flicker, it was as if we had turned a page in the book of our lives and once again left the Andersons behind us in a previous chapter. It seems odd to me how easily we file away yesterday into the past and place all our attention in the here and now, but that's how life trained us. Forever onward to new destinations, never looking back, like the crew in an episode of *Star Trek*, one of our favorite TV shows.

At that point, Dad hadn't quite established himself in business well enough for us to afford living on our own just yet, so we moved into another foster care living arrangement with a corpulent, dark-haired woman we called Miss Lucy. She lived somewhere else in Tacoma with her husband Myron, her teenaged daughter Connie and two adopted little girls, Alta and Lori. I remember a nice, big home where Mark, John and I shared a dark wood paneled bedroom at the top of the stairs on one side of the house, while Monica and Marguerite shared a room at the top of another staircase on the other side with Alta and Lori. Dad had a room just below our staircase next to Connie's room, and Lucy and Myron's room was across the hall. This household came with a brand new set of rules to abide by which we did our best to adhere to, but I was just doing time and didn't care if I was spoken to or not, trying to survive the nightmare of another major unwelcome change.

Miss Lucy's house was nestled in yet another school district, so Monica, Marguerite and I were quickly registered at Sheridan Elementary, which offered me yet a third sixth-grade class to attend that year. At that point, I was getting used to constantly changing schools and didn't care, since I hated every one I attended, comparing them all to Blessed Sacrament in Portland. Following suit from the first two schools I was enrolled in before this one, I didn't spawn any lasting friendships here, either.

Luckily for Mark and John, they were able to remain at Stewart Junior High with familiar friends and teachers. Mark had joined the Band class, where Mr.

Anderson (no relation to our foster family), the Band teacher, asked the students one day which instrument they'd like to play.

"The trumpet," Mark answered without missing a beat, remembering the story Dad told of playing the trumpet years ago in the family band his father required all his children participate in against their will.

Mr. Anderson looked at him.

"The trumpet, huh? Well, with big lips like yours, you ought to play the tuba."

So Mark played the tuba. We couldn't afford to purchase musical instruments, so Mr. Anderson kindly loaned Mark an old tuba to practice on at home. From that day onward, we shared space with the brass monstrosity that became a "toe stubber" and took up a whole corner of our bedroom collecting dust, as it almost never got played.

Going to Sheridan was like living in a total time warp. My teacher, whose name eludes me, was a kind, older man but I still didn't apply myself to learning anything. A singing class was included in my curriculum but I didn't care, as my heart wasn't in anything at all. I just took it one day at a time and was emotionally shell shocked from too many disturbances in my young life. I do remember how aggressive the kids were at Sheridan, as every recess consisted of playing a painful game of dodgeball, where getting hit in the face with multiple rubber balls was considered fair sport. If you didn't want to take the pain that game inflicted, tetherball was the only substitute, but those who chose to play that game were ostracized by the "in" crowd.

Dad was gone more often than not, but we knew he was around somewhere and he always kept a distant eye on his kids. He got up every day and drove off to Seattle, where he had recently quit his association with the Sporty Tops Company and was trying to start up his own business in a small garage on 75th and Aurora, providing the same services he had for Sporty Tops. Often on weekends, Dad would take Mark, John and me with him to lend a hand, and we'd run errands, sweep and clean up the small shop and wipe down the cars with a strong solvent to remove the excess glue stuck onto the cars that Dad was topping. At the end of the day he'd give us five dollars and then drive us home, making one religious stop on the way at the 48th street Tavern in Tacoma. We'd wait in the car while he poured down a cool pitcher of beer and then he'd come back to the car carrying fried chicken and Jojo's (deep fried potato quarters) for us to chomp down.

At home, Miss Lucy's routine consisted of faithfully watching *Hee-Haw* on TV each week as she had a schoolgirl crush on the singer Merle Haggard. She loved country music and rugged men, and we were expected to sit and enjoy the show along with her, which some of us pretended to do because she was always in a jolly mood during Hee-Haw. I liked the dancing animated pigs that slid across the TV screen, but didn't dare announce that I wasn't really a fan of the show. Some of the country songs were okay, but I knew the danger of sharing an honest opinion in someone else's home so I kept my mouth shut. Miss Lucy was an extremely gifted short-order cook, and worked as a part-time chef at Marilyn's Restaurant on Puyallup Avenue, near the Tacoma Dome. Lucky for us, she expressed her incredible cooking talents at home and prepared delicious meals every day, which we always devoured heartily, but she had an extremely grim and complicated marriage, to say the least.

Miss Lucy kept her dark side at bay and was congenial enough when we first moved in, but her true colors bled through the floral print fabric of her muumuu all too shortly thereafter, and they were not in soft pastels. She and Myron would bicker constantly and then sleep in separate bedrooms for a time during which she'd make crass, nasty complaints in a loud and tediously repetitious manner. She'd sit at the table and pick on all his faults, spewing them out as if she were itemizing a shopping list, to which he'd repeatedly threaten "Keep it up, Lucille." Their dour squabbles that would continue for hours, days, or sometimes weeks would pass before they'd finally make up and sleep together. When that happened, she would become sweet as a lamb, yet her positive disposition only lasted while they were sharing the same bed, which unfortunately for the rest of us, was of short duration. I had learned how to distance myself from the negativity surrounding me, but I was growing sick and tired of being forced to endure everyone else's emotional angst. I just wanted to go far away.

Once, when Miss Lucy and Myron were caught in one of their sparring spin cycles, she decided to hit the bars to chase other men in an effort to render Myron jealous. In preparation for the big night, Connie, an apprentice beautician, stood there in the dining room curling, ratting and styling her mother's long, dark hair under endless whimpering loud moans of "Connie, you're killin' me!…you're killin' me, Connie!". As soon as Connie finished pinning up the hair-do, Miss Lucy calmly looked into the mirror to admire herself, but after an hour or more of hearing "Connie, you're killing me", we all silently agreed that she was anything but the fairest of them all. Later that evening, returning from her manhunt, she collapsed her inebriated bulk into her La-Z-Boy recliner in the living room and snored away for hours on end, twisting and turning as Connie's hairdo came apart, all but engulfing Miss Lucy's face. Although the sight was comical, nobody dared make a sound that might awaken her into a nasty fit. Even poor Connie admitted to me that she was planning her own escape to run away as soon as she got her beauty license, sick and tired of being treated like a slave, trapped in her mother's hellhole.

There was no real laughter in that house that I can remember, aside from a few good quips from Myron when Miss Lucy wasn't home, although there was

Charlie, a very amusing talking mina bird who sat in his cage in the living room. He had the only real sense of humor in the house and offered comic relief all day long, slicing through the dense negative energy that permeated the walls. He'd cackle a laugh and speak full phrases at all the wrong moments. Miss Lucy and Myron would be shouting at the top of their lungs, and all of a sudden, good ole' Charlie would chirp out his punch line: "Caw, caw, did you ride your bicycle, asshole?" Charlie did his best but was unable to lighten the air for long.

One Friday afternoon at school, I dragged myself down the stairs and stood outside the music room in the school basement, lined up against the wall with my other classmates. One student was admitted at a time into the big room as soon as another came out. Whispers spread about a special choir we were auditioning for. Big deal, I thought. I just did whatever I had to do until the school day ended. When the student in front of me finally came out the door, I went in. Mrs. Kathryn Habedank, a tall, very pretty blond woman in her twenties, was sitting at the upright piano. She was writing something on a large notebook, but took a moment to direct her attention to me as she smiled with her heart in her eyes.

"Hello Matt, I'll be with you in a minute. Have a seat."

I sat down and couldn't take my eyes off her while

Matthew Gonder

she completed her notation. When she finished, she placed the notebook on top of the piano, then smiled again right at me as if I were someone special.

"Come on over to the piano, Matt. I'd like to hear you sing 'My Country 'Tis of Thee', but I want you to start on the note you hear me play on the piano. Will you try that for me?"

"Sure." I flew to her side like a mosquito to a porch lamp.

Well, I'd been there and done that before. She smiled and played the starting note she wanted me to sing and I took it from there. While I sang, her eyes beamed with such kindness that I felt as if someone had finally looked at me with love, the same way my aunts always did whenever I saw one of them, like family. I finished singing and she tapped the same piano key she had before, which matched the final note I sang.

"Good. Okay, now I'm going to play a few series of notes that I want you to sing back to me. Just listen and repeat them as best you can, okay?"

"Okay."

Easy as pie. Done that before, too. She played four notes. I sang them back to her "la la la la". The music part was boring, but she smiled so warmly with each series of notes she played, that I desired nothing more but to chirp them back to her just to watch her smile again. I think I fell in love and I wanted to crawl into her pocket, but suddenly the dream ended.

"Perfect. Thank you, Matt. I'll see you again soon. You can send the next student in on your way out, okay? Bye-bye."

"See ya."

She turned her attention to the notebook on the piano and began writing something, probably about me. I walked to the door and left the room as the next candidate entered, and like most sixth-grade boys with attention spans as fickle as those of fruit flies, immediately forgot about the whole incident.

Returning home that afternoon, I found Miss Lucy and Myron in the dining room throwing verbal daggers at each other from opposite sides of the table, this time more violently than ever. Myron stood up, leaned on his bad leg that he kept in a brace and limped out of the dining room, while Miss Lucy yelled constant obscenities at him.

"That's enough, Lucille. I'm movin' out! I ain't gonna take any more of this shit."

"Good! GO! Get outta here then, you good for nothing bastard! You ain't no good for nobody anyway, ya lazy, lousy sonofabitch, who the hell NEEDS ya?"

Myron slept in the small guest room that night, just

like he did every time they were fighting. The next morning, Saturday, he packed his bags and stomped out as best he could on his bum leg. Miss Lucy was unbearable to everyone, picking on anything that poured oil onto her foul, moody fire that flared throughout the entire day. Connie, Alta and Lori sat prostrated in silence, which was their usual reaction to Miss Lucy's bad moods. My siblings and I hid out in our rooms. Miss Lucy's storm didn't pass but seemed to get worse. I couldn't eat dinner and felt sick to my stomach.

I went to bed early that night and didn't feel any better the next day, waking up with stomach cramps that lasted into Sunday. The bad energy floating about the house was too much for me. I ran to the toilet to vomit, and then judging from everyone's caring reactions to my state, realized I had something here. Miss Lucy thought I had come down with the flu. I was afraid I might vomit again, so I didn't eat all day. That night, Miss Lucy told me I didn't have to go to school as long as I remained in my room, where, according to her, sick boys were supposed to stay put. I was content to know I could skip going to a school I hated anyway, and staying alone in my room was a good way to escape the hellfire energy in that house. So, I stretched out my fake symptoms and read alone in the peace and quiet of my room. I pretended not to be able to eat the first day, but in truth I had swiped a big bag of potato chips that I hid in a drawer and ate as sparingly as I could, just to kill the hunger pangs.

On the second day of my mock illness, I came downstairs as soon as I heard Miss Lucy drive off to go grocery shopping. The potato chips were gone, so I went to the fridge to sneak something to eat that wouldn't be noticed and went outside to get some fresh air in the back yard, all the while keeping my ears tuned in case I heard Miss Lucy drive up. Soon enough, her car came idling toward the house, and I ran back inside and up into my room. Although Miss Lucy began feeding me light meals, I followed this same routine for the rest of the week but quickly got bored. Saturday morning arrived and I was itching to play outside with my brothers. Mark and John were getting dressed in our room.

"Whatchyou' guys gonna do?" I asked.

"We're goin' out to shoot pop cans and targets with our BB guns in the vacant lot," Mark offered.

"Wish I could come with ya."

"But you can't, cuz' you're too busy fakin' it," John snorted.

"I puked, didn't I?"

"Yeah, a week ago. Big deal." He wouldn't have any of it.

They went outside, leaving me to spend my afternoon counting the knots in the wood paneling on the walls of our bedroom.

On Sunday, Mark, John, Monica and Marguerite were out playing as far away as they could get from the house without getting into trouble. Connie, Alta and Lori had to accompany their mother on her errand run. As soon as the rumble of Miss Lucy's car faded to silence once they drove away, I climbed down the stairs and heard the sounds of a typewriter tapping away in Dad's room. I knocked on the door.

"Yes?"

"Dad? It's me, Matt. Can I come in?"

"That must be Matt-sue from Kalamazoo, or is it Timbuktoo? Sure, c'mon in."

I opened the door and Dad sat smiling at his table in front of the typewriter. It was rare to see him there, as he worked such long hours in Seattle.

"How ya doin' Matt? You feelin' better?"

"I guess."

Dad pushed himself away from the typewriter and I jumped onto his lap hugging him, making him moan in pain.

"Ow! You're getting' too big for me, Matt-sue."

"Sorry, Dad. Just this time, okay?"

"Okay."

He poked me in the stomach. I laughed.

"Whatcha doin'?" I asked.

"I'm writing a poem."

"A poem? What for?"

He weighed his words and slowly made a tender announcement.

"I met someone, Matt."

Selfishly, all I could do was wonder if that meant another move was looming our way. I pressed my head into his chest.

"That's nice. Dad?" He knew something was up.

"What is it, Matt?"

"How much longer do we gotta stay here?"

"Well, I'd say about a month or so, that's all."

I pulled away and stared into his eyes.

"Really?"

"Yep. Business is going real good, Matt. I'm opening up my own shop next to the Duwamish river, south of Seattle, and as soon as that's up and runnin', I'll be lookin' for a house for us."

"Just for us? Nobody else? Honest? Our own house, ya promise?"

"I promise. You just hang tight and we'll be outta here PDQ."

"Pretty Damn Quick! Groovy!"

"Shhh. Keep it down! You promise me you'll feel better and I'll keep my promise and get us outta this goddamn den of iniquity."

"I'm fine! I swear! I'll go to school. I'm all better now!"

Dad laughed. He knew what was troubling me. I let out a sigh of relief and pressed myself against his chest. I hugged him tightly and then he tickled me, laughing.

"Get off me now, you're too big."

I slid off his knee and stood next to him.

"Hey Dad, does Mark and John and Monica and Marguerite know yet?"

"You're the first one I've told. You tell 'em for me, okay?"

"Okay but I'm not tellin' anyone else!"

"You do what you think is best, Matt."

"I will. I can't wait. Man, I wish we were leavin' today."

"Take it easy, chief. Dooon't get excited. It took me a little longer than I thought it would, but we'll be outta here and put all this happy horseshit behind us soon enough." He smiled and turned his eyes to the typewriter.

"Good. Wow. Ya wanna read me your poem?"

"Okay, if you like."

He rolled the paper out of the typewriter. I looked into his eyes. As he began to read his poetic words in honor of new love, I saw him as I never had before.

To Ann

I've never tried to make a poem,

I've never quite known how

From deep within me comes this urge

That makes me want to now

Matthew Gonder

Too long have I constrained myself,

Too long I've torn apart

A tragic figure unfulfilled,

An artist without an art.

I must unlock this soul of mine,

I must let me be known

How could I hope you'd understand,

Until you have been shown

The thoughts that surge within my mind;

The thoughts that you still share

The agonies that pierce my soul,

And at my heart does tear.

A poet, it seems, that you must love;

A poet --- I make my start.

My love for you does plagiarize,

The volumes of my heart.

J.J.G. 3/22/70

He looked at me as tears welled up in his eyes, humbly seeking approval from his eleven year-old son, and I loved him for it more than ever.

"Your poem's real good, Dad. What's plagiarize mean?"

But before he could answer, I heard the familiar rumble of Miss Lucy's car engine purring in the street.

"Wait! Tell me later. I gotta go. That's Miss Lucy's car! See ya later, alligator."

"After while, crocodile," he whispered back.

I ran upstairs as Dad grabbed his coat and went out the front door to his car. I stayed in my room and listened as Miss Lucy clamored noisily through the back door, with Connie, Alta and Lori in tow. I put on a tired face to hide my secret as I slithered downstairs and went to the kitchen. Alta and Lori ran up to their room as Miss Lucy placed a brown paper grocery bag on the countertop, tossed her car keys and purse next to the bag then turned to discover me standing nearby.

"Well lookee here! What's this, you up?"

"Yeah. I can help you carry in stuff, if you want."

She studied me sternly for a frozen moment.

"Hmm. 'Bout time someone around here was good for somethin'. Yeah, there's more out in the car. Put it all on the counter, right here."

Connie placed a bag on the counter.

"I can do it, Mom."

Miss Lucy barked back at her.

"Connie, goddammit, let HIM do it, will ya? You just empty the bags and put the stuff away after he brings 'em in!"

Miss Lucy passed by me and went into the living room to flop into her La-Z-Boy recliner while I carried in the bags from the car. I played it low, moving nice and slow, trying to appear as if I was feeling just a little better. Once I had finished, I smiled at Connie. She smiled back like an accomplice that knew I'd been faking all along. She quietly gestured me out of the kitchen, so I joined Miss Lucy in the living room.

"All done, Miss Lucy. Can I watch TV now?"

"I suppose, but keep it down low while I'm in there cookin', ya hear?"

"I will."

I sat down in front of the TV on the floor to watch *Gilligan's Island*. After a few minutes she brushed by me and returned to the kitchen to make dinner. Later that afternoon, as my brothers and sisters came in, I cloistered each one off individually to whisper the wonderful news. It was as if the clouds had parted and sunshine finally filled our hearts. I reminded them to keep the secret to ourselves, which they all promised to do. We were all so ecstatic that we ate like happy Gonder pigs that night, and nothing could destroy our good moods. Not even Miss Lucy in her doldrums over Myron's departure affected us. She tried her best, however, as she sat berating John, busy shoveling forkfuls of her delicious lasagne into his mouth in rapid tempo.

"Good God, John, slow down, will ya! Where're you puttin' it all? Jesus, I swear you'd eat horseshit if someone put milk and sugar on it."

We all cracked up, which surprised her, as she was not accustomed to reactions of laughter to her witticisms. Then she glared at me.

"What are you grinnin' at? The way you're stuffin' your face, looks like you're feeling better too, don't it?"

"Much better, Miss Lucy."

"Then I expect you'll to be goin' back to school tomorrow, hmm?"

"Sure. I feel great."

"I can see that. Damn near miraculous, ain't it?" She added suspiciously.

When Dad arrived that night, our eyes all focused in his direction. He could tell by the way we looked at him that I had shared the news with everyone, so he smiled and gave Mark, John, Monica, Marguerite and me each a secret wink in confirmation, and we kept it to ourselves, hiding our joy. I don't think anyone else caught on. We had learned to hide our feelings for the sake of survival. Besides, whenever Dad was there with us, Miss Lucy kept her snide remarks pretty much to herself. We watched TV and went to bed at our usual hour.

I went to school on Monday with a huge grin on my face, and got stopped a few times in the hallway by my classmates with words of congratulations. My first thought was "Yep, congratulations to me. I'm outta here soon and into my own house", but then I realized they couldn't know we were moving, so I stopped one classmate to ask.

"Hey, why is everyone congratulating me?"

"You got picked for the all-city choir, Matt," he answered.

"The all-city what?"

"Choir. Remember the auditions we did over a week ago?"

I'd completely forgotten.

"Oh, yeah."

I didn't really comprehend what everyone was talking about, but I didn't care. Nothing could possibly be better news to me than what Dad had announced yesterday.

At the appointed hour, I went down to the basement to the choir room with my fellow classmates for the singing class we all attended. Mrs. Habedank was so happy to see me she ran over to greet me personally as I entered the room.

"Matt! Where have you been? I've been worried about you. Are you okay?"

"I'm fine."

She looked at me with such deep concern that I fell in love all over again.

"Did you hear the news?"

"Well, kinda, but..."

"You're one of the singers chosen from Sheridan to participate in the all-city elementary choir. Isn't that wonderful?" she beamed. Man, she was pretty.

"I guess. I don't really get it. What am I supposed to do?" I asked.

My question got lost in the noisy shuffle of too many students rambling into the room.

"We rehearse tonight. I'll explain everything to you then, okay? Can you stay with me after school for just one hour?"

"Okay," I squeaked.

I would have given her two.

I took a seat with my classmates and rehearsed the normal school songs we were working on in unison or weak harmonies. When choir ended, Mrs. Habedank smiled at everyone then looked at me, saying "See you after school" with silent lips. I nodded an affirmation and walked back to my homeroom but couldn't stop dreaming of our new house. The wheels of inspiration churned overtime in my head. I imagined us living in another cozy Craftsman like we had in Portland, but didn't really care what it looked like, as long as it was ours and nobody else's. Finally I had something to look forward to. I found Monica during recess and told her to tell Miss Lucy that I had to stay after school and would be an hour late, and that I would explain later. She promised to deliver the message.

I was a clock-watcher the rest of the afternoon, as I grew more anxious by the minute to hear what the all-city songs sounded like. When school finally let out, I flew down the stairs to the basement choir room before anyone else arrived. Mrs. Habedank said how proud she was of me and explained that only the six best singers were chosen from every elementary sixth grade singing class throughout the city. All combined, close to 300 youngsters would be singing in a concert at Jason Lee Junior High School at the end of April. She handed me a big white envelope that contained the sheet music selections we were to perform, and a rehearsal schedule for the chosen six from Sheridan. We were to practice with Mrs. Habedank in the choir room three days each week after school for the first three weeks, and then she would drive us to the group rehearsals where we would meet and put it all together with the students from the other schools. Wow, I thought. This much good news in only two days was unbelievable. I was batting a thousand.

"And you've already missed three rehearsals, Matt, so you'll have to work real hard to catch up."

"I will, I promise. I won't miss another one. I'll be here for all of 'em from now on, you'll see."

"Good. Ah, here come the other singers."

"Thanks, Mrs. Habedank. This is – so cool!"

"Yes it is. We're going to have a wonderful time together."

47

I wanted to hug her. I couldn't have been happier.

"Come in, everyone. Take a seat."

I sat down in the chair closest to her and the piano. The five chosen singers entered and sat in chairs next to mine. I hadn't met most of them as we came from different homerooms. Mrs. Habedank smiled at everyone and introduced us, but I only had eyes for her.

"Let's get right to work, and start with 'This Lonesome Valley'."

I pulled the sheet music out of the envelope and sat eagerly awaiting. The others had an advantage on me as they knew the melody already, but I caught on right away. We went through the song a couple of times. Mrs. Habedank played the parts on the piano to help us iron out the complicated passages of half-tones, counter melodies and rhythms and I concentrated more on that music than I had on anything put before me the entire school year. I felt totally alive for the first time in a very long time as I sang:

Jesus Walked this Lonesome Valley

He had to walk it by himself

For nobody else could walk it for him

He had to walk it by himself.

Once we had worked that song to Mrs. Habedank's approval, she smiled again and instructed us to take out the music to *Dear World*. We followed her direction and after we worked through the song the first time, the words seemed like a poem that Dad had written just for me, because they mirrored the promises I made to him the day before.

Please take your medicine, Dear World

Please keep your pressure down, Dear World

Promise to thrive on each word your doctor speaks,

He'll bring the roses back to your cheeks.

I could tell that Mrs. Habedank was proud of me. I was lucky to possess a good ear for music even though I had no idea what those weird black dots and lines on the sheet music meant. Once she played the notes on the piano, I planted those melodies firmly in my brain. We then rehearsed a third song, *Yellow Bird*. Each song seemed to express facets of my personal life, and this song reminded me of my Mom, who had long since passed away.

Yellow bird up high in banana tree

Yellow bird, you sit all alone like me.

Did your lady friend, leave the nest again?

That is very sad, make me feel so bad,

You can fly away, in the sky away

You more lucky than me.

We worked on and eventually came to the end of the rehearsal. Time flew by in a heartbeat. I wanted to stay with her there and sing forever. Mrs. Habedank closed her sheet music and turned to us, smiling broadly.

"Now remember, you all have to memorize every song, so practice at home or with each other if you need to, okay?"

"We will, Mrs. Habedank," we replied in unison.

"And I'll see you all again on Wednesday after school," she concluded.

We stood up, grabbed our things and headed toward the door. As the others exited the room, I turned and ran over to Mrs. Habedank as she closed up the piano.

"Thanks, Mrs. Habedank. I'll be the first to memorize every song, I promise."

"Oh, Matt. I bet you will. See you Wednesday."

This time I knew her beautiful smile was only for me, because the other singers were gone. I left the room and danced and sang to myself outside the school. I couldn't wait to tell Dad about the choir. I hadn't given the audition a second thought and now, I felt like I'd won the raffle at the Puyallup Fair. A new home and a concert directed by this tall blond Amazon painted my world beautiful.

Knowing I was late, I ran as fast as I could to tell everyone the news. Miss Lucy was unimpressed and welcomed my announcement in her typical smarmy way at the dinner table.

"Well, ain't you somethin'? Looks like we got ourselves a little singin' angel here, everybody! Well, la-dee-dah."

She could have said anything she wanted to, because right then, nothing evil would have touched me. I only wished I could have told Dad first, but he arrived too late that night and was gone before we got up for school in the morning.

Tuesday dawned and I remember concentrating on my lessons in class that day for what seemed to be the first time ever. We ordered books from the book club and I drew a cartoon with singing carrots, celery stalks and beets about the importance of eating five vegetables per day. I played dodgeball at recess and didn't get hit once. I hummed the all-city choir melodies to myself throughout the day. I pulled my sheet music out that night to memorize the words. Those songs became my mission, the fuel that got me through the long school days and even longer dreary evenings. Thanks to the music, I became alert and aware of everything around me. The trees were exploding with budding leaves and colorful flowers bloomed in the gardens of the houses I passed on my way to and from school. I finally could see and take part in the beauty of the new spring life surrounding me.

Wednesday came, and Dad was still nowhere to be found, working non-stop to build his own business in Seattle that he christened Sporty Roofs, but we all forgave his absence because we knew the carrot he was chasing for our benefit. After school that day I attended my second rehearsal with Mrs. Habedank and the other singers in the choir room. I hadn't memorized all the words yet and I made some mistakes singing the half-tone harmonies in my part just like the others, but Mrs. Habedank steadily played each part out on the piano, correcting and working with us as she smothered us in her amazingly tender smiles. I was determined to prove my worthiness to her.

That night, after everyone had gone to bed, I couldn't sleep. I kept singing the songs quietly under my blanket until suddenly I heard Dad close his bedroom door behind him. I got up and slowly crept down the carpeted stairs to his room and opened the door, anxious to share my news of the all-city choir in whispers.

"That's great, Matt. No kiddin'? Only six singers from your school were chosen?"

"Yeah, six from every school in the city, and we gotta rehearse three times a week after school."

"Well, I'll be damned. Good for you, Matt-sue. I thought you might sing again. You just do what you have to, to make those rehearsals. If you have a problem with you know who, you just say the word and I'll take care of it."

"Okay, Dad."

"I'm proud of you, Matt-sue," he grinned, wiping a tear from his eye.

"Yeah."

"You better hit the sack, now. I'm going to re-read something I wrote this morning."

Then Dad picked up a page of typewritten words from his table and held it up to his eyes.

"Another poem?"

"Yes, it is, Matt."

"Wanna read it to me?"

"Sure."

And then he opened his heart completely, baring his soul as he read on. I watched silently, understanding him better than I ever had before as I listened to the rhyming words of James Joseph Gonder, the man, now poet; not my Dad who cared for me, my brothers and sisters, but simply a man who had lived, loved and lost. And right there, at that very moment, was a man who, only five days after he celebrated his forty-sixth birthday, taught me to believe in hope.

To My Autumn Love

If Autumn is a good time

In the seasons of one's life

Then one should have an Autumn love

And one's heart should not feel strife.

But grasp and hold her closely

Is the thing I cannot do.

I'm stricken with a loneliness,

In the fear that she's not true.

I hope she truly loves me,

And I pray that this be so.

Why does she torture me so much,

When she knows I can't let go.

If Autumn love is fickle,

Then it tears the heart of me.

How can I stand another loss,

When I need her desperately.

Oh! Once I had a Spring love,

In a season of my life.

I asked if she would marry me,

And this Spring love was my wife.

Too soon did she depart me,

In her death so suddenly.

Her loss seemed more than I could bear,

But time healed the scar in me.

A Summer love I did find,

In that season of my life.

Her love brought forth new hope for me,

But this too was full of strife.

For she was soon to leave me,

And her loss I could not stand.

My anguished heart did burst and bleed,

When she chose another man.

'Tis Autumn love I've found now,

In late season of my life.

Oh! Let me keep this love of mine,

For we all must face time's scythe.

I want this love so very much,

Oh! Let it linger here!

Don't take this love of mine again;

For 'tis loss again I fear.

A Winter love I hope for,

In last season of my life.

His love will shield my tortured soul,

And He'll take from me this strife.

His peace is everlasting,

And His love will set me free.

For He will take me as I am,

The way He created me.

All seasons' loves are needed;

But the one I hold most dear,

Is Autumn love that's with me now,

It's the one that's crystal clear.

My Spring love is over,

And my Summer love is past.

And Winter's love must bide His time,

I've found Autumn love at last.

J.J.G.

3/25/70

I stood there frozen for a moment, looking at him, unable to speak until finally I forced my tongue.

"Dad, what's scythe mean?"

"A scythe is a farmer's tool that he uses for cutting crops, and I use it poetically to say how time, sooner or later, cuts us all down."

"Oh. It's really – great, Dad."

My words deceived me. I wanted to praise him more but my tongue was emotionally tied. I knew who all the loves were that he had mentioned in his poem, which took my breath away.

"Ya like it?"

"Yeah. Is it for your lady again?" I choked out.

"Ann. Yes it is."

"Ann. Are you gonna marry her, Dad?"

"I don't know. We haven't crossed that bridge yet. All I know is that I feel better than I have in a long, long time, Matt, that's all I know."

"Me, too."

"Okay, what do you say we hit the hay now? I'm beat. Goodnight, Matt-sue."

"Goodnight, Dad. Oh, and nobody except us knows our big secret about our house, either. G'night, don't let the bedbugs bite."

I crept out his door quietly, climbed up to my room and into my bed, where I slept better than I had in months, knowing there were no scythes lurking in my world to cut me down.

Confident that the near future held good news in store, absolutely nothing got my goat. Everything became light and carefree. Each day brought me a little closer to the heaven awaiting. I paid attention at school and accomplished monotonous daily tasks with a happy "Hi-Ho" attitude like one of the Seven Dwarfs.

Throughout the rest of the week, school ran its course while my head and heart were filled with music, thanks to the after-school rehearsals. I kept my word to Mrs. Habedank and was one of the first to memorize the all-city songs and couldn't wait to meet the singers from the other schools. Meanwhile I counted down the days like a soldier in boot camp, knowing soon we'd be living our own lives in our own home.

The following Monday after school, we followed Mrs. Habedank to the parking lot over to her maroon Pontiac Firebird to drive to the first group rehearsal. I ran to the passenger side of the car, opened the door and jumped into the bucket seat next to her before one of the others had a chance. The other five crammed into the back seat. Fashion of the early '70s had blessed all men, as almost every female wore miniskirts and I was truly an apprentice leg fan. Mrs. Habedank, loyal to the current popular dress code, sat in the driver's seat in a colorful mini dress that hiked up her panty-hosed thighs, gracing a bucket seat beneath. She looked around at all of us, smiling like always, and I had to quickly raise my eyes to meet hers.

"Everyone in?"

"Yes," came our reply in choral unison.

"Okay, then, here we go."

She turned the key in the ignition, the engine rumbled and we were on our way. I had a fantastic view of those long legs extending from that short sheath sitting next to me. I couldn't keep my eyes away from them as we drove on, her feet pumping the brake and accelerator pedals during our journey through the Tacoma streets. We rehearsed our songs during the ride and I wanted to drive off with her forever and never look back, but unfortunately, there were the others in the back seat and oh yeah, I was eleven and she was already married. Rats!

We drove across town up north to Jason Lee Junior High School and pulled into the parking lot that had already filled up with cars. Hundreds of children and teachers were everywhere, scampering to the doors of the brick school building. We joined the noisy masses and walked down the halls to a huge auditorium completely filled with chairs all lined up in rows and divided into sections to group the Sopranos and the Altos together. There was a conductor's podium set up in front. Mrs. Habedank guided us to our respective sections to take a seat. Once all the singers filled the chairs, an attractive dark-haired woman entered the room and climbed onto the podium. She introduced herself as Lois Best, the director of the all-city annual concert series, and warmly welcomed everyone to what would certainly be an unforgettable musical event. She thanked us for working so hard and made a few announcements to make sure all useful information was properly dispatched. Then the rehearsal began. We were instructed to take out *This Lonesome Valley*. All eyes were glued onto Mrs. Best, as she gave the tempo to the pianist to play the introduction, and then we opened up and sang out. The music teachers from each school meandered through the sections, listening closely and singing along whenever necessary to help a student over a musical hurdle. All of a sudden I saw a familiar face walking toward me from across the room. As it drew closer I recognized Mrs. Brown, the choir teacher I had dumped at Horace Mann Elementary. She moved with purpose, making a beeline straight at me. Mortified, I froze my face forward, pretending not to see her and kept on singing as she stopped next to me, leaning in slowly to whisper just above my head.

"Well, hello Matt. It's nice to see THIS choir wasn't too impossibly early for you to attend."

I wanted to shrivel up, disappear and die. I gave her a wimpy smile and continued singing, not knowing what to say. Then she pulled away and walked off. I felt like

I'd been caught with my hand in the cookie jar. It had never dawned on me that Horace Mann would also have six singers in the concert. My past had finally come back to haunt me. We sang for an hour in the auditorium. The sound was amazing, hearing good voices singing on key all around me. I knew my parts well, but I wasn't prepared for the dizzying effect that came from crooning with three hundred of the best singers in a room with good acoustics. The counter melodies blended into smooth harmonies and the vibrations sent chills through my body. Mrs. Best guided us through nuances, crescendos, decrescendos, cut-offs and sustained notes. I was in nirvana, hearing my voice disappear into the vocal throng surrounding me. After rehearsal, we ran out of the school and jumped into Mrs. Habedank's Firebird, and I was relieved not to run into Mrs. Brown in the parking lot. Mrs. Habedank drove us back to Sheridan where we all said goodbye and went our separate ways home.

Once I arrived in front of the house, I prepared myself mentally to enter the Wicked Witch of the West's den, but as I entered I heard giggles and saw Myron sitting at the dining room table, enjoying a banquet of foods that Miss Lucy, giddy as a schoolgirl, had spread out for him.

"You want another roll, Myron honey?"

"No thank you, Lucille, that'll do it for me."

"How 'bout a slice 'a homemade apple pie?"

"That sounds good."

"I'll get it for ya. You just relax right there."

She jumped up and all but flew into the kitchen, eager to serve her man. Strangely enough, I stood there mesmerized, witnessing how blissful she was right then. I found myself feeling sorry for her for the first time as it finally struck me how badly she just wanted and needed to be loved. I could definitely relate to that. I silently threw a wish in her direction with hope that she would forever feel as happy as she did now. The next morning, Miss Lucy was on the phone laughing with a salesman at a mattress store, placing an order for a new, reinforced bed frame. I listened and smiled as she confessed how she and Myron had broken their bed during the night. I was sincerely happy for her and yet, when the new bed was delivered a few days later, the honeymoon once again had sadly come to an abrupt ending. Myron went back to sleeping in the guest room as Miss Lucy climbed aboard her emotional spinning wheel but it didn't faze me this time because although I now felt sorry for her, I knew our days there were numbered.

In the quiet of our room, my brothers and I would discuss all the things we were going to do in the freedom of our new home with no rules to bind us, coming and going whenever we pleased and doing whatever we chose when we decided. We didn't converse much with our sisters about it as their room was on the other side of the house, and we had to be careful that Alta and Lori didn't catch wind of our plans or they might tell their mother.

We had a couple more group choir rehearsals at Jason Lee, and although the music continued to feed my euphoric state, I was not happy to share the bucket seat in the front of Mrs. Habedank's Firebird with the other singers, but I begrudgingly gave them their turn to ride next to her, against my will.

On Saturday, Mark, John and I went outside to shoot at pop cans in a vacant lot behind Miss Lucy and Myron's house, where neighborhood kids loved to wander and play in the wild brush. There was an old caterpillar bulldozer parked in the lot. We climbed on top, sat on the big rubber wheels and in the seat, pretending to handle that engine like big men. Standing on the bulldozer, we shot a few rounds of BB's at the tin pop cans we lined up on a tree trunk in the distance, and then after a while we called it quits and returned to the house. Miss Lucy was planted in her recliner chair, watching TV.

Just before dinnertime there was an aggressive knock at the door. Miss Lucy did not welcome the disturbance.

"Jesus, who the hell is that? Connie, turn the sound down 'n answer the door, will ya? Good God."

Connie obeyed, jumping up, lowering the sound on

the TV and rushing to open the door. An older man stood there and began to shout at Connie.

"Your boys shot out all the gauges in my bulldozer with their BB Guns!"

Connie was insulted.

"My boys? I don't have any boys. I'm only nineteen."

Miss Lucy bellowed in.

"Tell him to come in here, Connie!"

Connie ushered the man in.

"Who the hell are you?" Miss Lucy snapped from her La-Z-Boy, semi-reclined position.

"I live in the house on the other side of the lot behind you. And your boys shot out all the gauges in my bulldozer with their BB Guns, and someone's gonna have to pay for it!"

"Connie, go get them boys, and get their Dad, too. He's in his room."

The man continued to wail, but Miss Lucy cut him off.

"Hold your horses, dammit, they ain't my boys neither."

Mark, John and I entered the living room. Miss Lucy began the interrogation.

"This man here says you shot out the gauges in his bulldozer out in the lot behind the house. Well, whatchya' got to say for yourselves?"

Mark stood fast in our defense.

"No we didn't. We played on your bulldozer but we shot pop cans, Sir."

"Yeah, that's what we always shoot," John offered in our defense.

"Uh-huh!" I added for team punctuation.

The man didn't buy. Just then, Connie came back, followed by Dad, who obviously had just been awakened from a nap.

"What's goin' on?" Dad yawned, trying to focus.

The man repeated his accusation in a firmer tone.

"You the father of these boys?"

"Yes I am." Dad, a two-time war veteran, always woke up fast when under attack.

"Well, those boys shot out the gauges in my bulldozer in the lot back there behind the house with their BB Guns, and..."

Dad cut him off.

"Now YOU wait just a cotton pickin' minute here before you jump to the wrong goddamn conclusion!"

He turned to us, asking firmly but fairly.

"Did you boys do what this man says you did?"

All three of us responded at the same time.

"No, Dad. Uh-uh. We played on the bulldozer but we only shot pop cans like always."

The man still didn't buy.

"They're lyin' to ya!" he charged.

Dad turned to the man and shot both barrels at him verbally, backing him out the door.

"That's what YOU think. If my boys SAY they didn't shoot out your goddamn gauges, then they DIDN'T shoot out your goddamn gauges. Period! Now GET OUTTA HERE and leave us alone, and if you don't want kids to play on your goddamn bulldozer, then don't PARK the sonofabitch where they PLAY!"

The man ran away in a huff. Dad slammed the door shut and turned to Miss Lucy, agitated.

"Anything ELSE you'd care to discuss?"

Miss Lucy didn't say a word, but just shook her head, frozen stiff by Dad's reaction. Dad turned away and shuffled off back to his room to continue his nap. As soon as he shut his door, Miss Lucy found her tongue.

"Connie, turn the damn TV back up."

April 24th, the day of the concert at Jason Lee Junior High School had finally arrived. As soon as the school day ended, I hurried back to Lucy's house to eat and change into the white shirt and dark pants we were all instructed to wear. At the scheduled time, I ran back to Sheridan to meet up with Mrs. Habedank and the other singers. We rode together across town in Mrs. Habedank's super cool Firebird and joined the mayhem in the parking lot at Jason Lee, where again everyone scrambled into the building. We all assembled in concert formation in a large room adjacent to the auditorium, and Mrs. Best came in and made a couple of announcements, reminding us to have fun in the concert and to not forget to smile. Afterwards, Mrs. Habedank pulled me aside to say that during the applause after the concert, I was to jump out of the risers, return to this room and pick up a huge bouquet of flowers to carry in and hand to Mrs. Best who would be standing on the podium.

"Okay" I said, thinking that was easy enough to do.

The auditorium began to fill with guests for the concert. I could hear the buzz of people's voices rumble and echo through the halls of the old brick building. We were instructed to make last-minute visits to the toilet and then remain in the waiting room, which took a good fifteen minutes to facilitate. Finally we lined up in proper single-file formation and were led out of the room and into the auditorium. We walked past the music teachers, and I could see from a distance that Mrs. Habedank, appearing worried, looked at each singer until she finally saw me, when she tilted her head with a big warm smile.

"Oh, there you are, Matt. Have fun."

Caught in the movement, I entered the auditorium that had filled with people, all of them applauding as we made our entrance. We climbed into the risers and waited. Once the applause died down, Mrs. Best entered to throngs of an even louder ovation.

The room finally grew silent. Mrs. Best thanked everyone for coming, explained our reason for being and then turned and raised her arms to give the tempo to the pianist, who in turn played the introduction. Then we began to sing. The acoustics in the auditorium pulled our voices out and filled every corner of the room, and I discovered what heaven sounded like. I only had one pang of sadness as each song ended, knowing I wouldn't be singing it again, at least not like this. We sang through the repertoire and time stood still each time the public showered us with appreciation.

Once we finished singing our last song, we were drowned in an ocean of applause. I wriggled my way through the alto section, jumped down from the risers and hurried to the assembly room, where Mrs. Brown stood holding the huge bouquet. Behind me, I heard the audience applaud louder than ever as Mrs. Lois Best bowed to the crowd. Mrs. Brown placed the bouquet in my arms. Smiling, she winked at me, and then I turned to enter the auditorium, carrying the enormous spray of fragrant blossoms to the podium where Mrs. Best stood. When asked to carry the bouquet before the concert began, I didn't really give it much thought, but right then, as hundreds of clapping people had their eyes on me, the flower delivery boy, I felt like the chosen one, as if I'd just won an election. I stood below the podium, smiled and raised the bouquet to Mrs. Best. She bent down, kissed me on one cheek, said thank you, then stood back up cradling the flowers like Miss America. I returned to my place in the risers as the applause continued. Finally we filed out the same way we had entered, one line at a time, returning to the assembly room to grab our coats and belongings. We were given an envelope addressed to each of us individually that enclosed a signed certificate/award in recognition of our participation, signed by Mrs. Lois V. Best, the Director of the all-city choir, Delwen B. Jones, the Director of Music Education, and Angelo Giaudrone, the Tacoma Superintendent. My school, Sheridan, also got billing on the certificate, but to my disappointment, Mrs. Habedank's name was omitted, which I found totally unfair. After all, she deserved an award more than anyone for having given so much of her own time and dedication smothered in warm smiles to prepare us, not to mention her great legs.

Parents and families began to join us in the room. Bravos and hugs were showered on all the singers. No one from my family attended the concert, but I didn't mind nor give it a thought. I knew the long hours Dad was putting in to get us out of Miss Lucy's, and besides, the concert was just an extracurricular activity for me. Who else could have really understood what I was experiencing at that moment? Mrs. Habedank found me standing alone in the chaos, and when she learned that I had no family members present, she felt sorry for me being there all by myself and said she'd drive me home. Groovy, I thought! Good thing my family wasn't there or this would never have happened. The two of us, she and I, together in her maroon sports car. What could be better?

We drove south on Pacific Highway, and unfortunately there was no traffic slowing us down. Darn! She had me back in a jiffy and pulled up in front of Miss Lucy's house. I thanked her for all she had done for me and she leaned over and kissed me on the cheek, telling me one more time how proud she was of me. Man, she smelled good. I opened the door and forced myself out of the bucket seat next to her, saying I'd see her at school, but knowing in my heart that our brief, yet beautiful musical moment was fading off into the sunset.

3. THE LONG AND WINDING ROAD

A final page of another chapter was being turned in our epic when almost a month later on May 23rd, four days after the eighth anniversary of Mom's death and true to Dad's promise, give or take a week, we were packing our belongings into boxes and stuffing them into Dad's car. When Dad had offered us the choice to finish out the last few weeks of the school year before moving, not one of us voted "yes". We eagerly climbed into the car, leaving the Andersons, Miss Lucy's family, Stewart Junior High, Sheridan Elementary and Mrs. Habedank behind without saying goodbye as we drove north on the freeway, past the old paper mill where we plugged our noses to avoid breathing the familiar stench of the "Tacoma Aroma". Our hearts were lighter than ever, the road to freedom beckoned loudly, and all we insisted Dad do was step on the gas.

Stuff was piled so high into our car to the point that Dad could only see behind our vehicle through the side view mirrors. There were suitcases and boxes along with Mark's tuba strapped to the roof, and with five kids crammed like sardines into the seats we looked like the Beverly Hillbillies as we headed north out of Tacoma on the Interstate-5 freeway. Mark eventually voiced the question that hadn't even crossed our minds.

"By the way, Dad, where we goin'?"

"Well, let me put it to ya this way, by the way. Federal Way," Dad rhymed musically.

"Federal Way? That sounds like a government thing," John conjured.

"Well if it is, Johnny, boy, this time we're runnin' TO the government instead of FROM 'em for once!" He chuckled. "No, it's a town between Seattle and Tacoma. It's closer to my new shop and real nice. You kids'll see soon enough."

"Long as it's far from Tacoma, I don't care," I threw in.

Monica and Marguerite began to chant the words "Federal Way" over and over as they played Cats Cradle in the back seat next to me. As usual when we were all in the car, it didn't take much to lead us into our favorite traveling hymns, often beginning with a colorful version of *Animal Fair* that Aunt Frances had taught us years earlier on previous car trips.

I went to the animal fair

The birds and the bees were there

The grey raccoon by the light of the moon

Was combin' his auburn hair.

The monkey, he got drunk

And fell on the elephant's trunk

The elephant sneezed and fell on his knees

And that was the end of the monk'!

Once we had sung that tune and laughed, a second Aunt Fran hit immediately followed:

Oh the moon shines bright on Charlie Chaplin

His shoes are lackin' for the need of blackin'

And his old grey slacks they need a patchin'

'cuz he was scratchin' mosquito bites.

Short, sweet, and to the point, these songs were among our favorites to help us pass the time on road trips. Caught in the giggles over the lyrics, we might then segue through a few choruses of *I love to go a*

Wandering to *Sing Me a Song, Carmelita, Five Hundred Miles* and John's favorite: *Ninety-Nine Bottles of Beer*. We'd run through our entire repertoire as the miles accumulated on the odometer until finally, we pestered Dad to perform the standard that he'd sing with his brothers whenever they assembled, reminding us of comic family reunions with inebriated uncles slurring in bellowed unison.

To the tables down at Mory's

To the place where Louie dwells

To the dear old Temple bar we love so well

Sing the Whiffenpoofs assembled with their glasses raised on high

And the magic of their singing casts its spell

Yes, the magic of their singing of the songs we love so well

"Shall I Wasting" and "Mavourneen" and the rest

We will serenade our Louie while life and voice shall last

Then we'll pass and be forgotten with the rest

We're poor little lambs who have lost our way

Baa, baa, baa

We're little black sheep who have gone astray

Baa, baa, baa

Gentleman songsters off on a spree

Doomed from here to eternity

Lord have mercy on such as we

Baa, baa, baa

And finally, from the ship's captain position he held firmly behind the wheel, he would end our road show with his showstopper, the famous Rudy Vallee jewel, *The Old Sow Song*:

There was an old man and he had an old sow

(grunt) ow (PFTHTTT) ow (whistle) Hi diddle dow,

There was an old man and he had an old sow,

La sa fa ral de ray.

Oh, Susanna's a funny old sow

(grunt) ow (PFTHTTT) ow (whistle) ow,

Susanna's a funny old sow.

And this old sow had nine little pigs

(grunt) igs (PFTHTTT) igs (whistle) Hi diddle jigs.

And this old sow had nine little pigs

La sa fa ral de ray.

Oh, Susanna's a funny old sow

(grunt) ow (PFTHTTT) ow (whistle) ow,

Susanna's a funny old sow.

They tried to get over the garden wall

(grunt) all (PFTHTTT) all (whistle) Hi diddle dall

They tried to get over the garden wall

La sa fa ral de ray.

Oh, Susanna's a funny old sow

(grunt) ow (PFTHTTT) ow (whistle) ow,

Susanna's a funny old sow.

Federal Way first saw life in the late 1800's as a logging settlement. A small town sandwiched between Tacoma and Seattle, due west of the I-5 freeway, Federal Way mushroomed out in the '50s and '60s with the arrival of Boeing engineers, Weyerhauser executives and their families to cut the commute between both cities at the halfway point. Driving north, Dad took the 320th exit off the freeway and we sailed into our new town. He cruised down to 8th Avenue and turned right. The houses, primarily 1950's one-level ramblers, were nestled in generous formations of luxurious trees and green shrubbery, like a Garden of Eden. Our long and winding road came to an end as we drove north five blocks, and then Dad spoke up.

"Thar' she blows!"

"Our house?" I tightened up in anticipation.

"Which one, Dad, where?" Monica shook her hands free of the string she was playing with to look around.

"The one right here on the corner," Dad teased.

"Which corner? There's FOUR of 'em," Marguerite complained.

"The first one here on the right," Dad chuckled.

Dad slowed the car down as we reached the end of the block so we could get a good look. Five young faces were instantly glued to the car windows. There, on the corner of 8th avenue South and 314th street proudly stood our new sanctum of liberty. The unassuming brown rambler at 31408 wasn't unlike any of the others on the street, an "L" shaped wooden home with high windows and a garage with a concrete walkway that invited you up three stairs to a small landing and the door to our new heaven. Dad slowly pulled into the driveway for full effect. Excited as a bunch of bees near a lavender flower bed, we all pulled the door handles and hopped out before the car came to a complete stop, racing each other to the front door.

"Hurry, Dad! Unlock the door," Marguerite pleaded, jumping up and down.

"Dooon't get excited, I'm comin'," Dad laughed. He parked the car, got out and forged a path through the five of us huddled at the door, taking forever to dig the key out of his pocket, then ever so slowly aimed the key at the lock but suddenly turned around, looking at us to prolong our excitement.

"Dad, hurry up!"

"C'mon!"

He laughed, opened the door and we all burst inside as if we'd entered the main gates at Disneyland. We exploded across the threshold and ran into an entry/hallway that separated the roomy living quarters off the left side of the hallway from the bedrooms down the hall to our right, buzzing throughout the house in all directions, squealing with delight as we discovered and explored each room. Dad was so tickled to see us express ourselves loudly and freely after all we'd been through that he laughed and squealed right along with us, adding momentum to our jubilation. The first door down the hall on the left opened to a smaller bedroom for Dad directly across from the door to the bathroom. Further down the hall next to Dad's room stood the door to the biggest room for Mark, John and me to share across from a built-in linen closet in the hallway, and Monica and Marguerite's bedroom was at the end of the hallway. Each room had built-in closets and plenty of room for storage and the entire house had been freshly painted a coat of pure white, symbolic of our new beginnings.

Magically, all the furniture from our Craftsman in Portland that had vanished between the two moves with the Andersons in Tacoma had now reappeared like long lost friends and were installed in our new home. Our bunk beds, Dad's bed, Monica and Marguerite's double bed were all assembled, set up and ready for use. Dad had purchased new thermal blankets, pillows and sheets that lay plastic-wrapped on top of each mattress, waiting to snuggle us into slumber.

The living quarters welcomed us into a large dining room, where our beloved yet slightly fraying red and black vinyl floral print chairs and our long linoleum dinner table we had eaten so many meals at were centered patiently in allegiance, awaiting the celebration of our first dinner that night. The dining room opened into a family room area with a full brick wall and a small fireplace, where nearby, our TV sat proudly on top of Mom's cedar hope chest. There were large picture windows along the walls of the family room and dining room with a door between them that led the way onto a patio in front of a huge grassy back yard. Our reliable white enamel push-button stove and refrigerator from Portland were installed and plugged into the kitchen, which boasted an open ledge above the stove offering a view into the family room and dining room. Further back from the kitchen, there was a half bathroom on the left side of a laundry room, where our faithful, worn-for-wear washer and dryer both stood greeting us, hanging on for dear life.

Not all the furniture from Portland made the move, however. The brown couch that Aunt Mary had sewn up too many times from shoe abuse and Dad's matching worn-out rocking chair apparently had both bitten the dust, as they were nowhere to be seen. On the right side of the dining room stood an open door to a spacious living room, which apart from the boxes Dad had piled in the middle of the floor was completely void of furniture, but what mattered most was the few furnishings that had survived the journey swathed us in reassuring comfort.

Once we had calmed down as much as could be expected under the circumstances, Dad turned on the radio perched on top of Mom's white, wooden desk standing on the left wall of the dining room next to the kitchen door and gave the order for us to empty out the car. Like worker ants, we carried in everything we had packed and spread it out on the living room floor. When that job was finished and the car emptied, Dad drove

Mark and John down to the grocery store while Monica, Marguerite and I busied ourselves emptying out the boxes of dishes, pots, cast iron skillets, pans, utensils, silverware, Mom's Sunbeam electric mixer, the toaster, Mom's pink Pyrex pie pans and serving dishes, and placed them in their new residences in the kitchen. I smiled when I found all of our beloved Christmas decorations snuggling together and set them aside to await Christmas future. Then from a big box, I ripped off the tape and pulled out Mom's framed Degas, Monet and Renoir prints and gave each one space, leaning them against the walls. I stood there silently for a moment, admiring each painting as it took its first breath in the light of day after being held captive in a cardboard prison for so long, and it seemed like the faces in the painted scenes were smiling at me in gratitude for liberating them. Everything that belonged to Mom was a priceless treasure for us. Since we only had a limited number of clear memories of her, we cherished the things she loved as a way to keep her alive and with us.

While Monica and Marguerite made all the beds and fluffed the pillows, I dragged the boxes of clothes and suitcases to each room depending on whom they belonged to. I crammed towels and washcloths into the deep linen closet, discovering that with all the room remaining behind the towels, that linen closet would make a great hiding place for Hide 'n Seek. After that job was done, we ran out the back door to discover our old rusty barbecue leaning hopeful on the patio. The three of us ran around the entire back yard playing tag, chasing each other like puppies to claim the ground and then returned inside. Soon enough, Dad's car drove up. He and Mark came in carrying sacks of groceries that they placed on the beige tiled kitchen countertops, sending us out to help bring in the rest. John carried in an armful of Pres-to-Logs from the car, stacking them next to the fireplace. Marguerite brought in a new mop, broom and dustpan as Mark, John, Monica and I grabbed more bags. We all put the groceries away, including our favorite "Swiss piss" chocolate powder, frozen pot pies and an array of TV dinners, Kraft Macaroni & Cheese, boxed cereals, flour, sugar, rice, canned vegetables and soups, spaghetti noodles, breads, Sunny Jim peanut butter, Empress jam; all the foods we had missed since leaving Portland. We stored the soaps, Brillo pads, Pine Sol and other cleaners under the sink next to a brand-new plastic garbage can.

We filled the fridge with eggs, milk, butter, cheese, luncheon meats, ice cream and a huge hunk of ham as Dad wiped out and turned on the oven then washed out "Old Faithful", our blue enamel turkey roaster pan that had finally returned after a year sabbatical. That roaster was the probably the most vital utensil in our kitchen, as in it Dad cooked almost everything from curry to stews, and now it gleamed shiny clean and ready for Dad to whip up his famous pork chops, rice and mushroom gravy, one of our favorite comfort-food dinners. We danced around the house as it filled with the wonderful cooking odors, and when the moment arrived, we sat around our table in a state of pure bliss eating a meal fit for a king. After dinner, although it wasn't really cold enough for a fire, John ignited a Pres-to-Log to claim the fireplace while Dad turned on the old black and white TV set and fiddled with the rabbit ear antennas until clear images of The Lawrence Welk Show filled the screen. We carried our vinyl chairs over, aligned them in front of the TV and sat there together happier than we had been in such a long time. Joe Feeney, the Irish tenor, famous for fathering an enormous family as well as his big tenor voice, was introduced and began to sing.

When Irish Eyes Are Smiling, sure 'tis like a morn in spring.

In the lilt of Irish laughter, you can hear the angels sing...

Loyal to his Irish heritage and paying homage to our O'Donnell ancestors from County Mayo, Dad hushed us to listen and share the moment with Joe. Near the end of the song, Feeney hit a high note and held it for what seemed like an eternity.

When Irish hearts are happy, all the world seems bright and gay,

And When Irish Eyes Are Smiiiiiiiiii...ling, sure, they steal your heart away.

Mark was impressed.

"Gee, Dad, how can that guy sing like that?"

Faster than lightening, Dad responded.

"Well HELL, Mark, you'd sing like that, too, if you had ten kids to feed!"

Exploding into laughter, everyone stretched the joke out throughout the evening, listing all the things you could do if you had ten kids to feed like Joe Feeney.

During a commercial break, Marguerite spoke up.

"Who wants ice cream?"

The party atmosphere carried on as Mark sliced the half-gallon block of Rocky Road ice cream into six equal portions before a jury of watchful eyes who insured that nobody get cheated out of his fair share. Marguerite and Monica handed out the bowls to everyone, and we sat there shoveling spoonfuls of ice cream into our mouths in front of the TV, while the Pres-to-Log flames danced on the walls in complete harmony with our hearts and we felt at long last, in the most complete sense of the word, home. Dorothy wasn't lying; there's no place like it. Later, when tucked in tightly in my bed, I slept that night as if we'd just returned from an exhausting and perilous journey fighting lions, tigers and bears in the Land of Oz.

We woke up the next morning to the familiar scent of ham and eggs wafting in from the kitchen. Dad was drinking coffee as he prepared breakfast. While we ate at the table, we planned our Sunday.

"What are we gonna do today, Dad?" John yawned.

"Well, I thought maybe we might all take a drive around, look at the town and get to know the place a little better. How's that sound?" Dad threw in for discussion.

He didn't have to ask twice. We gobbled up our food and for once, didn't fight over whose turn it was to do the dishes. Mark was to begin that chore cycle, age ruling, but Monica and I helped him put them away. We got dressed, ran outside and into the car. Dad took place behind the wheel and drove us slowly around the neighborhood to give us some bearings. Mirror Lake Elementary, a long, one-level school was only a block away from our house.

"Matt, Monica and Marguerite, this here's where you'll be going tomorrow."

"That's gonna be my FOURTH sixth-grade class this year." I counted aloud.

"Wow, it's only a block away," Monica said.

Dad again had a comeback.

"Sure is. Any closer 'n that and it would be in your front yard."

"Well, we sure won't get lost on our way to school," I added.

We drove around the flat, one-level building that spread out over the entire block. Slowly, Dad drove us past our house again to make sure the girls were well oriented.

"There's our house, and this street here's the quickest way to all the stores."

Dad drove through all the back roads to acquaint us with our neighborhood. We rode slowly past the side of our house on South 314th until we hit 10th, turned left and drove up to 313th, took a right and drove down to 12th Pl. South, turned left up to 312th, turned right and drove down to the corner, memorizing colors of the houses and other landmarks on each street as we turned, and finally we arrived at The Federal Way shopping mall, that spread up and down both sides of Pacific Highway South, the old Highway 99. We turned right and drove past the Thriftway grocery store, Woolworths, A&W Root Beer, down to Herfy's Hamburgers, Wigwam department store, and clear down to Dick Balch Chevrolet (the famous skinny car dealer in the devil costume on TV commercials who would bash up a car with a 12 lb. sledgehammer, laughing hysterically at himself as he asked "If you can't trust your car dealer, who can you trust?"). Dad made a U-turn and drove back up Pacific Highway to 304th, turned left up one street to 16th, turned right and drove 4 blocks and turned left onto Dash Point Road taking us past a small convenience store and a little further down the street, to Sacajawea Junior High School, another one-level campus that sprawled out over a block or two.

"Here's the school you'll be goin' to, Mark and John."

"Well, ours is more than a block away from home." John said.

"Dooon't get excited, Johnny boy. There's a school bus that stops right across the street from the house," Dad reassured him.

"That'll do," Mark nodded.

We drove back to the Thriftway to pick up more groceries, including apples, cookies, waxed paper and lunch bags in preparation for the next day. Dad slowly drove the back way home so we could test ourselves at how well we knew the way, telling him when to turn right or left at chosen landmarks we remembered. Back at home, we had more pork chops to finish off in the fridge, so Dad cooked more rice and stretched out the gravy for us that night. After dinner we all went to bed, knowing we'd have to be up early to register in school.

Early Monday morning, Dad called out down the hall.

"Up and at 'em, Atom Ant! C'mon kids, time to get

a move on!"

We pulled ourselves out of bed, got washed and dressed, ate cinnamon toast and milk, made our lunches and were out in the car at the appointed time. We drove first to Mirror Lake Elementary. Mark and John stayed in the car. Monica, Marguerite, Dad and I went into the office and approached the secretary at the counter.

"Good morning, can I help you?" The lady greeted.

"Yes, good morning. I'm Jim Gonder. We just moved here to Federal Way and live around the corner. I'm here to register my three kids in school."

The secretary just stood there with her jaw dropped.

"Now – I, I mean t-t-today?" she asked, stupefied.

"Why not? Any problem with that?" Dad challenged with a smile.

"No, but – there are only three weeks left before the end of the school year!"

"Well, better late than never," Dad said, quick as ever, impossible to be topped.

Dad filled out and signed the forms for the secretary. Afterwards, Monica, Marguerite and I said goodbye to him and were ushered to our classrooms. I entered Miss Karen Steele's sixth grade room and was introduced to a brunette teacher in a miniskirt that looked like a cross between Ali MacGraw and Marlo Thomas. Nice. Something told me I could learn a lot here and I knew I'd even be willing to stay after school to earn extra credit points, if necessary. Miss Steele presented me to the class and told me there wasn't going to be much to do but enjoy the last few weeks of school, which was okay by me. The major tests had all been taken and were waiting final grading, so we basically only had to wind down the year with fun and games. Ali-Marlo-I mean Miss Steele laughed all the time. Everyone and everything amused her and she had eyes that sparkled through her long, dark locks of silky dark brown hair that she whipped over her shoulder in a most arousing way. During those few weeks, Miss Steele gave me Math, English and other quick exams (not on the subjects I really wanted her to teach-test me on) to check my education level, which I whizzed through effortlessly; happy to get on with the fun and games she had planned for the entire class.

Meanwhile, Mark and John, busy integrating themselves at Sacajawea Junior High, met a guy named Snorky MacLean, who not only was in John's seventh grade class at school, but lived a block away from us. They met up everyday as they rode the bus to and from school during the last two weeks remaining, and we would get together in the late afternoon to hang out before everyone split up to run back to their respective homes at dinnertime. Snorky, in turn, introduced us to Rich Williams, another neighborhood comrade. Rich lived just further down our street and was in my grade at Mirror Lake but a different class than mine. We all became inseparable buddies. Marguerite and Monica made a slew of girlfriends as well, including Lori Moss, who lived next door with her sister Sally and their three brothers, Anita and her sister Barbie who lived down the street in addition to other stray kids from all over the neighborhood.

We took to Federal Way like fish to water, swimming freely in a brand new sea of joy. Towards the end of the first week in Federal Way, Dad woke us up for school but told us he'd be going in late for work, as he had to stay home and wait for the telephone company to come by and hook up our phone. When we arrived home from school that afternoon, Dad had long gone to his shop in Seattle and we discovered a yellow telephone sitting on top of a phone book on the floor of the dining room, reminding us that our newfound freedom came with the means to communicate, even though we had no clue yet as to who we could call. Monica and Marguerite ran over and played pretend with the receiver, taking turns flirting with imaginary boyfriends.

"Oh, I love you, too." Monica toyed into the receiver.

"Um hmm. Yeah. Um hmm." She continued.

Marguerite grew impatient.

"Gimme the phone, Monica, it's my turn."

"Just a minute," she answered. And then, into the receiver she added, "I'll call you back or you call me tomorrow, honey, will ya? My sister has to call somebody. Okay, I love you, too. G'bye."

Marguerite grabbed the phone, dialing a fake number and cooed to the dial tone.

"Hi honey, you love me?" (pause) "How much?" (pause) "Well then buy me something, okay? Get me some perfume and jewelry and buy me a bag o' popcorn, oh, and take me roller-skating too, okay? Okay, honey, g'bye."

She hung up the phone, giggling with Monica.

We started making our dinner and suddenly the phone rang, making us all jump out of our skin.

"HOLY SHIT!" Mark yelled, jumping at the loud noise.

"What's that?" Marguerite asked, frightened.

"The phone, dummy." I told her as it rang a second time.

"God, we don't even know the number. How could anybody else?" John asked.

"You answer it, Matt." Monica said.

"Geez, it's not gonna kill us." I told her.

As it rang a third time, I picked up the receiver.

"Hello?"

"Hi Matt, it's Dad."

"Hi Dad." I said, turning to everyone, rolling my eyes.

Monica and Marguerite let out sighs of relief. Dad said he just wanted to check in on us and see if the number worked.

"So, what's our phone number, Dad?" I asked.

"VE9..."

"Wait a minute. Monica, get me some paper and a pen, quick."

Monica grabbed my Pee-Chee sitting on the table. I grabbed the pen inside.

"Okay, Dad, what is it?"

"V E 9 - 4 3 5 8," he answered, articulating clearly.

"VE9-4358," I sang back to him as I wrote it down.

"Okay, I got it, Dad... Okay then, see ya later. Bye."

I hung up the phone, turning to my siblings.

"Dad's on his way home. VE9-4358." I chanted.

Dad didn't realize when he innocently gave me the phone number that it would be the beginning of his undoing. We were all coming of an age where the phone would become a favorite pastime for some of us. And it all began that night. After dinner, Marguerite ran next door to Lori Moss's house to give her our number, telling her to call, then came running back into the house just as the phone began to ring.

"I'll get it," she yelled out, sprinting over to the phone to pick up the receiver.

"Hello?...Hi Lori, it works!" She squealed.

"Yeah! Okay, I'll see ya tomorrow at school, okay? ...G'bye."

And that ended her first conversation on the new phone. She hung up the receiver and ran out the back door, returning five minutes later just as the phone rang again.

"I'll get it," she announced, picking up the receiver.

"Hello? Hey Anita, ya see, it works!"

Thus ended our calm and peaceful household, as that phone seemed to never stop ringing. We gave our number to everyone we knew and kept the Federal Way phone company in business from that day forward.

The last week of school breezed by. We were happy guppies in our new home but there was one fly in the ointment, we all felt embarrassed to invite our friends inside our house. We had all been to our friends' homes on occasion and had seen their well-furnished dwellings, but aware that we had no place for anyone to sit except on one of the six dining room chairs that multi-tasked as our TV chairs in the evenings made us feel as if someone might judge us as too poor to be worthy of befriending. So, whenever someone came to the door, we'd peer out a small crack to see who was there, and then make the party wait outside behind a closed door while we called out the person requested, who then came running to join the guest outside. Dad wasn't aware of our procedure or he would have told us we had nothing to be ashamed of, but we somehow banded together and adopted this absurd routine.

The day before school let out for summer, my brothers and I were hanging out with Snorky and Rich in our yard, when Dad drove up and parked the car, jumped out of the driver's seat and came over to say hello as we huddled like a gang on the corner of the front lawn.

"Hey Dad," Mark, John and I greeted in unison.

"Howdy," Dad sang out in response. "What's goin' on?"

"Nothin'. Just hangin' out with our friends Snorky and Rich."

"Hi Rich" Dad said, and then he turned to Snorky.

"Hi Mr. Gonder," Rich responded politely.

"Snorky?" Dad asked. "Either that's gotta be a nickname or you're puttin' me on. What's your real name?"

"Harold," Snorky confessed.

"Harold, huh?"

Faster than the speed of light, he responded.

"No wonder they call you Snorky."

Dad broke up the gang laughter with the usual everyday interrogation he served to the first person he saw in his path whenever he arrived home. He didn't mind what we were doing or where we were as long as we could be accounted for.

"Where are the girls?"

"Next door at the Moss's," I informed.

"Well, go tell 'em to come home for dinner."

"Ah, feed 'em beans!" Mark said, coining the vernacular of the day.

"Snorky and Rich, you two wanna join us?" Dad extended. Mark, John and I cringed at the thought that they'd come inside, but luckily they didn't accept his invitation.

"No thanks, Mr. Gonder. We gotta get home," Snorky said.

"Yeah, we'll see you guys." Rich added, putting an end to that.

Relieved to not have dinner guests standing up to eat in our empty house, Mark and John grabbed the sacks of groceries from Dad's car and carried them into the kitchen, while I ran next door to retrieve my sisters. I climbed onto the porch and knocked. Lori, a boy-crazy fifth-grader, answered the door.

"Hi Matt, ya wanna come in?" She invited with an overexcited grin.

"No thanks, Lori. Just tell my sisters that Dad wants 'em to come home for dinner."

"Oh, okay," she answered sadly, then turned to call out to my sisters.

"Monica! Marguerite! Your Dad wants you to go home for dinner!"

"Thanks. See ya." I turned to walk away. She yelled after me.

"Hey Matt, you wanna come over and swim

tomorrow?"

The Moss's were the only neighbors who had a built-in swimming pool in their back yard. My sisters had been invited a few times over for a swim and with summer coming up, Lori knew she had bargaining power to snag me into her Venus boy trap.

"Sure, why not? Thanks." My sisters ran to catch up with me as I walked down the driveway, heading home for Dad's comforting chicken curry dinner.

4. IN THE SUMMERTIME

The school year was over in a heartbeat. Our house was finally in order the day I hung Mom's impressionist prints on the walls, spreading her love of classic art throughout the house, while the radio piped out all the current Top 40 hits. Summer vacation finally had arrived and we found ourselves with all the time in the world to do anything we wanted with all the new friends we had made. Dad would often say: "In the words of Mark Twain: The sooner you start treating your child like an adult, the sooner they'll become an adult", and so he left us to our own devices, unless of course we strayed too far, when only a few of his colorfully choice words sent in our direction would get us to toe the line once again. He never found need for discipline, as we had been weaned on his ever so quick mind that taught us to consider the consequences before an act was committed. Don't get me wrong; we didn't live in a state of fear at all. There were only a couple of house rules to follow, and the first and foremost was to attend school, which we all did with no resistance. The second was to honor our turn at washing the dishes, which, if left undone could send Dad into an exaggerated blind rage, especially if after work he had oiled up at King's Restaurant bar prior to coming home, which, on most nights, was a given. The problem was that he never kept strict hours and could arrive at any time, catching us off guard. The usual response to "Why aren't the goddamn dishes done?" would be a wimpy "they're soaking", which on occasion could buy time until whoever was supposed to do them rushed in and got them done. But one night Dad appeared out of the blue in a sour drunken mood and yours truly happened to be the first kid within range so I got the third degree.

"You kids have some dinner?"

"Yeah, we had ham and eggs."

"I see that. But why aren't the goddamn dishes done, huh?"

"It's John's turn, Dad."

"Well, where the hell is he?"

"Outside."

"Go tell him to get his ass in here!"

I ran outside and told John Dad wanted to see him

front and center, warning him of the storm cloud that hovered over the egg-encrusted dishes piled high in the kitchen sink. By the time John came into the house, Dad was frying up a steak on the stove and had lost all control of his calm. He took one look at John and exploded.

"There you are! Why the HELL didn't you do the dishes?"

John tried to defend himself, aware that it was too late.

"I was gonna do 'em, Dad."

Dad jumped onto that one and ran a mile with it.

"Oh you WAS gonna do 'em, huh? You WAS gonna wash the goddamn dishes, you say? Well let me tell you a few things I WAS gonna do for you, Johnny boy! I WAS gonna put your ass on a plane and fly you off to a safari in Africa! Yep, sure WAS! I WAS gonna cook you a goddamn steak and lobster dinner! I WAS gonna fly you to the moon! I WAS gonna buy you a trip around the world! I WAS gonna do a million goddamn things for you! Yes I WAS! You can't IMAGINE all the things I WAS gonna do for you!"

John took the verbal beating and washed the dishes as Dad continued his tongue-lashing, repeating all the things he "was" gonna do for John. Dad eventually ran out of gas and calmed down once his steak was cooked blood rare, but his point, as usual, was loudly and clearly made. I made a mental note to never use the word "was" in Dad's presence in the future.

Aside from the occasional dirty dish episode or getting yelled at for "rough-housing" with each other, our lives were bathed in warm summer rays and Dad was always eager to listen to us recount or reenact our daily adventures when he got home from work. He never meddled into our affairs, ever, but was right there if you wanted to talk to him about something and he always had time for a conversation. He was all about the truth with no happy horseshit, as he would say. Honest to a fault, you knew what he was thinking or feeling at any given moment, be it joy, sorrow, anger or pain because he wore his heart on his sleeve. What you saw was what you got, and everyone admired him for his integrity. He courageously called a spade a spade, whether you wanted to hear it or not. His vocabulary was full of dirty words, but they sounded more comical than threatening the way he delivered them.

Mark, after having worked his butt off the previous summer to earn his gold, 3-speed bike, realized he had sold himself short, so he offered his full summer services this time around to Dad for a salary of fifty dollars per week at Dad's new shop near the Duwamish River area. Dad laughed and accepted the new deal, proud that Mark had, on his own, learned a lesson in the art of negotiation.

"So you figure you were underpaid last summer, huh, Mark?"

"I'm not complainin' but yeah, you got me once, but I'd be stupid if you got me twice for that much."

"Okey dokey, Mark, you just named your price. Fifty dollars per week it is. You'll start on Monday, okay?"

"Okay, Dad."

And the matter was settled there. So Mark had a summer job lined up, but for the rest of us, Dad gave John, Monica, Marguerite and me a small weekly allowance, informing us that if we wanted more we had to earn it by babysitting or running errands for people. As we were newcomers to town, we weren't very well acquainted with many people so jobs came few and far between. Snorky had a job; he went around the neighborhood dragging his lawn mower and knocking on doors to ask if he could mow the lawn in exchange for a few bucks. We didn't own a lawn mower yet, so Dad hired Snorky to mow our lawn whenever it grew knee-high.

We ran down to the mall every Saturday as soon as Dad gave us our allowance. I remember roller-skating at the Federal Way Rinks and spinning around to the bellowing organ music. There were pinball machines at the roller rink that I loved to play but I got "tilt" more often than not from banging out my frustration on the machine. On other days, I'd walk to the mall with my sisters. Woolworth's had a popcorn machine and all the penny candy you could imagine, in addition to the perfumes and make-up that my sisters favored. Marguerite bought a small bottle of "Soir de Paris" perfume in a cobalt blue bottle and thought she was so exotic and continental. Monica bought new pink foam hair curlers and other sundry girlie items.

As Monica, Marguerite and I were walking a long way home from the mall one afternoon we ran into Lori, who joined us for the walk. As soon as we passed a big house, Lori stopped in her tracks.

"Oh my God, that's where Jerry Leavenworth lives," Lori squealed.

"Who?" I asked.

"Jerry Leavenworth. Don't you know him?"

"Never heard of him," I answered.

"How could you not know Jerry Leavenworth? He's so cute."

"Why should I know him?"

"Does he go to our school?" Marguerite asked.

"You're in love with him, aren't you?" Monica pointed her finger, just as she and Marguerite began to chant:

Lori and Jerry sittin' in a tree, K I S S I N G

First comes love, then comes marriage,

Then comes baby in a baby carriage.

"Yes, I am. Jerry, I love you, I love you, I love you," Lori chanted as we passed his house. She couldn't keep her eyes focused on the street as she walked mesmerized in front of Jerry's house, hoping he would run out and into her arms.

One sunny morning, when her allowance had all been spent, Marguerite decided she was going to sell lemonade. She carried a TV tray and a chair outside, made a big pitcher of Kool-Aid lemonade with ice cubes, grabbed a few plastic cups and set up shop on the corner of our yard, certain she had selected the perfect spot to attract business. Eventually her friends Anita, Barbie and Lori came by the stand and chatted with her for a while, hoping she'd give in and just offer them some for free. They didn't have any money to purchase a glass, but definitely wanted to sample the product.

"Ah c'mon, Marguerite, just lemme have some." Anita begged.

"I'll give you some, but you gotta pay for it first." Marguerite, the saleslady informed.

"I want some, too, Marguerite, and if ya gimme some, I'll go get my brothers to buy some from ya." Lori schemed.

"Okay, I'll give you guys a little, but I'm tryin' to make some money, ya know."

Marguerite poured them each a small glass and they stood there drinking it down and chatting up a storm. Then, right as I walked up with Rich, Marguerite saw us as potential approaching customers.

"Quick, gimme your cups," she warned to her girlfriends, snatching the cups out of their hands and pouring the remaining lemonade back into the pitcher as if no one saw her do it.

"Hi Matt. Hi Rich, ya wanna buy some lemonade. Five cents a cup!"

Lori and Anita wanted to help the sale.

"It's real good, Matt. I had some," Anita testified.

"Me, too. It's really yummy," Lori threw in. Marguerite appeared content with her sales staff. I couldn't hold back.

"Yeah, sure. You poured what they didn't drink back into the pitcher." I told Marguerite.

"We saw you! So go poison someone else with your

germs," Rich scoffed as we walked away, laughing.

Marguerite didn't make much money but deserved a medal for tenacity, holding court at her stand for hours and hours, grilling her skin under the sun and flirting with the cars that drove by. After a while, when she realized her blond pigtails weren't drawing customers, she put on a sad, flushed face, eventually enticing a couple of suckers that felt sorry for her and bought some of her semi-regurgitated refreshment.

John, Monica, Marguerite and I may not have had jobs but our summer days were filled with plenty of things to do. Marguerite and Monica had crushes on Bobby Sherman and sang *Julie, Do Ya Love Me* until we were all haunted by and sick of the song. While the radio churned Five Stairsteps *Ooh Child*, Bread's *Make It With You* and Three Dog Night's *Mama Told Me Not To Come* and other tunes, we had water balloon fights in the back yard to cool off and grilled hamburgers and hot dogs on the barbecue. Dad always came home with a couple of sacks of groceries in his arms, and you could bet money he'd be toting a watermelon in one sack that we would slice and gobble up on the patio. One afternoon, Mark, John and I went down to the Jerry Lewis Cinema with Snorky and Rich to watch *Little Big Man* with Dustin Hoffman and all wished Faye Dunaway was around to teach us the tricks she taught the happy men in the movie.

Rich introduced me to his sister, Nancy, who was

one year younger than I. Nancy often invited me over to listen to 45's in her bedroom. Mrs. Williams would always open the door to check on us carrying a platter of Kool-aid and cookies free of charge, unlike Marguerite. The Carpenters' *Close to You* was number one on the radio at that time, and after singing along with it in Nancy's bedroom, we'd go hide out in the tool shed in her back yard to neck. Nancy had her own horse and showed up on the street one day offering rides to the neighbor kids at Mirror Lake School. Monica finally got her turn to ride that horse, but not five minutes after she mounted, she experienced her first public feminine accident. Red faced, she slid off the horse and ran home, hiding her stained jeans as best she could from everyone.

Another day, Dad pulled a brand new croquet set from the trunk of his car. He had John and me carry it to the back yard where he proceeded to teach us how to set up the wickets and play the game. By the time we had it down, we'd drawn a crowd of neighborhood kids and once we taught everyone how to play, we were hosting daily tournaments in our large back yard. Soon enough, the Moss boys couldn't get enough of the game and would show up at our door almost every day, asking:

"Can we play croquet?"

I knew we had our own trump card for barter negotiation and used it whenever I could.

"Sure, if we can come later and swim in your pool."

"Okay," was always their eager response. We'd send them around the back and they'd be out there for hours playing game after game. After all, they had long grown accustomed to having a kidney-shaped pool in their back yard to cool off in, but they had neither lawn nor croquet set like we did, so we bartered our game against afternoons in their pool. Fair trades.

One night, Dad came home from work and rounded us up, announcing he needed to speak to us about something. We gathered together, all a bit worried that some new upheaval was about to occur in our lives.

"Kids, my new partner Lyle is lookin' for a place to live but needs a place to shack up for a month or two until he finds a place of his own. Any objections?"

Silence filled the air. Dad had already told us he had a new partner that was going to help him build his business, but nobody expected to hear he would also be living with us.

"How long is he gonna stay?" Monica asked.

"Just until he finds his own apartment, that's all," Dad answered.

"Long as he doesn't give us any rules," I said, breaking the silence.

"Yeah. No more rules from anybody but us!" My siblings all immediately joined forces with me.

"There ain't gonna be no more rules. Lyle will be OUR guest. The sonofabitch'll have to abide by OUR goddamn rules," Dad teased.

"But, what if he tries to make some anyway?" Marguerite worried.

"Feed 'em beans!" Mark said, reusing the popular phrase, making us all laugh.

"That's right," Dad affirmed. "We'll feed him beans."

"Good, then sure, Lyle can come stay with us," I concurred.

Monica opened her arms, waving around the room.

"But where's he gonna sleep?"

"Yeah, we don't got any more beds," Marguerite said.

"He'll bring his own mattress and can park it in the living room. How's that sound?" Dad asked.

"Living room's empty anyway," John stated dryly.

Lyle came home with Dad the next day, dragging in a single bed mattress, blanket and pillow and flopped it on the floor of the empty living room, under two of Mom's paintings. After that first night he asked permission to move the mattress into the family room near the door to get more air during the night. Nobody cared so he did just that. Dad and Lyle got up every morning, drank down a cup of coffee and drove off to work with Mark in tow. We got along with Lyle, whom we didn't see much of, really, as he was often out chasing women after work, but whenever he was home with us, he would laugh and act silly with us just like Dad. Mark would come home from the shop and tell John and me about all the cars he worked on, totally enamored with a yellow 1970 Mercury Cougar with a Black Vinyl Top, the cat's meow as far as he was concerned.

Soon after Lyle moved in we had another tenant come to reside with us. Someone had given us a pet rabbit that we quickly named Chomp-Chomp, due to the loud crunching sound he made while eating vegetables. One night Dad was cooking up a spaghetti dinner for us and asked if Chomp-Chomp had eaten.

"Anybody feed ole' Chomp-Chomp today?"

"Feed 'em greens," I answered. Dad and Lyle enjoyed the twist I gave to Mark's phrase.

Chomp-Chomp, like everyone else, had no rules to abide by and ran freely around the house as he pleased. He loved to sleep in Lyle's bed during the day, but after the first week Lyle begged us to put Chomp-Chomp in a cage so he wouldn't have to wake up every morning to find "bunny biscuits" on his pillow and in his sheets. Chomp-Chomp, however, hated his cage and one day scuttled out the back door, never to be seen again. Dad wished Chomp-Chomp would have run into the turkey roaster, but he chose Mirror Lake Park as his new residence, never to be heard from again. Along with Chomp-Chomp, we had a couple of dogs and some cats as well take up residence with us at other moments in our lives. Although we enjoyed their company and never abused them, we weren't mature enough to give proper care to our animals, and so, feeling neglected, they ventured out on their own to seek better lodgings and never returned, a truth I am not proud of but one that fortunately remedied itself in time.

We all liked Lyle because he and Dad were good buddies. Business partners, they spent long hours together working at the shop in Seattle and got along famously. One night they announced they would endeavor to get into top physical shape and lose the beer-bellies they both were sporting by signing up at a local gym, vowing to work out a few times each week once their work day was over, a no-brainer for two strong men in their prime. So, sign up they did; they proudly bought the requisite shoes, clothing gear and attended their first grueling workout session, giving their all to the exercise program designed for middle-aged single men who weren't ready to relinquish their powers of seduction. They came home later than usual Monday night carrying their bags of sweaty gym gear, bouncing about and feeling terrific, convinced they had found a new religion and way of life that would attract single ladies to them like bees to honey. Watching the two of them carry on about how invincible they were that evening with such enthusiasm and confidence really impressed me.

The next morning was a totally different story. Dad and Lyle became the brunt of unending teasing as they writhed in comic agony with every movement they made. They walked around like crippled old men as they slowly got ready for work and it took many painful maneuvers to wrench themselves into the driver's seats of their respective cars. On Wednesday, they reluctantly returned to the gym for another bout with torture, to afterwards pour their pain into a few pitchers of well-earned suds at King's Tavern before swerving home to their beds. Come Friday, after the third workout (followed by another ale quencher) I heard Dad's car pull into the driveway and figured he'd be coming into the house shortly. A few long minutes passed and I began to worry, so I ran outside to see what was the matter. Dad had turned off the ignition, but had completely passed out and was snoring with his face crushed and distorted against the steering wheel. I laughed, woke him up and helped him into the house. He threw his 'goddamn sweats' into the trash and never mentioned the gym again, opting instead to refer to his midriff paunch as an "investment", adding that the ladies would get an even better deal, him and his gut, or two men for the price of one.

Not long after that episode, our loyal clothes washer and dryer that had traveled to hell and back during our two years in Portland and barely survived the subsequent moves to Tacoma and now to Federal Way, had finally spun their last cycles and "threw in the towel" once and for all. From that day onward, our laundry room turned into a cemetery for the broken machines while Sunday afternoons became our laundromat expedition days, where we'd squat a row of clothes washers and spend a few hours washing, drying and folding our clothes in preparation for the following week. One Sunday afternoon the phone had rung one too many times, waking Dad up in a grumpy mood from his nap. He gave the order and we ran to our rooms and grabbed all the dirty laundry we could muster, then piled it up on the floor of the dining room like always, proudly announcing to Dad we had finished. Dad sauntered over in a sleepy haze to check out the heap and almost went through the ceiling as he reached down and pulled out an old Cub Scout shirt.

"What the hell is this doing down there? Not one of you sonsobitches ever WEARS the goddamn thing, so why the hell do I gotta keep payin' to WASH the sonofabitch?"

He tossed it to John.

"Sorry, Dad." Mark tried to appease Dad's anger, unsuccessfully.

"Je-sus Christ! Nobody's even BEEN to a goddamn Boy Scout meeting for years but every week I'm still washing the goddamn SHIRT!"

"We'll throw it away, Dad," Mark offered as a solution.

Silently, we separated the rest of the clothes into white and color mounds, bagged it up and stuffed it into the car along with our box of Tide soap and Clorox Bleach.

"All ready, Dad," Mark announced, but Dad had not quite cooled off.

"LOOK at this place. Goddamn pigsty!" Dad wailed.

"We'll clean it up, Dad. C'mon everyone, I'll sweep," Mark announced.

Quiet as church mice, we all began to pick up our coats, toys and junk that lay strewn all over the house. Mark grabbed the broom and began sweeping everything that had been left on the floor into a big pile in the middle. Monopoly game pieces, homework, floor dirt, dust bunnies, anything and everything could be found in that big mountain of debris, and once Mark had swept it all into a heap in the center of the floor, the rest of us scrounged through it, digging out whatever was important to retrieve. As soon as nothing remained but a pile of waste, Mark tried to enlist Dad's authority in the process, hoping his eagerness would appease Dad's anger.

"See, Dad? All done sweeping. What should I do

with it now?'"

Dad exploded, jumping and pointing at the pile of debris through his screeches.

"PISS ON IT! PISS ON IT!"

Without another word, Mark swept the dirt into the dustpan, and we climbed into the car and drove to the laundromat in total silence. By the time we had arrived, Dad's anger had completely subsided and we were already laughing at the episode, and as soon as we finished the laundry, we had replaced our usual phrase of "feed 'em beans" with "Piss on it" as a solution for everything we could imagine.

One afternoon I sat watching TV on one of our dining room chairs and all of a sudden Snorky came bursting through the front door, walking over to the dining room table. Stunned, I looked at him coming at me.

"Hi Matt! Yeah, I been inside your house," he said."

"So," I responded, shocked.

"Who cares if you don't have any furniture. Every time I came to the door and had to wait outside, I thought you had a bunch of nudie's runnin' around here all the time," Snorky confessed.

And that ended our embarrassment issue. From that

moment on, ours was an open, if not practically empty house where all our friends met up every day. Monica and Marguerite danced long happy afternoons in the empty family room with Anita, Barbie and Lori to another favorite tune, *The Lion Sleeps Tonight*.

As June drew to a close, makeshift wooden firework stands were installed in the parking lot at the mall, and the promise of a big show of sparkling pyrotechnical gadgets "Made in China" enticed us to dig deep into our pockets. We bought what we could afford and complained about the prices, eventually talking Dad into becoming a better patriot by raising our allowance to ensure we would, like good citizens, justly honor the national holiday. We bought firecrackers and all sorts of cheap sparklers, bottle rockets and fountains that we stored in Mom's desk, waiting for the national holiday. However, excitement got the best of us one night before the big day. Mark, John and I, with Snorky and Rich in tow, shot the bottle rockets from our bedroom window at the cars whizzing past our house, causing a few drivers to swerve in the street.

On the afternoon of the fourth of July, the weather climbed to a sunny eighty-one degrees while the charbroiled smells of barbecued meat filled the neighborhood air. Everyone seemed to be outside, engaged in various summer meal activities. We grilled burgers and hot dogs and ate watermelon during the day, and when evening fell, ran throughout the neighborhood to watch the fireworks displays at each of our friends' houses.

While Mark was off working with Dad and Lyle, John and I took turns riding Mark's gold bike to join our pals, Snorky and Rich. Mark, feeling sorry for John, bought him a brand new green Alta 10-speed, allowing us the freedom to ride off together for the first time without having to borrow a bike from one of our friends' brothers. Jeff Allen, another pal in John's class, rode over one day on a brand new racing bike. We stood there admiring the expensive two-wheeler.

"Nice bike, Jeff."

"Yeah, I guess it's okay," he mumbled.

"Okay? Just okay? Whaddya talkin' about?" I asked.

"Yeah, that thing must a cost a fortune," John added.

"Who cares," Jeff answered.

We didn't understand his response.

"If I bang it up, he'll just get me a new one."

"Who?" John asked.

"My Dad."

"He will? Man, you're lucky." I said.

"I'm lucky? No I'm not, you guys are. I get stuff all the time. Don't ever see my Dad, though. He's always gone somewhere n' he buys me things 'cuz he feels guilty."

"What's wrong with that?" John asked.

"You guy's Dad is here. He works but he comes home. Wish mine was home once in a while. Rather see him. I'll see ya later."

He rode off, leaving us pondering the value of a father present in our lives as opposed to lots of cool gifts. Thinking of Dad coming home late and often drunk, we wondered who got the better deal.

For the most part, people lived behind unlocked doors, and trusted their fellow man to respect the territorial rights of each citizen. There were, however, according to rumor, a couple of strange men who would comb the neighborhood streets in a van at night, stealing bikes from people's yards. We didn't adhere to the paranoia and foolishly, like everyone else in our neighborhood, carelessly left our bikes anywhere completely unchained. Soon enough, both Mark's and John's were picked up and found weeks later in some ditch; the bike frame carcasses completely stripped of their gears, wheels and parts. Sadly, certain lessons in life are learned the hard way. We pulled the bicycle remains out of the ditch and brought them home. John's was easy to fix up and within a few days, John had his bike up and running again, the new scratches just adding character to the two-wheeler. Mark's bike however, had suffered badly. He hung the gold frame on a hook in the garage, figuring he'd buy parts for the crucified body and resurrect it some other day. Yeah, right.

The month of August arrived and the day dawned to bid farewell to Lyle. He had found a new apartment for himself and it was time for him to move on. We had enjoyed his company for those short months and Dad and Mark still worked with him every day, so it didn't seem like he was going anywhere. He threw his bedding and the few items he owned into his car, bid us goodbye and drove off as if he was a guest that had just finished dinner and was on his way back home.

Towards the middle of the month, Mark, John and I received an envelope in the mail from Sacajawea Junior High School full of pre-registration documents that included maps of the buildings and schoolroom layout, forms to fill out, class lists and a host of rules and instructions to follow in preparation for the upcoming school year. I felt so grown up, eager to leave elementary school behind me in the kiddie dust and enter the big man adult world of junior high. We each filled out the forms, choosing the elective classes we wanted to take. All seventh graders were allowed to choose one class on the list in addition to English, Math, Science, History and other classes we would be required to attend. I read through the list, discovering that Sacajawea offered wood shop classes, typing, and various music and Art classes. I stopped right there. I read in the description how the art students would be working with clay, painting and drawing and working in a host of other crafty mediums. My decision was made without hesitation. I put an "X" in the Art class box, placed my form with Mark's and John's in the envelope and off they went back to the school for processing and scheduling.

One of the less exciting requirements we were to fulfill was to undergo a complete physical examination by a doctor prior to the first day of school, in order to participate in Physical Education classes and extra-curricular sports. The letter contained a list of neighborhood doctors and the addresses and phone numbers of their offices. That afternoon, we got together with Snorky and Rich who had also received their envelopes from school and found themselves in the same boat, however Mark, John and Snorky had already been through the process and naturally ribbed Rich and me as we worried about our first experience in the matter.

"I don't want no doctor touchin' my balls," Rich said

"Don't be stupid. It's just a physical to hear your heartbeat n' check your reflexes n' stuff," Snorky answered.

"And pee in a jar." John added.

"Yeah, but THEN he's gonna touch your balls," Mark warned.

"Whaddya mean?" I inquired.

"He's gonna stick his finger under your balls and tell you to cough." Mark primed.

"What for?" I cringed.

To see if you got a hernia." John answered. Rich had the next question.

"What's a hernia?"

"I dunno, somethin'. Some sort of rip or tear, and if you got one, you can't do sports," Mark said.

"You're kiddin' me," I frowned.

"No we ain't," Mark, John, and Snorky piped in unison.

"The doctor finds out if you can do sports by stickin' his finger down there?" I asked.

"Yeah, and try not get a boner when the doctor does it!" Snorky challenged.

We all shuddered at our predicament.

We made the appointments with the doctor in our neighborhood for the following week. On the fated day, I arrived at the doctor's office. There were a couple other boys accompanied by their mothers in the waiting room, but I just walked in and sat down by myself, humming along to the canned Muzak that was piped into every room of the office. One boy finally came out of the examination room carrying a document signed by the doctor, and as he walked out the door with his mother, a nurse called out my name.

"Matt Gonder?"

"Here," I said, raising my hand automatically like at school.

"The doctor will see you now. Take this cup into the bathroom to give us a urine sample and then wait for the doctor."

I went through the door into a small bathroom, peed into the paper cup, and then waited. The doctor opened the door and shook my hand.

"Matt Gonder? C'mon in. Strip down to your underwear and socks and sit on the edge of the table."

I followed orders. He took the cup from me, told me to stick out my tongue and say "AH", pressing my tongue down with a popsicle stick and looking down my throat. Easy enough. Then he looked into my ears with a flashlight, took my pulse, temperature, blood pressure, listened to my heart through a stethoscope and had me breathe heavily as he listened to my lungs, tapped my knees to check my reflexes with a small hammer, and then said:

"Lie back on the table." I swallowed hard and laid back. He pressed my stomach in a few areas and then quickly slid his hand in my underwear and tucked a finger under my balls. Apparently used to witnessing the fear on young boy's faces at this moment, he smiled as he told me to cough. I coughed. He pulled his hand out and snapped the underwear elastic against my belly, making me cramp up on the table as he laughed.

"All done. You're in good shape, Matt. You can get dressed now."

It was over as quickly as that. I jumped off the table and got back into my clothes as the doctor filled out some papers on his desk.

"These are the documents you need for school. Have a fun year, Matt."

I thanked him, took my documents and ran out of the office. I couldn't wait to tell Snorky that I didn't get a boner.

Pre-school excitement began to get the best of us all. My brothers, sisters and I combed through the stores at the mall, looking for the cheapest deals to purchase new clothes, underwear and socks along with the Pee-Chee folders, Bic pens, pencils, paper and other school supplies we needed.

As summer vacation finally drew to an end, I began to feel like a full-fledged adult heading into the seventh grade. In 'no way' whatsoever could I continue dating Nancy Williams. After all, everyone knew she was still an "elementary" school girl so I dumped her, aware that it was simply time to move on to more mature women my age. I wondered how old Faye Dunaway was.

5. ABC

"Mark, John, Matt, Monica, Marguerite...Up and at 'em," Dad called out from the end of the hall, waking us from our slumber. Dad was always the first one up, had already shaved and was dressed and drinking coffee by the time he woke up the rest of us.

We all rolled out of bed, jumpy as fleas for the first day of school, took turns in the bathroom and then without a second thought Mark, John and I got dressed in our new jeans and white t-shirts, standard wear for the "grown men" of junior high in the early '70s. Marguerite and Monica however, took forever to get ready, unable to decide what dress to wear, making last-minute changes to the wardrobes they had decided upon the night before but somehow hated in the light of day. Finally after changing God knows how many times, they were clothed and then Marguerite ran up to me as I sat at the table finishing my bowl of Wheaties with Mark and John.

"Matt, will you make me some pigtails? Please, will ya'?"

"I'm eatin'. Ask Monica."

"She's still gettin' dressed. You do it for me, please?"

"Oh, geez, okay," I caved in.

I gulped down the milk at the bottom of my bowl and before I had time to place the bowl back onto the table, Marguerite shoved the hairbrush in my face, turning her back to me. I grabbed it and pulled the brush through her blond hair, but got caught on a huge balled-up clump at the nape of her neck. I tried to brush through the snag, but her fine hair wouldn't cooperate. I pulled harder.

"Ouch! Don't yank! That hurts, Matt!"

"Well, I can't help it. If you'd brush your hair more often, there wouldn't be a big 'ole rat in the back."

I tried to brush out the big wad of natty hair but finally gave up the battle and parted what I could of her hair that wasn't snagged up. I made two pigtails and bound each in a rubber band, leaving the big 'rat' hanging more exposed than ever in the part line on her scalp that pointed directly at the prominent baby dreadlock formed on her neck. I figured she couldn't see it, so why worry about it. Dad looked at his watch.

"Okay, kids, you better get goin'. Don't want to be late on your first day of school. Monica, you dressed yet?" He called down the hall.

Monica came running out from the bathroom, pulling the last curlers from her hair.

"I'm almost ready, Dad, I just gotta brush my hair and eat breakfast." she answered.

"Too late for breakfast now. Just grab a piece of bread and let's get a move on." Dad said.

"Quick, gimme the brush, Matt," Monica screeched.

I handed her the brush and she whipped it through her hair in rapid strokes. We all collected our Pee-Chees crammed full of our class schedules that had been mailed to each one of us, various documents and paper, pens and the lunch bags we had prepared and Dad shuffled us out the door, giving us each five cents for milk as he closed the door behind us.

"Have a good day, kids." Dad called out as we walked passed the car in the driveway.

"Bye, Dad, see ya tonight," we all replied.

Monica and Marguerite crossed the street and walked the block to Mirror Lake Elementary. I saw them join up with their friends Anita and Lori on their way. As I watched my sisters, I remembered foxy Miss Steele from the three weeks I spent with her last year in sixth grade, but my nostalgia fled as I heard Snorky, Rich, Dan and Don Hilderbrand, John Smith and our entire neighborhood gang waiting at the bus stop calling out to us.

"Hey, Gonders, hurry up, the bus is coming!"

We ran across the street to the bus stop. As soon as we arrived, the yellow school bus quickly appeared, screeching to a full stop. I felt nervous and ready for adventure as we climbed inside and took seats, but I quickly learned that it wasn't cool to show excitement on the first day of school. The eighth and ninth graders were discussing who their teachers were and sharing comments from last year's experiences with the frightened seventh graders.

"John, you sign up for Metal Shop?" Snorky chewed through his gum.

"Yep."

"Hey Matt, who'd you get for Social Studies?" Dan Hilderbrand asked.

"Mr. Sarver."

"I had him last year. He's boring, gives tons of homework. Who'd you get for Math?"

"Mrs. Scott."

"Oh God, old Vernet, tough luck for you." Snorky said between chews.

"I know." Mark added. "She choked me last year."

"She choked you?" I asked. Mark recounted the story.

"Yeah. There I was, mindin' my own business, just jokin' around with someone in class last year and old Vernet heard me, came running over and told me to be quiet. Then she started to walk away so I turned back to the person I was talking to and said 'now as I was saying before I was most rudely interrupted'. Vernet turned around, came running back at me and wrapped her wrinkly old fingers around my neck and started squeezing, but I didn't feel a thing! Swear to God! She stood there shakin' and chokin' me but she was so old and weak I could hardly feel her grip!"

Mark acted out the scene, leaving us all roaring with laughter.

"Hey Gonder, you playin' tuba in Band again this year?" John Smith asked Mark.

"Yep. B Band," Mark answered.

"Unless he gets thrown out." John joked.

"You were supposed to practice this summer, but I never saw you play it," Snorky chewed.

"No shit! That tuba just sat in the garage all summer." John tattled.

"Whaddya mean? I played it." Mark fibbed.

"Yeah right, how many times? Don Hilderbrand inquired.

"We never saw you touch it." Rich added.

Mark thought hard, stretching out the moment.

"Hmm lemme see now, I played it once or twice," Mark lied.

We all laughed.

"You big liar." I said.

"Well, I got a little busy," Mark offered in his defense.

"Tell that to Hart," John Smith added, making us all laugh even harder.

"Ah, feed 'em beans" was Mark's final word on the subject.

By that time, I wasn't sure if I should dread Junior High or not but I couldn't wait for my Art class. Our bus driver was a lady who chewed gum and wore her hair tied in a big, neatly combed bun on her head. I thought of Marguerite's rat hanging on her neck on the first day of fourth grade and felt sorry for her. We drove on through the streets and finally arrived at Sacajawea Junior High, a newer school built of cinder blocks and concrete that had opened in 1968, named after the Lemhi Shoshone Indian girl who joined the Lewis and Clark expedition. The school was divided into sections for each department, be it Math, English, Music, Science etcetera that were contained in their own freestanding building connected to the other structures by a covered concrete walkway. The campus boasted a large atrium in the center where students gathered between classes or at lunch.

One by one, we funneled out of the bus and joined the throng of kids arriving at the same time in their school buses. The seventh graders were all scurrying to the gymnasium to attend the first teacher-student meeting of the year. I followed the pack and quickly climbed to a seat in the bleachers. There was an overhead projector facing a large screen that displayed an aerial view of the school with all the departments labeled next to long tables with chairs that had been set up on the floor of the gym. Seated behind the table sat Mr. Pocrnich, the principal, Mr. McIntyre, the assistant principal, and a few other people. After Mr. Pocrnich welcomed us to Sacajawea and made a short speech introducing everyone around him, he passed the floor to another man, who stood up behind the table.

"Good morning and welcome to Sacajawea Junior High School. I'm Mr. Gish, and I'm one of the counselor's here. Now you all have been given smaller copies of the map you see projected here to help you find your classrooms. I know it might be confusing for you today, but by tomorrow none of you should get lost or be late for your classes. My office is inside the administration building, so if you need anything, come by and see me."

The gymnasium hummed with mumbling voices. Mr. Gish held up a small pad of yellow notes stuck together.

"Now listen up everyone and look here. This is important. These are Hall Passes. Since the campus is a large group of separate buildings, the only way to keep track of you all is with one of these. Every teacher keeps these under lock and key, and if you are caught running around the campus during school hours, you'll be required to present a hall pass signed by one of the teachers. If you get stopped by someone and are not carrying a signed hall pass, you will be taken immediately to the school office, where you will have to explain to one of the counselors like me what you're up to. Chances are I won't believe you, and if I don't, you may get suspended and sent home from school. And then you'll have to explain why to your parents. Also, if I or another teacher or anyone else needs to see you during class, one of these will be delivered to your teacher and handed to you, telling you where to go and explaining further instructions if necessary. Is that clear?"

"Yes," the whole group responded together.

"Okay then, when the bell rings, off you go to your first class. Have fun and work hard."

The bell rang a moment later, and we all stood up and scrambled off to our first seventh grade class.

My first class was Social Studies/English with Mr. Sarver, a thin man who wore glasses. Some of the desks were lined up against the walls so I nabbed one near the window next to a boy who introduced himself.

"Hi, I'm Jerry Leavenworth."

"Hi Jerry. I'm Matt Gonder."

A light went off. Could it be the name I heard all summer? I couldn't help myself.

"Hey Jerry, you know a girl named Lori Moss?"

"Um, brown hair, kinda…"

"Weird? Yeah, she's my next-door neighbor and she's really in love with you. She talked about you all summer."

"Oh God," he moaned.

We shared a laugh and on that common ground, our friendship was secured. Mr. Sarver explained that instead of having us work from a book, he would be handing out individual lessons printed on one or two sheets of paper or units for us to work on and then hand in for grading. This new method appealed to me, and seemed more like a game than an English lesson.

As I went to my classes throughout the day, I knew I was going to have fun in junior high which was doubly confirmed the moment I walked into Mrs. Jensen's Art class. I entered the room and smelled the paint, plaster, clay and art supplies that filled the air like perfume, permeating the walls and feeding my desire to create and make all kinds of cool stuff. Mrs. Jensen announced that we'd be working in many mediums during the quarter but in separate groups. One group would be drawing while another painted and another group would work with clay and ceramics, and then we'd all switch to another medium after a few weeks. I raised my hand and joined the ceramics group first, eager to learn how to throw something on the potter's wheel that sat in the corner of the room.

While I was lost in the nirvana of my Art class, Mark was in the Music building next to the parking lot in his B Band class, blaring out hideous sounds on his tuba, making Mr. Hart furrow his brow. Mr. Hart stopped everyone.

"That's fine. Mark Gonder, can I see you for a moment?"

Mark knew he was in trouble as he approached Mr. Hart.

"Mark, tell me the truth. Did you practice your tuba at all this summer?"

"A couple times, but I had to work at my Dad's shop in Seattle five days a week. I bought my brother John a new bike." He said, hoping to buy points with his brotherly kindness, but Mr. Hart didn't bite.

"That was nice of you, but what's a bike got to do with your practicing the tuba?"

"Sorry Mr. Hart. I kinda got a little busy."

"I can hear that. You're making lots of noise but not much music."

"Well, if it's music you wanna hear, you should listen to my little brother Matt, he sang in the all-city elementary choir last year in Tacoma."

"Again, what's that got to do with your tuba playing?"

"He was one of the six singers they picked from his school for the choir," Mark continued, hoping he'd buy his own redemption. Mr. Hart was intrigued.

"Oh? Where is he now?"

"Right here at Sac. He's a seventh grader."

"Well, I'm sure Mr. Warner is happy to have him in choir, but…"

"Oh, Matt's not in choir," Mark interrupted.

"Why not?"

"He took Art for his elective class."

"Well, it's too bad he couldn't give you his musicality to help you play the tuba before he ran off to Art class. Okay, Mark, we have no other choice but to have you come after school for a half hour twice a week to practice with me."

"Okay, Mr. Hart, but is that gonna interfere with football practice?" Mark asked, frightened.

"If it does, then you'll just have to come practice before school."

"Okay. See ya tomorrow."

We had five minutes between each class that allowed us ample time to rush to the next class across the campus. In the atrium, I ran into Jerry Leavenworth, who was coming out from P.E. as I headed in.

"Hey Matt. How's it goin'?"

"Okay. You?"

"Pretty good."

"You like your classes?"

I couldn't contain myself.

"My Art class is my favorite. Tomorrow we start working in clay."

I could see by the look on his face that he didn't get it.

Suddenly, one girl came running out of the girl's side of the Gym, sobbing loudly as she flew passed Jerry and me standing together in the atrium.

"What's wrong with her?" I frowned at Jerry. He cupped his hand and whispered.

"Oh man, she must be the girl everyone was talkin' about that went to P.E. wearing a training bra."

"What's wrong with that?"

"Training bras are for elementary school girls, dummy. Everyone was makin' fun and pickin' on her."

"Oh." I made a mental note to tell Monica to avoid having my sister live through that humiliation next year.

I went into the locker room and met Mr. Zuck, my P.E. teacher. We all quickly got dressed in our gym clothes and rallied in the gym, standing directly across from the girls who stood in their one-piece, light blue gym outfits. Mr. Zuck took roll call and began making announcements.

"Anyone caught snapping towels in the locker room will have to do laps in the gym wearing nothing but a jock strap. Understood?" Mr. Zuck cautioned.

"YES SIR," we all responded.

"Okay now, I want to collect all the forms you had signed by your doctors."

We took them out and handed them to him. There were two guys who hadn't had a physical completed by a doctor, so Mr. Zuck announced that they couldn't attend P.E. or sports until they had taken care of the matter. Then Mr. Zuck made us all do push-ups, sit-ups and run laps around the back of the school yard before he sent us off to the showers, where no one dared snap a towel at anyone.

After P.E., I went to Mrs. Scott's Math class, expecting to encounter a monster after hearing Mark's story on the bus, but she turned out to be nothing more than a harmless little grey sparrow. Ancient in years in comparison to the other teachers, she moved about at a slow pace and looked like she might keel over at any moment. Yet, when she began to warble on about Properties of Operations, Ratios, Equations or Decimal Points, she instantly became animated, alert and giddy as a schoolgirl, her wrinkled arms flailing about as she evangelistically tried to baptize us into her formulaic religion through a grey-toothed grin, all but foaming at the mouth. Listening to her, you'd think Math was better than food. Apparently we didn't share the same priorities. At one point, I walked over to grind my pencil in the sharpener hanging on the wall near the door, and saw a few signed yellow hall passes that Mr. Gish spoke about tossed into the garbage can beneath the sharpener. Discreetly, I took one out to get a good look at it, noticed that it was signed by "V. Scott" and then tossed it back in before taking my seat. We finished out the day, rode the bus home and that night, told Dad all about our classes and the people we had met, squirrelly as monkeys to return the following day.

6. EVIL WAYS

The next day, I had the routine down and couldn't wait to get back to school. The strange newness had worn off everything from the bus ride to the layout of the campus and I knew my way around. When I finally arrived at my beloved Art class, I felt like I had literally found paradise. Mrs. Jensen gave each of us in the ceramics group a ball of reddish-brown clay; teaching us the pinch method and inviting us all make a bowl or an ashtray. I loved feeling the clay that took form under my pressing fingers and found myself concentrating to the point of losing all notion of time.

Eventually, some girl entered the room and handed a yellow hall pass to Mrs. Jensen. She took it and announced:

"Matt Gonder?"

I turned my head to her and raised a beautifully

clay-stained hand.

"Over here."

She walked over and placed the hall pass on the table in front of me. I noticed the signature; a slanted, left-handed scribble of the initials "M.F.W."

"You're wanted in the Music department." She informed.

"What for?" I asked.

"Mr. Warner wants to see you. Cover your work with wet cheesecloth then wash your hands. As long as your work stays moist, you can pick up where you left off when you return."

I did as instructed, but did not welcome the interruption. I exited the classroom carrying the hall pass in my hand to avoid getting caught unarmed in the outdoor hallways. As I walked on, I reread the hall pass again and wondered what M.F.W. meant. I figured the "W" stood for Warner, since Mrs. Jensen mentioned his name in passing, but why did he want to see me? I crossed through the empty atrium, strolling through the school campus that appeared like a ghost town as everyone was indoors in his or her respective classes. I arrived at the Music department building and opened the door, entering a big room with wooden acoustic booms hanging from the ceiling. The floor plan was designed in levels climbing upwards with seats lined in rows. There was an upright piano on one side of the room, a music stand with a bar chair behind it in the middle of the room, and leaning over a big black grand piano near the door stood a dark-haired man busy writing notes with his left hand. Without looking up, he heard me come in.

"Yes?"

"Are you M...F...W?" I asked, reading the signed initials on the hall pass.

"Yes, I'm Mr. Warner," he answered, head lowered, eyes fixed on his notation.

"Oh, hi. I think I'm supposed to see you. I'm Matt Gonder."

He raised his head and focused on me with interest, dropping his pen onto the piano. He walked over to greet me with a smile, his eyes unblinking.

"Oh, yes. Hello, Matt Gonder."

I held up the hall pass for him to take. He showed no desire to retrieve it, so I stuffed it into my pocket.

"Hi. So what do you wanna see me for?" I stood guard near the door.

"I've heard a lot about you," he grinned with a twinkle in his eye.

"Ya' did?" I studied him, worried.

"Yes, I did. Mr. Hart told me you were in the all-city choir last year in Tacoma."

"Yeah. So?" My mind began to wander. Who was Mr. Hart and how did he know what I did last year? Mr. Warner pulled my attention away from my thoughts and back to the predicament at hand.

"Was that fun?" He appeared genuinely interested.

"Yeah." I answered, my mind flashing back to Mrs. Habedank's legs in the Pontiac.

"Well, Matt, I'd like you to sing something for me."

"What? Now? But, I'm supposed to be workin' on my ceramic bowl," I protested.

"This won't take long," he unsuccessfully assured me.

"But my clay's dryin' out!"

"It can wait."

"I wanna go back to my art class," I whimpered.

"You will, but first sing 'My Country 'tis of Thee' for me."

"Oh geez. Do I gotta?"

"Yes, Matt, you gotta," he reiterated my words,

holding his ground, leaving me no choice. I glared at him as I suddenly had a good idea what the 'M.F.' stood for in his signature.

"Okay then, gimme the note," I acquiesced with a moan, just wanting the torture to be over and get out of there.

"What?" he asked.

"Aren't you gonna gimme the note you want me to start out on? Everybody else does."

"They do, huh? Oh, okay then, start here."

He crossed over to the piano and tapped a key. I took the note and started to sing out the patriotic song very rapidly without conviction, all the while retaining my strategic get-away position near the door.

"Mycountry'tisoftheesweetlandoflibertyoftheeIsing."

"Slow down, Matt. Start again and this time, follow me."

I gave in and followed the tempo he conducted with his hands to make me hold certain notes, just like Mrs. Best and Mrs. Habedank had done last year. I did it his way and then finished on the exact note he played once I stopped singing, like always. Big deal. His eyes lit up as he smiled. I didn't give him the chance to speak out.

"Okay, you got your song, can I go now?" I asked, irritated.

"Yes, you can," he answered slowly, still grinning.

"Well, aren't you gonna gimme another hall pass to get back?"

"Not this time, Matt, because I'm going with you."

"Oh, okay." I stupidly trusted him.

We left the choir room together and walked down the concrete hallway. Mr. Warner walked uncomfortably close to me and just as I started to turn left past the music building to return to Art class, he grabbed me firmly by the arm.

"This way, Matt."

"What? But Art's over that way!"

"You're not going back to Art, Matt. You're coming with me and we're going to sign you up for Boy's Chorus."

"I don't wanna be in Boy's Chorus! I'm sick of singing, I wanna make some art!"

"With a voice like yours, it's a crime to not use it."

He kept dragging me towards the office. I tried to pull away from him without success. Mr. Warner, unlike

146

Mrs. Scott, definitely had a strong, firm grip and wouldn't let go of my arm. I had no choice but to go where he led me.

"You can't change my elective class. It's MY choice and I chose ART!"

"Well, Matt, you chose wrong. You've got to sing." He said calmly, pulling onwards.

"Well I 'ain't singin' and YOU can't make me!"

"We'll see about that."

He guided me through the doors and into the office. Mrs. Paige, the school secretary, sat behind a desk but smiled and stood up to greet us as we walked in.

"Hi Mr. Warner."

"Hello Mrs. Paige. This is Matt Gonder."

She looked at me and smiled broadly, full of warmth.

"Hi Matt Gonder. I'm glad to meet you. I'm Mrs. Paige, one of the school secretaries here."

"Hi," I answered coldly, rubbing my sore arm while glaring at Mr. Warner.

"Matt is a seventh grader. He signed up for Art class and we have to change that and put him into Boy's

Chorus," Mr. Warner instructed.

Mrs. Paige tried to be kind about the matter as best she could under the circumstances, but she could see I was not a happy camper.

"Oh, okay, but we'll have to take a look at his schedule. That might change a few of his other classes due to the rescheduling," she noted.

"Well, it has to be done. He's a talented singer."

"He is? Why, that's wonderful, Matt!" Mrs. Paige offered with a big smile.

"Is not," I mumbled under my breath.

Frozen, I watched as my Art class was scythed away with no consideration as to what I might have to say about the matter. I stood there silently in shock, unable to defend myself or fathom what was happening to me. I felt numb. Mrs. Paige combed through my schedule and only needed to make two changes. One of them was to place me in Mr. Dunham's Social Studies class and the other into Boy's Chorus, taking me out of Art and away from Mrs. Jensen and Mr. Sarver. She handed me the new schedule with a warm smile.

"Here you are, Matt. You can return to your regular classes today, but this new schedule will start tomorrow, okay? I'm sure you'll have lots of fun in Boy's Chorus with Mr. Warner."

"I doubt it," I answered with clenched teeth as I took the new schedule from her. I read the note she handed me.

"And there's two t's in my name," I said dryly. She looked mortified.

"Oh dear, let me fix that right away," she said, reaching out for the paper.

Mrs. Paige added one more 't' to my name and handed it back to me, looking at me with such remorse that I had to forgive her.

"Here you are, Matt with two t's. I'll never forget that again, I promise."

"Thanks, I guess," I said, taking the note back.

"Thank you, Mrs. Paige," Mr. Warner said with a victorious, shit-eating grin on his face.

"You're welcome," Mrs. Paige answered, adding "And here's a hall pass to get you back to Mrs. Jensen's Art class. Goodbye, Matt, see you soon."

"G'bye," I muttered deadly.

I took the hall pass from her. Mr. Warner and I turned and walked out of the office together. As soon as we crossed the threshold and were outdoors, I let him have it.

"Okay you win. Maybe you can make me GO to Boy's Chorus, but you can't make me SING! I'll never sing for you. NEVER!"

Mr. Warner sighed in my direction as he tried to reason with me but I would have nothing of it.

"Matt, calm down. I'm just trying to do what's best for you. You have a very special instrument. Our job here is to make sure you use your talents and develop them. You'll thank me later."

"That's what YOU think," I spouted as a final word before I ran away towards my beloved Art class.

I ran through the campus, entered Mrs. Jensen's classroom and held out the hall pass for her to retrieve.

"Hi Matt, just throw it in the wastebasket and take your seat," she instructed.

Don't ask me why, but instead of following directions, I folded the hall pass and tucked it into my pocket as a souvenir that sent me "to" Art class instead of "from". I returned to my worktable, removed the wet cheesecloth from my clay masterpiece and wanted to cry out in anger and injustice. I smashed my clay bowl with a clenched fist and Mrs. Jensen heard the noise and rushed over.

"Matt, what's wrong? Look what you've done. That was good work."

"Who cares? I can't come back tomorrow anyway," I answered sadly.

"Why not?" Mrs. Jensen asked.

"They changed my schedule. Startin' tomorrow I gotta go to stupid ole' Boy's Chorus instead of comin' here."

"Oh, I see. Well, there must be a good reason," Mrs. Jensen stated.

"A lousy one if you ask me."

The bell rang and we all grabbed our things and left the room. I looked around once before I walked out, silently saying goodbye to my ceramic dreams.

The rest of the afternoon was a fog to me. I went through the motions in my last two classes, too pissed off to really concentrate. When school let out, I climbed onto the school bus to go home and met up with my brothers, Snorky and Rich. I told them all about the hellish episode I went through with Mr. Warner, and how he just took me out of Art class.

"Can he do that?" Snorky asked.

"I thought it was an elective, your choice," John added in my defense.

"Yeah, really." Snorky didn't know what to say.

"What I don't get is how did he find out I was in all-city chorus last year?" I said.

Mark just shook his head, remaining completely silent, and was relieved when Rich finally put his two cents in.

"Well, I'm in Boy's Chorus, Matt. It's fun."

Mark took the bait.

"Yeah, Matt, listen to Rich, you'll have fun. You like singin'," he said, hoping to convince me.

"Not when somebody forces me to," I countered.

After a silent moment, Mark thought it best to change the subject.

"Hey, you guys wanna play some touch football down at Mirror Lake?"

His diversion was successful. We all ran home respectively once we had arrived at our stop, dumped our things and met up on the lawn in front of Mirror Lake Elementary. The grass spread out all along the school driveway, offering a soft green field to play on. We tossed the ball and chased each other until it began to get dark, when we split up and went our separate ways home.

"See ya tomorrow, Snork and Rich," Mark, John

and I yelled out.

"Yeah, see ya guys," they called back.

Dad wasn't home yet from work but we were used to fending for ourselves. Monica was eating a TV dinner and Marguerite was chatting on the phone as we walked into the house, and by the time Dad came home, he was too tired to discuss my choral predicament so I let it slide, determined to find my own solution.

I woke up the next morning and dragged myself from bed. The thrill of junior high school was definitely gone. In only two days after I had the routine down, I no longer wanted anything to do with it. I got dressed against my will and rode the bus in a daze. I went to my first few classes and went through the motions and met Mr. Dunham, who, as rumor would have it had been a Catholic Priest prior to becoming a teacher. A talented orator, he welcomed me into his Social Studies class and got on with the lesson at hand. I ran into Jerry in the atrium between classes and explained why I wasn't in Sarver's class anymore, promising to meet up with him after school. I ran to my next class, which, once that hour drew to a close, I knew my next class would be my first trip into the hellhole of Boy's Chorus. My heart sank and I longed for the nirvana of Art class. The bell rang at the end of Mr. Dunham's class and I knew I had but five minutes to get to the choir room but I took my time, dragging myself slowly through the outside halls against my will. I bumped into Rich outside the Music department.

"Hi Matt. C'mon in. You'll see, it's okay," Rich tried to convince me.

I slid into the room with a scowl on my face, feeling like a prisoner walking the last mile to stand before a firing squad and face death. Mr. Warner smiled as he handed me a folder full of sheet music.

"Hello, Matt. Welcome. Take this and grab a chair on the far left side of the room in the first tenor section."

I didn't respond. I followed instructions and took the folder, found a vacant chair and sat down glaring at him while repeating over and over in my head:

"I'm not singing and you can't make me. You can't make me, you can't MAKE me!"

Mr. Warner took control of the class.

"Okay now, take your seats everyone. Let's get to work. Please take out 'The Water is Wide'."

Everyone noisily yanked the song he requested from the music folders. Mr. Warner just stood there behind his music stand in the middle of the room with his arms raised in the air like a dictator, waiting for everyone to quiet and settle down in preparation to sing. As soon as all eyes were focused on him, Mr. Warner counted the tempo for Anita Glasford, a curly-haired ninth-grader who sat at the upright piano, while the big black grand piano stood near the door, untouched. Strange, I thought. Why doesn't she play the big piano? Oh who cares, not my problem, I told myself. As soon as the boys began to sing, I noticed they weren't singing in two part harmony but three, which surprised me, yet I just sat there with a zipped lip and a bored look on my face, pissed off to not be working my clay. I glanced at the sheet music, and sure enough, there were three distinct groups of black dots and lines that the three sections of boys more or less managed to comprehend and perform as they sang:

The Water is Wide I cannot get o'er

And neither have I wings to fly

Give me a boat that can carry two

And both shall row, my love and I...

I couldn't believe the sappy lyrics my poor ears were hearing. No way was I ever going to sing a word of that music from Hell, but now he wants me to row? Yeah, right. He's not gonna make up MY rules! I was sick of people telling me what to do. Anita played the vocal parts on the piano, one by one for each section, as requested by the M.F. tyrant. It was cool how she rarely peeked at the keys while she played, and secretly wished I could do the same. I thought of Aunt Mary, who had studied years to become a concert pianist, and wondered where she was. Mr. Warner looked at me a couple of times and I could tell he was disappointed that I wasn't singing along with everyone else. Good, I thought, that'll show him! He stopped the song many times to have Anita pound out sections where attention was required, and then finally he announced:

"Okay, let's run through it from the beginning with the accompaniment."

He waved the tempo with his hands for Anita, who effortlessly played the intro until finally the boys came in, singing their respective parts. It was kinda cool to hear three distinct vocal parts for the first time, but they didn't sing half as well as we did in Tacoma last year so why was I wasting my time? Once that song ended, Mr. Warner spoke out.

"Everyone! Hold that last note until I cut you off."

Yeah, he's good at cutting people off, I thought.

"Now let's take a look at Santy Anno," Mr. Warner announced.

Everyone pulled the music from their folders and sat in silent allegiance to the slave driver. Again, he counted the faster tempo for Anita, who took his direction like an obedient servant and played alone until the boys joined in, singing out:

We're sailin' cross the river from Liverpool

Heave away, Santy Anno

Around Cape Hope to Frisco Bay

Way out in Californio

I wished they'd sail away without delay. I was quietly intrigued by the melody sung in three-part harmonies, but I kept my mouth firmly shut. I could hear that most of the singers were mediocre anyway, singing off-key and not in sync with each other, nothing like the quality All-City choir I had grown accustomed to last year, and M.F.W. thinks I'm gonna THANK him for taking me out of Art class and forcing me to come here for this? Over my dead body! The hour seemed to drag on forever as they finished that song then worked on *Sloop John B* and *Fast Freight*, yet I held my silent ground, refusing to take part in Mr. Warner's evil ways.

As soon as the bell rang, I left the music folder on my seat and ran out of the choir room, proud of myself for not giving in, off to my next class. I found Jerry near the buses after school and we rode back home together. He said he missed me in Sarver's class but told me his family was moving to a new town in a week anyway. I sure knew what that felt like, the loneliness and constant changes that came from moving so often in my own life. He asked me if I wanted to have his yellow parakeet he named Katie. I accepted right away, went over to his house and picked up Katie and her cage. I wished Jerry luck in his new school, knowing I'd probably never see my new friend again. I brought Katie home, and she chirped and bounced around and quickly became a new family member.

Against my will, I attended Boy's Chorus each day, acting the part of an angry inmate without singing one note and instead of participating vocally, I yawned or cast frosty looks to publicly feed my battle against Mr. Warner. My bad attitude routine went on for what seemed like an eternity to a twelve year-old boy; close to three whole weeks. However, whenever there was a problem in a song, rhythmic or melodic, Mr. Warner did something no other teacher I had ever seen do before. He walked over to the chalkboard, wrote out and worked through the problem in music theory terms and symbols. Against my better judgment, I found myself fascinated as he explained what all those black notes and squiggly things meant on the printed sheet music above the words we -they- were singing.

Up until then, I had been given no formal music training whatsoever and just sang by ear, but Mr. Warner firmly believed in teaching the scholastics of music education, against the wishes of his peers who wanted him to 'entertain' the students by basically babysitting them with a song or two. Unable to follow their directives, he explained every facet of the language of music to his pupils, making us -them- work as hard in choir as one might in Math. I couldn't help but welcome the challenge. The cracks in my anger foundation began to appear and crumble as he taught how a whole note equals two "half notes" that in turn equal four "quarter notes" which multiply into "eighth notes" or "sixteenth notes", and how the dot after a note gives it one half more value, and the different rests we -they- had to respect. All of a sudden, music began to mean something that required thinking and concentration, not just a good ear. The more Mr. Warner explained music theory to us, the more I wanted to put the logic to test. It was like learning a new language, rendering it more difficult for me to feign boredom as he opened a new door in my world. I loved the tricks he gave us: FACE was the trick to remember the notes in the spaces on the music staff. "Fast Cars Go Down Another Extra Bump" was the trick phrase he gave us to remember how sharps FCGDAEB are always patterned at the beginning of the key signature. It all amazed me.

I wanted to master this new language and decided to participate silently, but then Mr. Warner passed out more sheet music for us -them- to sing. He gave the tempo to Anita and she began to play the intro to *Five Hundred Miles*, one of the songs we'd sing in the car with Dad, and here we -they- were singing it again, but this time in harmony. I couldn't help myself so I began to sing through clenched teeth with the other boys in my Tenor 1 section, yet when Mr. Warner looked my direction, I clammed up and displayed a cold face that showed him I didn't care. But damn it, I loved that song so I figured what the hell, I could sing this one song but I would never give in and sing any of the others.

If you miss the train I'm on

Matthew Gonder

You will know that I am gone

You can hear the whistle blow

A hundred miles

Mr. Warner wore me down slowly, writing more music theory stuff on the chalkboard every day, capturing my undivided attention. He explained more and more symbols printed onto the sheet music: fermatas, crescendos, decrescendos and accents. It was candy to me. That was neat enough, but then he'd scare the shit out of us by randomly choosing one student to count out a measure. Then he'd ask another to count out the following measure. I'd sit there working up a sweat as I silently figured it all out in my brain. I'm sure he noticed that I was interested in the theory because he finally chose me. Nervously, I slowly counted out my measure and was relieved to not make one mistake. He smiled at me, happy to see that I had finally bit his musically baited hook and appeared hungry for more.

"Good, Matt."

I was relieved to not blunder and look stupid in front of everyone else. Soon enough I was singing everything he handed us, putting to test the new information I had soaked up like a thirsty sponge. I was actually learning to read music, no longer was I just listening and repeating what I heard from memory. Singing a fourth interval on paper became as easy as singing "Here comes the bride". Mr. Warner had awakened the insatiable music monster in me, and I couldn't get enough. I would nab him after class, hold up the sheet music and point at a symbol I didn't understand.

"Mr. Warner, what's this thing here for?"

Ever patient and accommodating, he'd grin and answer my unending questions.

"That's the time meter, Matt. The top number tells you how many counts there are per measure and the bottom number tells you what kind of note gets one full count. This meter says 4-4, which means there are four counts per measure and a quarter note gets one full count.

"Oh, okay," I said, ready to run out the door, but he wouldn't leave well enough alone. He had to go for blood.

"So tell me, Matt, if the meter says 6-8, then what does that mean?"

Refusing to look stupid in his eyes, I concentrated hard before answering.

"Um...six counts in a measure and...a eighth note gets a count?"

"That's right, Matt. How about 3-2?"

"Three counts a measure and a half note gets a count?"

"That's it," he smiled at me proudly with those twinkling eyes.

"Oh, okay," I answered, refusing to say the words 'thank you' to him, God forbid. The bastard became my favorite teacher but I staunchly refused to give him the satisfaction of knowing it. I turned and ran through the double doors en route to my next class.

As time passed, my incorrigible student persona completely waned. I participated fully in Boy's Chorus, proudly singing out while insatiably consuming the printed black ink music symbols like licorice as Mr. Warner explained them in detail on the chalkboard in his slanted, left-handed scroll. Once I began applying myself in class, it became apparent that I was one of the best singers, thanks to comments made by some of the other singers and Anita, the pianist, yet I knew that Eric Hamre was considered the number one tenor and had a strong vocal technique that I didn't possess, where I had something raw and emotional in my voice that he didn't have. Eric was a nice boy who didn't have a competitive bone in his body and just appeared to enjoy singing with ease, while Mr. Warner was obliviously contented to have good singers in his classes and to teach us all what he knew without playing favorites. I became a happy contender.

One day, a tall man came into the choir room while

we were singing, and handed Mr. Warner a pile of sheet music. I turned to Ted Slaeker, another singer, sitting near me.

"Who's that guy?"

"The Band teacher, Mr. Hart."

"HART?"

It suddenly all made sense. I had found the missing link. My very own big brother, Mark, had sold me off to his band teacher. Traitor. My blood began to boil. Initially, I swore I'd get even, but by that time I was having so much fun in choir that I let go of my feelings of fratricide.

While Mark the traitor was "playing" the tuba in "B-Band" (his lame musicality did not allow him membership in the better "Concert Band") and I was in Boy's Chorus learning music theory and songs for the upcoming concert, John was up to his own tricks in Metal Shop class, where a gang of boys had been ordained in the current fashion of making Kung-Fu throwing stars that they cut from the sheet metal in class. The small group of crafty metal workers secretly gathered outside the gymnasium after school, where naturally a contest of "who can get his star stuck the highest on the siding" took place. John and his buddies threw until their Kung-Fu star stock was depleted and the poor cedar gymnasium wall was littered with silver stars penetrated into its flesh, gleaming in the sunlight.

There they remained, 20 feet up until the day they fell out on their own, which was months later, while some remained forever. We admired the handiwork as we ran laps during Mr. Zuck's gym class, proud of our brothers and their craftsmanship.

Meanwhile, back at Mirror Lake Elementary, Monica and Marguerite were caught up in their own scholastic affairs. Monica loved to sketch and paint, and seemed to be always drawing a portrait of someone or a landscape. Marguerite joined a beginning band class, announcing to us all that she would follow in her big brother Mark's footsteps into the world of brass by playing the trombone. Follow she did. She had an ear just like her brother, made of the same tin as the instruments. Dad rented the shiny new trombone for her to take to school and practice on at home, but aside from one or two painful evenings on which she blared out screeching noises that sounded like an animal's foot was caught in a hunting trap, that poor instrument collected dust in her closet and rarely saw the light of day, not unlike like Mark's tuba that shacked up in the garage, begging for air. In essence, her dream came true as her musical ability perfectly emulated that of her big brother.

Along with the school classes we attended, extracurricular activities also began to fill up our agendas. John would run down to the convenience store at the end of the street from the school to buy all-day suckers for five cents a piece and sell them on campus for ten cents each, making a good profit from a simple one block jaunt. This routine went on for a time, until one day he got caught and was taken to the office and immediately suspended from school. That night, being the "artiste" of the family, as Dad called me, I forged Dad's signature onto the paper John needed to return to school the next day. My siblings always came to me whenever they needed Dad's signature for school, as you never knew what time he would come home, so we figured why bother him with the petty issues we could easily handle ourselves?

Very soon and quite organically, my gift for calligraphy rapidly developed at Sacajawea Junior High as well. I had collected signed hall passes from many of the teachers and would practice their signatures at home, choosing the simplest ones to copy. Teachers often forgot to lock the virgin hall pass pads away, so swiping one from their desks was easier than taking candy from a baby. I always carried a pad in my pocket and earned a good reputation throughout the school for forging both Mrs. Scott's and Mr. Warner's signatures for friends who wanted to skip a class. Since hundreds of hall passes circulated throughout the school each day, the teachers barely glanced at them once they were handed out and nobody ever questioned the fact that Mr. Warner urgently needed to see so many students who weren't even members of his choirs. Needless to say, he never found out about my scam either, because once a student got the hall pass to go see M.F.W., they most certainly did whatever they freely chose to do without setting foot anywhere near the choir room.

Mark and John had both signed up to play on the football team. Dad paid their uniform fees and they both talked often about the thrill of battling it out on the field. I was uninterested in contact sports, being the scrawny one of our litter. After witnessing a few students around school coping with injuries from football, I couldn't comprehend what all the fuss was about. I had no desire to hobble about on crutches or break my back and knees, so when asked if I wanted to partake, I went so far as to show up for the first practice until I saw a group of boys run at the tackle sled as if they had just run against a brick wall. I immediately declined, imagining the poor boys that would replace the apparatus during the game. A few gave me grief for not 'being a man' like my two brothers, but I didn't cave in to the peer pressure. I liked Mr. Zuck's P.E. class with the physicality that gymnastics, track and wrestling offered, where I got a good workout without breaking any bones and was mainly competing with myself for improvement, but I did not have a taste for the aggressive contact sports. If some thought that made me less than a man, then so be it. For a brief moment I wondered if something was wrong with me for not wanting to play football like my brothers. I asked Dad, who told me not to pay heed or "give a good God damn" what anybody else thought I should do, but instead to do what was right for me.

7. GIMME DAT DING

In the early '70s, schools had funds to offer a variety of clubs young people could join to expose them to anything from sailing to cooking or music and sports. There was always something to keep everyone busy. Boredom wasn't a word in our vocabulary. We flourished on our own individual activity schedules as the warm Indian summer days cycled into autumn chills, the green vegetation surrounding us turning hues of yellow, orange, brown and red. After school, if and when we were home and not running around with friends, we'd sit in front of the black and white TV screen watching our favorite shows: *Bonanza, Mannix, The Odd Couple, Mod Squad, Room 222, Hawaii Five-O, Marcus Welby, M.D.* (that we nicknamed "Marcus Welby, V.D."), *Here's Lucy, Ironside,* or *Gunsmoke.* Many shows had a popular theme song that opened each episode, and I knew them all by heart:

Come ride the little train that is rollin' down the tracks to the junction...

Just sit right back and you'll hear a tale, a tale of a fateful trip...

The bluest skies you've ever seen are in Seattle...

Who's the girl with sunshine in her smile?...

Here's the story, of a lovely lady, who was bringing up three very lovely girls...

Green Acres is the place to be, farm livin' is the life for me!...

I'm so glad we had this time together, just to have a laugh or sing a song...

Hello world, hear the song that we're singin', c'mon get happy...

Come and listen to my story 'bout a man named Jed...

Diamonds, Daisies, snowflakes...

Love American style, truer than the red, white and blue woo, Wooo, WOOO!...

People let me tell you 'bout my best friend...

In any given week, a long list of popular stars hosted their own weekly variety show extravaganzas full of comedic skits and musical numbers. Pick a night, and you might see one or more of the following hour-long variety shows of entertainment: Ed Sullivan, Rowan and Martin's Laugh-In, Dean Martin, Jackie Gleason, Don Knotts, Andy Williams, Carol Burnett, Tim Conway, Jim Nabors, Tom Jones, Glenn Campbell, Flip Wilson, Johnny Cash, Pearl Bailey, Red Skelton, Debbie Reynolds, and Lawrence Welk. Music and comedy flowed into American homes every night, entertaining millions of families. And then there were the commercials. Coca Cola wanted to "Teach the World to Sing" while McDonalds preached "You Deserve a Break Today". Another commercial in particular ran all the time promoting the Polaroid Swinger instant camera. I'd sing along with Barry Manilow as he chimed:

Meet the swinger, Polaroid swinger

Meet the swinger, Polaroid swinger

It's more than a camera, it's almost alive

It's only nineteen dollars and ninety-five

Swing it up, it says "yes"

Take the shot, count it down, zip it off!

The idea of having my own camera to capture our lives on film really did it for me. I instantly knew what I wanted for Christmas and I began dropping daily hints by singing the commercial song at the top of my lungs every time the damn thing aired to make sure my wish was clear to everyone. Okay, so I announced it outright and often.

Sporty Roofs was growing so rapidly as the vinyl trend reached its zenith. Hundreds of vinyl-topped cars could be seen driving all over Seattle and the vicinity, while Dad and Lyle barely had enough time to top the cars and stay on top of all the paperwork and billing that piled high on the desks in the office. The cost Dad and Lyle charged per car varied between $125-$175, depending on vinyl grade choices, which could be anything from a mono-colored naugahyde to a paisley pattern that matched the interior. Cars lined up the parking lot every day of the week, anxiously waiting their turn to be dolled up. Word of mouth had spread to the point where car dealers just dropped another car off as soon as there was space available on the lot. Dad and Lyle met a man in his sixties named Gordy at King's, and brought him in to handle all the special upholstery headliner, interior and vinyl seat covering jobs that came through the shop. Gordy, very qualified at his craft, had just refurbished the booths at King's Restaurant in diamond-tucked dark red vinyl with gold buttons.

One night after oiling up with Lyle and Gordy, Dad brought home a special pen from King's that, by turning the barrel, displayed many photos of naked ladies inside. Rumor had it they were photos of the waitresses at

King's. John swiped it from Dad's room and showed it to Mark and me. The next day he took it to school and became popular for a week until teachers began to ask what it was he was showing everyone. John, to save himself from getting in trouble, quickly put the pen back on the nightstand in Dad's bedroom. We were all in bed one night when I heard Dad fumble through the front door, banging into the entry hall wall. I called out.

"Dad, is that you?"

"Howdy!" he slurred. I could tell he was oiled up, but I knew he'd sleep it off like always, so it didn't worry me. He usually just hobbled off to bed, but this time, he crept into my room and sat on the edge of my bed and spoke to me in whispers.

"Matt-sue, you asleep?"

"Nope."

"I need to talk to you 'bout somethin'."

"Okay, Dad, what's up?"

He sat on the edge of my bed and writhed out his remark.

"I'm in love, Matt."

"With that lady you wrote the poems for?"

"Yes, Ann, but I don't know what to do," eeked out

his whisky-laced reply.

I could tell he was gonna pour out his heart so I just waited.

"She's a good woman and I think I want to get married again. Would that be okay with you, chief?"

I couldn't remain silent.

"If you're happy, then, yeah, do it, Dad."

"Ya think I oughta do it?"

"Sure. Where's she live?"

"Tacoma."

Oh God, not Tacoma again, I thought. My stomach cramped.

"We don't have to move back to Tacoma, do we?"

"No," he smiled. "She'd come here. What do you think about having a new mother?"

"I don't know, okay."

"Well, would you take a drive down with me to meet her on Sunday?"

"I'll go with ya, Dad," which triggered the Tacoma treat he used to get for us in my mind.

"Can we get fried chicken and jojo's after?"

"Sure we can. Okay, Matt-sue, then Sunday it is."

He got up to leave but stopped, turning back.

"You remember the poems I wrote?"

"Sure I do."

"Well, I started to write another one tonight."

"Read it to me."

"It's not finished, but here's the first lines."

He pulled a cocktail napkin from him breast pocket, cleared his throat and began to recite.

To Kathy

A toast I drink to Kathy

Who tends a cocktail bar

A surface smile she gives me

That says, "don't go too far..."

He stopped the recitation abruptly, shoving the cocktail napkin back into his pocket.

"It's not all there, and besides, I just got carried

away at King's tonight, talking to the bartender about Ann."

"Who's Kathy?" I asked, wondering if her photo was in the pen John swiped.

"The bartender. Whaddya' say we get some shut-eye, Matt-sue?" He stood up and headed for the door.

"G'night."

"G'night. Don't let the bedbugs bite."

The following Sunday, Dad and I drove down together to Tacoma. I don't know why he only chose me, maybe because he read his poems to me, but there we were, Dad and me alone in the car. I told him all about Boy's Chorus and Mr. Warner as we drove into town and up to her house, a run-down old Craftsman that reminded me of our house in Portland. We walked up to the porch. The front door was wide open, a radio blared Three Dog Night's *Black and White* and we could see clear through the living room into the kitchen, where Ann stood hovering over her open stove. She waved us in and we crossed her threshold, walking through her sparsely furnished living room and dining room to join her in the kitchen. She smiled but didn't budge from her stove. Dad spoke first.

"Howdy! This here's my number three son, Matt."

"Hi, Matt," she answered softly.

"Are you a football player, too?" she asked. Dad came to my rescue.

"No, Mark and John are the football players. This here's Matt, my 'artiste'," Dad announced, patting me on the back.

"Hi. Where are your kids?" I couldn't think of anything else to say. I liked her immediately because she didn't seem to put on airs to impress me. She just stood over the stove with her foot on the open door, clutching her sweater while she turned her head to talk to us, as if we'd known each other forever.

"Oh, they're all out playing or running around somewhere. I don't really know. I'm here alone and too cold to do anything but stand right where I am."

"Oh."

Dad smiled and cut the visit short.

"Well, we'll let you get on with your day. We just wanted to stop by and say hello."

"Okay, Jim. Nice to meet you, Matt," she said softly.

"You, too. See ya."

"I'll call you later," Dad whispered, leaning in to kiss her. It was strange to see Dad like that, all mushy.

She remained right there, hugging her stove. We turned and headed through the rooms back to the front door. Dad turned to wave at her as I walked to the car. Our visit was over so quickly that I had to say something about it as soon as we drove away.

"That was quick, Dad. I thought we were gonna stay there longer."

"I wanted to surprise her so you could see how she really is."

"Oh, okay. She's nice. Can we get chicken and jojo's now?"

"Okey dokey," he smiled.

Dad had me wait in the car while he poured down a couple of beers at the 48th street Tavern, and then he showed up at the car, carrying my deep-fried poultry and potato treat that I gobbled up while he drove us back home.

I was a good student in my other subjects and breezed through almost every lesson except for Mrs. Scott's math class which was full of boring stuff to learn like "Properties of Operations" and "Decimals", which my brain barely digested, but after learning music theory, thanks to Mr. Warner, I wanted to play the piano as easily as Anita Glasford played. She showed me where middle C was on the keyboard, explained the octave runs and the black keys and how they all referred to the notes on the sheet music, and I took it from there, "squatting" one of the two practice music rooms every day as soon as school let out. After all, the school had a night bus available for students who remained on campus late and there stood an upright piano in a soundproof room that was all mine for a couple of hours. I lost track of time as I fumbled through the simple piano accompaniment to *The Water Is Wide* that I plucked on endlessly, vowing to master. Eventually, Mr. Warner opened the door to stick his head in.

"Matt, it's time to go home now."

I folded up my sheet music, said goodnight and caught the late bus. I wanted to play the piano more than anything and was jealous of all those who had their own at home. I stayed late at school almost every day for the following few weeks in one of the practice rooms to play until Mr. Warner popped his head in to send me home on the late bus. I was hooked. One night at home, I finally got the gumption to ask Dad.

"Dad, I REALLY wanna play the piano."

"Ya do, huh?"

"Yeah, more than anything. Can ya get me one, please, please?"

"A piano, huh?" He looked a bit worried by my request.

"Yeah!"

"Well! I guess it's in your blood. Grandma was a piano teacher, ya know."

"I remember. She used to play Grandpa Gonder's favorite song *Beautiful Dreamer* for us all the time in Spokane."

"I'll be damned. You remember that?"

"Yeah. And Aunt Mary was a concert pianist, right?"

"Well she gave it a shot, worked hard at it for years and damn near made it, too, but I guess it wasn't in the cards."

"But it is in mine! Please can we get one, please?"

He was happy to see me so excited over something.

"Tell ya what, Matt-sue, we'll see what we can do."

"Thanks, Dad."

That was good enough for me. Whenever Dad pronounced those words, you knew your request was a sure thing. I ran around telling everyone I'd have my own piano real soon. I announced the news to all my friends. I proudly told Mr. Warner that soon I wouldn't have to stay late after school to play on the practice room piano because I'd have my own at home. Every night, if

Dad's car pulled into the driveway, I'd run out to greet him and ask if he had any news.

"I'm still workin' on it, Matt-sue," he said with a laugh.

In preparation for the arrival of my coveted instrument, I grabbed the allowance money I had saved and ran to the mall that Saturday, where a grey-haired man gave piano lessons in a heavy German accent for five dollars a shot in a small music store near Woolworth's. I pushed open the glass door and walked in with confidence to introduce myself. The man was very kind and could plainly see I possessed a budding passion to master the percussion instrument. He had me fill out an information form that needed to be signed by my parents and gave me an appointment the following Tuesday afternoon for my first class.

I told no one about my lessons. Tuesday arrived and I showed up on time with the information document bearing Dad's freshly forged signature, no other questions asked. He handed me a beginning piano book, invited me to sit at his baby grand in the seat next to him and began my first professional lesson.

"The piano is made up of 88 keys and the first key to recognize on the piano is middle C," he informed.

"You mean this one?" I proudly responded, reaching out to tap the white middle C key, having learned from Anita Glasford in Boy's Chorus. After all, I couldn't let him think I was a total beginner.

"Very good," he said.

He then showed me how to play a running major scale with the correct fingering, using the thumb to play the fourth note on the right hand and the middle finger to play the sixth note of the climbing scale on the left hand. He did it real fast and whizzed up and down the keyboard as if it were nothing. Wow, I thought, how cool was this? I played a bit bumpy at first, but quickly caught on to what he intended me to do, certain that I'd fearlessly master it soon on my own piano. Then we opened the book and he chose the first piece I was to play with both hands at the same time following the fingering numbers written above the notes. The hour went by in a flash. He told me to practice minimum one hour every day until I could play the scale smoothly with no breaks and to work on the piece he had selected for me, adding that he'd see me next Tuesday. I paid him the five dollars and bid him farewell, leaving the store in a state of bliss, finally having found my calling.

Dad drove us all to Ann's house that night for dinner in an effort for everyone to get acquainted. She prepared and served a simple meat and potatoes meal that we ate surrounded by her five kids who seemed nice enough, but with no affinities to bind us, we felt more like guests than family, rendering conversation stiff and clumsy. No one had much to say outside the same questions everyone asked.

"How's school going?"

"Fine."

"More potatoes?"

"Sure, thanks."

Although Ann and her kids seemed normal, thoughts of living under someone else's rules like we did at the Anderson's and Miss Lucy's flooded my head. I remained silent, observing everyone without saying a word, because more than anything I wanted Dad to be happy. Dad tried to lighten the moment with his usual humor, but Ann's kids didn't know him well so his comic efforts were in vain. I knew what he was trying to do, but I felt paralyzed and unable to jump in the conversation. We finished dinner and drove home silently, tired and wondering how we were going to adapt to having new brothers and sisters living with us.

I carried the music book to Sacajawea every day and ran to the two soundproof practice rooms after school, which were offered to students on a first-come first-served basis, but someone else had arrived before me, taking both rooms on three occasions, As a result, I only practiced my lessons twice that week, and was not able to master the scales or the two-handed piece for my next lesson. I couldn't practice throughout the weekend, having no access to a piano, and when Monday rolled around I got lucky to nab the practice room after school, but it wasn't enough to make up for the lost time.

When Tuesday afternoon came around, I returned to the piano store at the appointed hour, confident I could bluff my way through. As soon as I sat down behind the baby grand, I was instructed what to do.

"Let's begin with your major scales, Matt."

"Okay."

I played through the scale with my right hand and got through it okay with only a slight hesitation where my thumb was supposed to reach under and play the F key.

"Hmm. Now with the left hand," he announced eerily.

I took a deep breath, aware that he had just kicked me in the balls. I played. The first five notes flowed smoothly, but there was a definite lull when my middle finger rolled over to play the sixth note. The man sighed.

"And now with both hands."

God help me, I thought. I tottered through the task like an epileptic on a roller coaster, starting over several times until my teacher placed his hands over mine to make me stop the torture.

"Tell me, Matt, did you practice every day?"

"Yeah," I lied, afraid he'd throw me out.

"Well, you certainly need to practice more."

Oh God, I thought. Now he thinks I'm a dummy no-talent and he's wasting his time.

"I will. I'll get it," I promised, swearing I'd find a way to step up to the challenge quickly.

I fumbled through the rest of the lesson, paid him and told him I'd see him next Tuesday as I went through the glass door, running over to Woolworth's for a bag of popcorn to snack on the walk home. That night, Dad came home from work and wasn't smiling. After dinner I broached the piano subject once more, anxious and impatient as ever. But this time, Dad looked at me with tears in his eyes.

"Matt, I'm so sorry. I've called every goddamn piano store from here to Tacoma and Seattle and no one will let me buy one on credit. Pianos 'aint cheap and I can't afford to lay out a thousand bucks like that. I just don't have it. Everything I got, and it 'aint much, is invested in building the business right now. I even called the bank for a loan and them cocksuckers won't help me, either. I tried everything, but right now, I just can't do it."

I hid my disappointment from him, forcing a smile.

"It's okay, Dad. No biggie," I lied, hoping to make him feel better.

"I'll be a sonofabitch. The one goddamn thing you ask me for and I can't give it to you. Maybe next year things'll be different, but right now, Matt, I just can't swing it and it pisses me off. Dammit, I can do for everyone else but I can't seem to help you the one time you ask for something important. I'm real sorry, Matt."

"Don't worry about it, Dad."

I decided to change the subject to make him feel better.

"Hey Dad, how's it goin' with Ann? When are you guys gonna get married?"

He stirred a bit and I knew I'd laid a bomb.

"We're not, Matt."

"What?" I was surprised.

"Well, Ann has her five kids and I've got mine, and she has her way of raisin' hers and I've got mine, so we just decided to let it be."

"Oh. Okay. I'm sorry, Dad."

"Don't be. Chalk it up to something that happened on the move out west; that's all it is."

He didn't want to continue the discussion, so he went into the kitchen to fry up a steak. I went out to the back yard and sat on the patio. Marguerite was playing with her friend Anita and could tell I was upset about something. I made the sad announcement that I wasn't getting a piano, and instantly, Anita came to my rescue.

"We got a piano at our house you can come play if you want."

I could hardly believe my ears.

"Really?"

"Sure. There's one in the basement nobody plays and I'll ask my mom but I'm sure she'll let ya."

She knew what my next question was and answered it before I could open my mouth.

"I'll go ask her now. I'll come right back and tell ya. Come with me, Marguerite."

She lived a couple houses away from ours down on 314th Street in one of the few split-level homes in our neighborhood. I sat back on the patio and waited impatiently. After the longest quarter hour in my life, Marguerite and Anita returned, walking slowly, sucking on popsicles. I was fit to be tied.

"What took ya so long?" I yelled, waiting for the verdict.

"Sorry, my mom said yes, you can come over. How about tomorrow night?"

"Sure, great!" I accepted with joy.

I jumped at the offer and couldn't wait until the next school day let out. I rode the bus home and ran over to Anita's. She escorted me down into her basement, where sure enough, a dusty old mahogany upright piano hid against the wall behind boxes of junk.

"Just put all that stuff on the floor," Anita invited.

I uncovered the keys and sat on an old kitchen chair. The piano was horrendously out of tune, but it was a piano and as such had earned my respect. I practiced my scales and two-handed piece for over an hour, then shut the piano, feeling elated as I climbed upstairs to thank Anita's mom. Anita met me at the top of the stairs, informing me that her mom wasn't home. She led me to the door and said I could come back the next day.

I showed up on time the next day, but there was no one home so I kicked pebbles on the way back to my house feeling abandoned, jealous that they had a piano that nobody wanted just rotting away in the basement. I stalked Anita's house everyday and got lucky a few times, finding someone home who would let me play my annoying music scales, but I soon realized that the noise coming from the basement was more of a nuisance to them than anything else and they were just being polite. My schedule didn't mesh with Anita's or her mom's, so I decided to put my piano hopes on hold for the time being until I could find another solution. I didn't return for my piano lessons anymore, either, as I figured what's the use if I couldn't practice. I would avoid walking past the piano teacher's store whenever I went to the mall, and resorted to the practice rooms at school whenever I felt the need to tickle the ivories, resolving myself to the fact that having my own piano simply wasn't meant to be.

But I didn't let it get me down. Throughout autumn, outside of football practice or other extracurricular activities, Mark, John and I would hook up with our neighborhood buddies, Snorky and Rich, looking for some new activity to engage in. On occasion, our band of neighborhood pals expanded to include John Smith, John Fernandez, Jeff Allen, Rusty Franseen, Marty Rymes, Chris Artman, or Dave and Dan Hilderbrand, who would eagerly join in our mischief. One evening, just as darkness set in, John Smith taught us something we never forgot. 8th Avenue South, the street we lived on, was a fairly busy street, acting as an easy access between 312th and 320th, so instead of fighting the traffic lights on Pacific Highway, drivers would often choose to cruise past our house. Knowing this, John Smith gave us all jobs to perform individually. He and my brother John rode their bikes down to 320th to the huge garbage bin behind the Safeway store, where dozens of eggs - past their shelf life - were piled up. They each grabbed a dozen and rode back to our house, where the rest of us waited with the items we were to pick up at home. Everyone parked his bike in our back yard, where John Smith warned us to think and act fast or the prank wouldn't work.

Each of us, prepared to do our part of the job, lined up and headed out to the front yard in the dark, waiting until no cars were coming down the street. Holding a small pebble taped to the end of a long piece of kite string, John Smith ran out and threw the rock over the telephone wire that crossed the busy 8th Avenue that ran in front of our house. The rock whipped around the wire a few times, creating a secure bind and leaving the long thin string hanging down in the middle of the street. Then, as fast as we could in sequential formation, Rich and Snorky taped an egg to the hanging end of the string right at windshield height, then I spread mayonnaise on the egg, Mark and John covered it in ground coffee and then we all ran back and hid behind the bushes to watch.

Soon enough, a car came whizzing through the intersection, colliding into the egg that splattered all over the windshield, the driver slammed on the brakes and cursed as they looked around until, realizing they'd been had, slowly drove off. Needless to say, this was thrilling to us. We spent the whole evening repeating our prank, egging cars and laughing in the bushes, never once getting caught by the furious drivers. Finally, when we ran out of eggs, we congratulated ourselves as we recounted our amazing exploits, then said goodnight and went home, setting a date to get together the following evening to do it again. We became addicted to scaring the drivers and watching them swerve and screech to a halt before swearing and driving off, and found ourselves engaged in our rotten egg hanging shenanigan almost every night for a couple of weeks.

Each day, the whole adventure gained momentum, finally reaching its acme when the Federal Way newspaper printed a warning to drivers something to the effect of "...if you don't need to travel between 320th and 312th after dark on 8th Avenue South, avoid it. There has been a great deal of vandalism to passing cars in that neighborhood..." We had been immortalized. We were stars, celebrities in our town forever. With our copy of the newspaper in hand, Mark, John and I were laughing at our exploits in the family room when Dad came in.

"What's got you three in such a good mood?"

Mark held the paper up to Dad.

"Look, Dad, they're talkin' about us in the newspaper," Mark announced proudly.

"Right there in black and white," John added, guiding Dad's eyes to the article on the page.

Dad read the article and then looked at us.

"What the hell is this all about?"

All together, we gave him the whole story, explaining in detail where we got the eggs to our techniques for hanging them. Once we finished, we looked at Dad expecting him to congratulate his three boys with the "shit-eating" grins on their faces. After all, we'd heard him chuckle as he smugly told us the story of how, many years ago, he and his brothers scooped fresh, steamy cow pies into brown paper bags, deposited the bags on the threshold of somebody's front door, poured lighter fluid on the bag, knocked on the door, ignited the sack, ran and hid to watch some person open the door and stomp out the fire, splattering cow shit everywhere. We were certain he'd appreciate our story, but Dad surprised us, calmly reacting with no emotion or smiles at all.

"Did it ever occur to you boys that egg white might eat the paint off of those cars?"

We were dumbfounded.

"What?"

"You're kiddin'."

He spoke calmly with purpose.

"No I'm not. Egg whites are protein, and just like bird shit, burn like acid through car paint. Well, I don't know 'bout you, but I sure as hell wouldn't be happy if someone did that to my car."

And that was the end of it. Our smiles turned to frowns as our fifteen minutes of fame vanished with Dad's words. Dad kept the paper and we flopped down in front of the TV without a word, knowing we would never hang eggs again.

At school, Sacajawea announced a big PTA Open

House, inviting all the parents to visit the school, meet the teachers and see what their kids were up to. We were given a printed program to pass on to our parents, inviting everyone to attend. I handed it to Dad, not thinking he'd even be interested as he was busy enough with his shop, but on the night of the big day, there I was in the school atrium with my pals, when Dad rushed by.

"Dad, what are you doin' here? I mean, I didn't think you'd wanna come."

"Hi Matt. I'm looking for Mr. Dunham's philosophy class. I'd kinda like to see what he's all about. Where the hell is it?"

His breath told he had been to King's prior to his arrival, and I had a feeling something might be up. I pointed to the room and Dad bid me farewell, joining the other parents in the classroom where Mr. Dunham welcomed everyone. I stood there in the atrium, amazed to find my Dad here at school. Dad took a seat in the chairs as Mr. Dunham closed the doors. A half hour later, the parents filed out of the classroom. Dad rushed by me with a satisfied look on his face and said he'd see me later at home. Word got out that Dad had raked Mr. Dunham over the coals, debating philosophical ideas with him until Mr. Dunham crumbled before the entire room. Oh God, how were we ever going to survive this, I wondered.

The next day, heads held low in shame, Mark, John and I walked through the halls, embarrassed as everyone talked about what had happened the night before. Mr. Dunham saw me and stopped me in my tracks.

"Hey Matt, I just want to say I was so happy to meet your Dad last night at the open house. What an amazing mind he has. You boys are really lucky to have a father like him."

I couldn't believe it. My shame turned to pride in an instant.

When Halloween Day arrived on October 31st, Marguerite, Monica and their girlfriends were tearing up the house, busy making last minute princess and witch costumes with whatever accoutrements they could find. We knew we were technically too old to partake in the holiday kiddy ritual, but we were still young enough to feel entitled to our share of free candy. So, instead of missing out, Mark, John, Snorky, Rich and I dressed up like hobos in baggy clothes, fake beards and ventured out into the streets as soon night fell, and developed what we thought to be a foolproof method to avoid getting caught. Before approaching a house, we simply waited until a group of smaller kids arrived. Being kind young gentlemen, we let them pass in front of us, only to follow them closely a few paces behind. As soon as one small kid rang the doorbell, we bent down behind them at the knees to appear smaller than we were and join in the chorus of "Trick or Treat" in high-pitched voices once the door was opened. We retrieved our sweets, stood up tall and said "Thank you" in our normal voices, often times elated to catch the candy donor off guard and enjoy the reaction. We kept this up all night, running through the neighborhood, house to house, until finally our thighs began to get sore, so we stood on the porch of the last house assuming our real height, rang the doorbell and a lady answered the door, holding a bowl of candy.

"Trick or Treat," we chimed in our normal, tired voices.

Peering out her front door in disbelief at five tall boys, she said:

"Aren't you boys a little old for this?"

Not missing a beat, John, in a show of brawn, grabbed the bowl, emptied the entire contents into his pillow case, handed back the bowl and answered:

"Ah, shut up, lady!"

The lady just stood there with a stunned look on her face, her mouth hanging wide and an empty candy bowl in her hands. We ran away from the door laughing at the incident, returning home with pillowcases full of sweet undeserved rewards.

November brought us to our first choir concert of the year. We had rehearsed everything to perfection, or as well as seventh graders could, I should say. Excited as clams at high water, we all assembled in rows and entered the gymnasium, packed full of family members, friends and teachers. The student orchestra played followed by the different bands that played numbers, and finally it was time for the choirs to perform. Each choir took their turn on the risers to sing the songs they had rehearsed under Mr. Warner's direction. The Boy's Chorus followed the Girl's Chorus, mainly composed of seventh graders like me who were gaining their first choral experiences, and then the Concert Choir finished the concert, performing more complicated music arranged for mixed voices of eighth and ninth grade boys and girls. Although I don't remember the songs everyone sang, I do remember wanting to be older to sing in the mixed choir. As soon as that performance was behind us, Mr. Warner passed out Christmas music to each choir to rehearse, in preparation for the upcoming holiday concert in December.

Dad wasn't home much during the weeknights to buy groceries and take care of issues on the home front. We all pretty much took care of ourselves, as we were all old enough to require less adult supervision. Whenever asked how he raised his kids, Dad would always answer "I try to BE there when they need me, and stay the hell AWAY from 'em when they don't!" and that's how our ship stayed afloat. If we were hungry, we cooked our own dinners, baked our own birthday cakes and made our own lunches or snacks on our own time schedules. We nostalgically imagined how wonderful it would have been to come home after school and find Mom in the kitchen cooking a hot meal for us like our friend's moms did for them, but instead of having that luxury in our cards, we were taught the power of self-sufficiency.

There were days, however, when we would run out of certain food staples or find ourselves facing an issue that needed quick attention that Dad would address "a day late and a dollar short", as he would say. To remedy the situation, he decided the best solution would be to put my name on his checking account, thus giving me the responsibility to handle certain facets of our lives. It made me feel like a grownup, making runs to the grocery store whenever necessary for the things we needed, and I would also handle certain bills when they arrived in the mail. Financially, some weeks were more difficult than others and when the money well ran dry, Dad would simply ask me to hold off writing any checks for a few days, until he could replenish the account.

Our system worked just fine, until one evening in November, I was watching TV with Monica and Marguerite when the doorbell rang. I got up and answered the door to find a man in a helmet clutching a clipboard in his hands.

"Hi," I said to the man.

"Howdy. I'm from the Puget Sound Energy Company. Is your mom home?"

What else could I say but the truth?

"My mom's deceased."

The man wasn't ready for that response. He gathered himself and continued.

"Oh, I'm sorry, I didn't...is your Dad home?"

"He's working, but he'll be home later."

"Later, huh. What time later?"

"I dunno. Just later. You never know. Anytime."

He forged on painfully.

"Well, we sent you notices, you're over two months behind on the bill."

"Yeah, I saw 'em."

"Then you knew we were coming by. Did your Dad leave a check with you or anything?"

"No. He doesn't have to. I write the checks."

"You write 'em?" He asked, completely amazed.

"Yeah."

"How old are you?"

"Thirteen," I answered, proud to be a full-fledged teenager.

"Well, can you write me one?"

"My Dad told me not to write any until next week, cuz' there's no money left in the account."

He was completely lost.

"If someone doesn't give me a check, I'm supposed to shut off your electricity."

"Yeah, I know. Go ahead," I answered without emotion.

The man looked around. I could tell he was disturbed by his task at hand.

"I tell ya what, I have other houses on my run to go to. I can do them first. I'll drop by again later, and by that time, maybe your Dad will be here and I can figure something out with him."

"Okay, see ya later." I closed the door and joined my sisters in front of the TV, not giving the matter another thought. A couple of hours later, as darkness began to set, the man returned, ringing the doorbell. Monica and Marguerite answered the door this time, calling out to me once they discovered it wasn't one of their friends. I went to the door.

"Oh, it's you again. Hi."

"Hi. Are those your sisters?"

"Yeah."

"How many kids live here?"

"Five."

"Five, huh? Did your Dad come home yet?"

"Nope. Sorry."

By now the poor man's heart was aching.

"I don't want to do this to you guys, but I'll lose my job if I don't shut off your electricity."

"So do it."

"I don't want to leave five kids in a dark house in the middle of November!"

"It's okay. Ya don't wanna get in trouble with your boss," I pointed out.

"Can't you call your Dad?"

I knew Dad wouldn't be at his shop at this hour. He and Lyle would be at King's, swimming in suds.

"No, I can't. Go ahead and turn it off."

"I have to do it. I'm really sorry."

"No biggie," I answered.

The man stood by his van for a few minutes,

stewing on the idea of leaving a bunch of kids in a dark house alone but finally did his job. We lit a few candles and took it in stride, making the best of the situation. When Dad came home later, he crossed the threshold into a house as dark inside as out. Marguerite and Monica were playing Old Maid with a flashlight.

"What the hell's goin' on? Why's everything shut off?"

"Hi Dad. Some guy came and turned off the electricity. You didn't pay the bill," I said.

"Sonofabitch!" he moaned, then changed his tune. "You kids get somethin' to eat?"

"Yeah. We had peanut butter sandwiches, cuz' we couldn't cook the potpies," Monica replied.

"Okay, well shit! I'll call the goddamn electric people tomorrow."

And the next day when we came home from school, everything was back to normal, electrically speaking. Marguerite had to call a few of her friends to find out what happened to Jan and Marcia the night before on the Brady Bunch, since the episode ended abruptly right in the middle when the electricity got shut off.

It snowed a little during the first week of December, but it was washed away by drizzle as soon as it fell, annihilating any thoughts of hooky bobbing, my brothers' and my favorite winter sport. One day after school, I was on dish duty, and while I stood at the kitchen sink scrubbing away at the pots and pans, I saw Dad's car pull in to the driveway. Instead of carrying an armful of grocery sacks, I watched him pull out a big TV set from the back seat of his car. Intrigued, I peered out and saw him smile at me as he passed the window and entered the front door. I turned and yelled throughout the house.

"Dad's home, you guys, and he's carryin' somethin' big. I think it's a TV."

Monica and Marguerite jumped up from their chairs in front of the black and white screen they were watching in the family room and beelined it for the door just as Dad entered.

"What's that, Dad?"

"Well...I brought home an early Christmas present for you kids."

Marguerite was perplexed.

"But we already got a TV, Dad."

Dad proudly made his announcement.

"Not like this one, you don't. This here's a *color* TV."

"WOW! A color one? Hurry up, Dad, plug it in!"

"I will. Dooon't get excited," he laughed.

Dad lifted the old TV and put it on the floor, then he placed the new TV on Mom's hope chest and plugged the cord into the socket on the wall. After adjusting the antenna, the picture came through in living color to everyone's elation. Marguerite bounced around the room.

"Hey Monica, tomorrow night Charlie Brown is on. We get to watch it in color!"

"Yeah, and the Grinch is gonna be on next week!" Monica added.

We grabbed the TV Guide and combed through the pages, circling in ink the shows we didn't want to miss. Christmas variety shows abound. Bing Crosby, Perry Como, Bob Hope, Carol Burnett, Andy Williams; a different show was announced almost daily, and now in color.

We performed our Christmas concert at school, and although I remember having a good time singing all the traditional songs in harmony, nothing could compare to the daily anticipation leading up to Christmas at our house.

At long last we were about to spend Christmas together with all the traditions we had adopted and cherished in Portland and hadn't been able to enjoy since then. It seemed like an eternity had passed but here we were, celebrating Christmas as if it were the very first time. Monica and Marguerite made tons of sugar cookies and decorated them in colored frosting, displaying a huge platter piled high on the dining room table for everyone to gobble up. On another night, Dad came into the house carrying a brand new plastic laundry basket and bags full of fruits, nuts and candies to recreate the cornucopia of snacks that we would munch on throughout the winter holidays, complete with the inimitable boxes of chocolate-covered cherries we all hated but couldn't bring ourselves to confess and hurt Dad's feelings.

Every night we'd all wonder what Dad would be bringing home, and would jump up to find out what he was carrying each time he came through the front door. Sure enough, he had something else in his arms almost every day to add to the holiday excitement. Dad was so tickled to see our reactions to the abundant gifts he carried home. He'd worked extra hard to build his business and really went all out to make Christmas memorable, and when the big day finally dawned, we all woke up and scurried to the tree to open our gifts.

Sure enough, Dad had bought me the Polaroid Swinger instant black-n-white camera I longed for. I ran out and snapped a photo of our house from the street, then took a few shots of everyone before I used up that first packet of film that only took eight photos. All throughout the morning, Dad prepared our traditional stuffed turkey with all the trimmings and our favorite pineapple upside-down cake, which we scarfed down like happy pigs later that afternoon, enjoying our Christmas feast exactly the way we liked it.

The only thing missing was the constant flow of Christmas music, but all the records and the stereo had remained with Aunt Mary when we moved from Portland. We didn't feel deprived, however, as there was Christmas music on every channel of our new color TV, and I sang carols along with all the major stars of the day, right in the comfort of my own home. All throughout the holidays, I proudly carried my Swinger around and took photos of my neighborhood pals, my family, our house and the things I wanted to record for posterity. I liked manipulating the strong, pungent chemicals on the developer stick I had to squeeze and spread onto each photo once the countdown was over and I'd peeled back the negative. Sadly, reality sank in quickly when I soon realized it cost almost two week's allowance money to purchase one packet of film. My new gift, however fun it was to operate and play with, was sadly too expensive to use every day.

8. I AM, I SAID

The day we returned to school from Christmas vacation in early January, the collection of holiday music we performed at the concert in December had become a distant memory belonging to Christmas past, and the New Year 1971 brought new songs for Boy's Chorus to learn, including a new favorite of mine: *Good News.* Mr. Warner made an announcement the day we returned to school that we could, if we wished, participate in the annual vocal and ensemble competition that would take place in February. He explained how we could sing solos, duets or quartets and enjoy the experience of performing before an adjudicator who would grade us between 1 and 5, with a 1 being the coveted superior rating of musical excellence. Mr. Warner pointed to the sign-up sheet he had attached to the wall, inviting anyone interested to write his or her name up there, adding that he would help select an appropriate song for them to practice and then perform. I listened but paid no heed, remembering all too suddenly my first and painful solo experience on New Year's Eve 1970 at the Anderson's party. I filed the whole idea into my mental waste bin, not giving it another thought. However the next day, Anita Glasford nabbed me before choir started.

"Hey Matt, what song did Mr. Warner give you for the contest?"

"What song? Nothin'! I'm not singin' in the contest. You crazy? No Way."

"Yeah you are. I saw your name right there on the list."

I hurried over to the sign-up sheet and sure enough, in that all-too familiar left-handed scrawl was my name etched as only M.F.W. could have done it. Immediately, I grabbed a pencil from my music folder and drew thick black lines through my name, making it clear that my gesture was a decision and not a clerical error and then I walked over and sat down as if nothing had happened. The next day, I glanced at the sign-up sheet, happy to see that the aggressive black lines I had pulled through my name still clearly destroyed any possibility of my name attached to that contest, yet once again, a few lines below other fresh signatures, my name had been rewritten in that "M.F." scrawl once again. I grabbed my pencil and scribbled "Matt Gonder" out so fast that I tore a small hole in the sheet. Undaunted, I didn't let the sleeping dogs lie and walked right over to Mr. "M.F." and stood before him, trying unsuccessfully to keep cool.

"Mr. Warner, I'm NOT singin' in the contest."

He looked at me, smiling the same way he did on the first day I met him, making me worry.

"Really? You should think about it, Matt. It would be a good experience for you."

"I don't care. I'm singin' in choir, that's enough for me. I don't want any more."

"I really think you'd be missing out on something fun and a good challenge for you."

"Well, I don't wanna do it, so stop puttin' my name on the list, will ya?"

"We'll talk about it later, Matt. It's time for class to begin."

I left his side, walked to my chair and sat down, my blood boiling just like when he forced me into choir. I sang through the new songs, reading the music much better than I had in the fall, but I kept a wary eye on him, wondering what he thought he was cooking up for me. However this time, I stood warned and was determined to win the battle. A few more days went by and I figured the message was received, as Mr. Warner respected my wish and hadn't put my name on the list again. Then, just as I began to think the matter was over and done with, Mr. Warner whizzed by me and handed me some sheet music as I was climbing to my chair in the risers.

"Here's the solo I think you should sing for the contest, Matt."

Before I had time to protest, I looked down at the sheet music and read the title:

Sometimes I Feel Like A Motherless Child

I choked on the lump that formed in my throat. Shocked, I crammed the music folder so nobody else would see as I sat down. How could Mr. Warner know this about me? Who told him? Mark? After all, he was the big mouth that got me into choir in the first place, but I couldn't imagine him having a conversation with Mr. Warner about our personal lives. I swallowed hard and hid the music in my folder behind the other songs we were working on. Once class was over, I ran outside and into the atrium, where I took the sheet music out to read the lyrics, away from anyone else's snooping eyes.

Sometimes I feel like a motherless child

Sometimes I feel like a motherless child

Sometimes I feel like a motherless child

A long way from home

A long way from home

Sometimes I feel like I'm almost gone

Matthew Gonder

Sometimes I feel like I'm almost gone

Sometimes I feel like I'm almost gone

A long way from home

A long way from home

Feeling vulnerably exposed, I wanted to run away but I couldn't leave in the middle of the school day. There weren't many lyrics to the song, but the few words there were hurt me deeply, mirroring the truth of my own life; a motherless child a long way from home. I went to my other classes in a daze, and once school let out for the day, I hurried to one of the practice rooms to play and hear the melody of the song. Once I had plucked it out on the keyboard, I turned off the lights and cried in the dark for a few moments. I found the melody as painful as the lyrics were and wondered how a song could exist that hit so close to home. It had never dawned on me that someone else could have lived what I was living and that was too much for me to comprehend. I let the tears pour out. A few minutes later, I collected myself and peered out the door to make sure that Mr. Warner nor anyone else was in sight, then ran out to catch the late bus home without saying a word to anyone.

That night, lying awake in my lower bunk bed, the song cycled over and over in my head, haunting me. I willed it to disappear from my mind when, just before I fell asleep, another perspective came to me. I could sing that song in honor of Mom. I woke up the next morning and the song ran through my head again, but this time, instead of trying to erase it from my mind, I decided I would sing it as an ode to my deceased mother, who might, in turn, break the painful silence and respond in one way or another. I began to sing the song to Katie when I fed or cleaned her cage, and she would gaze at me without moving a muscle.

Throughout the following few weeks, I practiced in turn with the others at the group rehearsals Mr. Warner had set up after school to run through everyone's numbers, one by one. He gave pointers to those who needed his guidance, but I had made the song mine and needed no help from anyone. He just smiled at me. I even lost all stage fright, standing calmly in front of the others and singing out my solo as if they weren't even there, feeling so connected to the music, and secretly to my Mom. Mr. Warner gave us the performance schedule a few days prior to the contest, telling us each the time of day we would be "on". I was scheduled at 11:30. Others complained when they learned that they were scheduled too early in the morning, afraid of not having a clear voice, but Mr. Warner announced publicly that anyone could sing just as good in the morning as they could later in the afternoon, and that was the end of that, no time changes would be possible.

The day of the contest had finally arrived, a Saturday in February. I stood making breakfast toast, leaning half asleep against the counter in the kitchen for support when Dad bounced in, reciting one of his familiar phrases he'd chime to tease us whenever one of us wore a sour morning face.

"Good morning, sunshine! Rise and shine!" he said with a snicker.

"Very funny, Dad. G'mornin'."

"Today's the big day!" he announced, smiling.

"Yeah," I yawned.

"Well, I'll be thinkin' about you up there singin'. Sorry I can't be there, but somebody's gotta work to keep a roof over our heads."

"I know, Dad. No biggie."

"You'll do fine, Matt."

With that, he went to the bathroom to shave for work.

Hosted at some other school, we arrived by bus or car and ran to the cafeteria where the grade sheets and maps were posted on a wall, indicating where everyone was to perform. I found my name on the list next to the room number and located it on the map. Rushing out to find my room, I discovered that pianos had been installed in selected rooms all over the school. Music flooded the halls. I was in seventh heaven. I found my room, entered and sat down, joining the crowd that had come to listen to one singer perform his solo. Ironically, it was a Math room that had a screen pulled down over a chalkboard to hide weird algebra equations. The singer, some boy, sang a song about a sailor. He did a good job and afterwards, while the adjudicator spoke to the singer privately at his desk, the room emptied out and filled with more people who wanted to hear the next performer. Joining the mayhem, I hopped between different rooms, listening to my friends and checking out the big board in the cafeteria every once in a while. Some were happy with the marks they received, some jumped with joy, some cried, others were shocked and complained how hard a certain judge was being or how "such and such" cramped up or got nervous while he/she was singing.

I kept an eye on the clock and returned to my room at the required fifteen minutes prior to my appointed hour. I didn't feel nervous at all. When my name was called, I stood up with Anita Glasford, my accompanist, and we stood before the hanging screen in front of the chalkboard. I was happy to see that I'd drawn quite a crowd. As soon as the adjudicator lifted his head and gave us the cue, Anita sat at the piano and began playing the introduction, and I sang out as calmly as if I was saying "Hi everyone, who wants to go get ice cream with me?" Once I had reached the end of my song, I walked up and sat next to the adjudicator while everyone applauded. The adjudicator talked me through the categories we were being judged on, saying I had excellent intonation, good phrasing, breath control, then told me to keep on singing. That was it. I stood up and left the room, not really feeling anything, it was over so fast. I went to a few other rooms to watch more friends perform their solos, returned to the cafeteria and ate the peanut butter sandwich and apple I had packed for lunch.

About an hour later, an assistant came in to add grades to the board. She gave me the highest mark possible: a "1". Mr. Warner was standing right there as my grade was posted. He smiled broadly and patted me on the back.

"Congratulations, Matt! I knew you could do it."

"Thanks."

At that very instant, something changed in me. Prior to then, I always knew I could sing, but it was just another activity I participated in along with many other students at Mass in Portland and had enjoyed in every other school as one of the subjects taught throughout the years, like English or Social Studies. Sure, Mrs. Habedank chose me as one of the six from Sheridan to participate in the all-city choir of three hundred voices last year and I really enjoyed that experience, but I had never taken singing or music seriously as a personal gift or talent until I was standing right there next to Mr. Marshall Warner and saw that "1" posted on the big board next to my name. I looked over at him. He was right. It had been more than a wonderful experience for me. I suddenly felt bad for being so mean to him in choir at the beginning of the year, but fortunately there was a group of classmates milling all around, pestering him for advice or receiving reassurance after obtaining a bad mark for their solo, so I didn't have an opportunity to apologize for my bad behavior verbally. I just looked at him under student attack and realized what a generous man he was, sharing his knowledge with each one of his students. I felt so lucky to know him. He not only taught me to read music but to believe in myself as an individual with capabilities all my own, and there I stood, thanks to him, as one of the stars of the day.

The school thinned out as many people often left for home once their grade was posted, but Mr. Warner remained at the contest until every one of his singers had performed and received their mark, running throughout the school as if on a marathon, carrying his clip-board with the entire program under his arm. I followed him around to watch other singers, but couldn't take my eyes off him, full of admiration and gratitude for my mentor. When the day was all over, we all said goodbye and went home. Mr. Warner was so exhausted and covered in sweat you'd have thought he'd been playing football all day. On the way home, I thought of what Dad had said to me after I sang at the New Year's party at the Anderson's: "Your job is to sing if that's what you want to do and those goddamn sonsobitches' job is to LISTEN to you when you do". He knew it all along. As soon as he came through the door that night, I ran to him and spewed out the news.

"Dad, I got a '1', I got a '1'!"

"Ya did?"

"Yeah, a '1'!"

He looked at me and could tell I had gained more confidence than ever. He started to laugh and asked me to describe all the events of the day, point by point, laughing along with and making me repeat certain sequences for extra emphasis to make my moment of glory last even longer.

"Matt-sue, my artiste!" he said to punctuate the moment.

The following Monday at school, I felt like a conquering hero, receiving words of congratulation all day long. I was in my element and music became the key to heaven. At that point, I didn't think music was my fate, but I remember feeling like I'd found something that made me stand out of the crowd and belonged only to me. Back in choir, I participated fully from that day forward. Anything Mr. Warner wanted me to do, I did. I asked him more questions than ever, soaking up his knowledge like a sponge, vowing to be a good boy from that day forward with no resistance. Well, as much as could be expected.

The month of March brought us into the spring quarter at school and new classes. Every discipline, be it Math or Science, offered an array of subjects we could choose from, depending on personal inclinations and tastes. The thought never occurred to me to not sign up for Boy's Chorus with Mr. Warner, which only got better thanks to my newly gained confidence. Choir also became easier for me as my sight-reading skills improved. My Science requirement gave me the opportunity to sign up for Photography class, where I hoped to learn how to develop my own photos and thus avoid paying a fortune for the Polaroid film I needed for my Swinger camera. I enjoyed working in the dark room with all the chemicals to develop my photos until one day, while goofing off, another student slammed the door on my hand that cut deep into the ring finger on my right hand. Spewing blood, I ran to the office, where Mrs. Paige jumped up from behind her desk to my rescue. She grabbed my hand, wrapped it in paper towels, took me into the bathroom to clean it and accompanied me to the school nurse, where I was given one big stitch to hold the skin on my finger together until it was healed. For the next month or so, I couldn't play the piano, as my finger was too swollen to move.

John, forever building something, had signed up again for the Woodshop class, and in it he fashioned a router-engraved wooden plaque with my name dug deep into the wood, offering it to me as a gift. I felt like a celebrity. For the Language arts requirement, I took a drama class with Mrs. Gorne, who laughed at all the students dramatic exploits, while Mark and John were in Typing class with Miss Maki. I liked Mrs. Threlkheld as well, my English teacher who resembled Grace Kelly, and there was also Mrs. Squire, who taught some subject nobody remembers because the only thing we learned from her was how to focus our eyes and attention. An attractive short woman who wore only Micro-miniskirts, she would stand on her tiptoes and stretch her arm way up to write on the upper section of the chalkboard, which made her dress climb up her backside and gave students who paid close attention to her lessons an occasional fleeting glimpse of her buttocks. Naturally, we kept the secret from her, because had she found out, she would have put an end to it. Mark, John and I would share notes on what she was wearing from one day to the next whenever we crossed each other in the halls. Mrs. Squire was obviously an excellent teacher because rarely, if ever, did boys miss her classes.

The last quarter of school whizzed by. On sunny days, many students gathered to sunbathe or eat their lunch in the atrium. Professional school photos were taken, and I smiled proudly for posterity when the photographer snapped the shutter, capturing me in the grinning group shot of Boy's Chorus. When our final concert took place in May, our musical knowledge had grown throughout the year and it showed in our performance. As soon as that concert was behind us, everyone started getting antsy for summer vacation to arrive. Final tests were taken, scored and handed back to each student until the only writing exercises that took place during that last week of school were the souvenir notes inked or penciled by friendly faces onto the pages of our yearbooks.

9. JOY TO THE WORLD

Three Dog Night rocked on every radio, telling the world that "Jeremiah was a bullfrog" while my sisters danced with their girlfriends to the Osmonds, imagining that Donny was singing personally to them each time he crooned *Go Away Little Girl* as summer 1971 came around bearing new promises of sunny fun for all. One full year had passed since we had moved to Federal Way, and by now we each had our own long list of friends to play with and knew the layout of our fair city like the backs of our hands. Mark, John and I went fishing at Steel Lake with Snorky and Rich, while Marguerite and Monica chatted with their girlfriends on our phone that rang constantly and drove Dad crazy whenever he was home trying to nap. We had become acquainted with many of our neighbors, so babysitting, gardening and odd job offers poured in keeping Monica, Marguerite, John and me busy.

Now that we were settled and thriving in Federal

Way, our aunts, uncles and cousins began to visit from time to time. Both Mom and Dad came from families where most married and had kids of their own, so we numbered thirty-nine cousins on the Gonder side of the family and thirty-five on the Kraft side.

One of the first relatives to show up that summer was Aunt Frances, Mom's eldest sister, who made spontaneous appearances throughout our lives, purchasing a Greyhound bus ticket and showing up at the door wherever we lived to check up on us. Aunt Fran believed in the importance of remaining connected to every one of her nieces and nephews. Whenever apart, she wrote newsy letters and you would be chastised if you didn't write back. She joyfully distributed hand-me-down gifts that she collected from the Kraft family home where Mom was born at 517 W. Longfellow in Spokane and would explain the history of each object in detail, sharing who the prior owner was and where it came from. Most of the gifts were useless, truth be told, but the stories she would tell about each item would transform them into living treasures you'd want to keep forever.

In Aunt Fran's eyes, everyone and everything held special meaning and a reason for being. She would stand in front of the stove, making stuffed cabbage for us, following the ancient recipe our Grandfather Kraft brought from Odessa, and share family history while she lovingly blanched each cabbage leaf. Once prepared, we finally sat down to enjoy the meal and got the impression we were being fed by our ancestors. The next day, apron strings tightly tied, she'd round us all up to clean the house, and God forbid you should forget to scrub one of the corners of the floor, for which she had an obsession. She jumped in and helped with whatever task required her German concentrated attention. A cross between General Rommel and Erma Bombeck, she'd magically turn household chores into games as magically as Mary Poppins, and our house would be sparkling clean when finished. She washed everything in Clorox Bleach that she comically called "Clorex", and Dad would laugh at her by saying "Well, it's a good thing you didn't use 'Purox'". We all adored Aunt Fran; she was a living reminder that we were part of and loved by a big family, while Dad appreciated his sister in-law's total lack of judgment, her gifts of tolerance, kindness, love and especially the way she became silly after drinking one beer. If the Lawrence Welk Show aired while she was in town, we'd be enlisted to take turns dancing with her in front of the TV screen.

Mom's brother, Uncle Joe and his wife Aunt Lorraine also drove up from Tacoma one day to drive us to Lake Morton for a sunny day of barbecue and swimming, telling us the stories of how our Mom used to spend time there in summers when she was a girl. The land parcel had belonged to someone in the family for decades and had been developed into a comfortable lakeside haven, open for family members to enjoy. An old A-frame beach house stood on a hill that swept down to the lake. We ran down to the boat landing, across the wooden slats and jumped into the cool lake all afternoon until evening set in, when Uncle Joe started the barbecue. There was an outhouse in a secluded area of the yard and other amenities including beaten pathways to run along. Knowing Mom had frolicked on the same trails many years ago strangely made it feel as if she were there laughing and having fun with us.

Not long after our trip to Lake Morton, just when boredom set in to the point where we had contests counting our mosquito bites after spending hours combing through the pages of Mom's photo albums of high school girlfriends we didn't know, Aunt Maryann (another of Mom's sisters) and Uncle Alex came through Federal Way, bearing a bottle of homemade balloon wine. Aunt Maryann had long ago earned her reputation in the family as a virtuoso by resonating her humming voice into her nasal passages while plucking her nose like a guitar string and sounding just like a Hawaiian ukulele. Never has a reunion or family gathering occurred without reaching the culminating moment where Aunt Maryann gave one of her hilarious, show-stopping schnoz recitals on her "Snoutivarius". This visit however, before her show began, Aunt Maryann told us all proudly how she made the wine herself.

"It's so easy, really. Kid stuff. All ya do is take one glass gallon A&W jug, one large can of frozen Welch's Grape Juice, four cups of sugar, one packet of Fleischmann's Yeast, you know, the kind you use for baking bread, add how much water the can tells ya to make juice, about a gallon, then ya stir it all up real good, and put the balloon on top of the jug opening. Then ya fasten that rubber band good n' tight around the top of the bottle to hold the balloon on. Ya put it in a dark cupboard and just wait," Aunt Maryann instructed.

John was more than intrigued.

"Wow, really?" he said, his eyes bigger than his mouth. Aunt Maryann continued.

"Yeah, that's it. Now, that balloon's gonna blow up and expand, but that's normal 'cause it's just the yeast doing what it's supposed to do, so anyway ya wait the whole month and then ya pour it through some cheesecloth and you got your own delicious homemade wine, cheaper than in the stores. Here, taste it."

John took a gulp of the grapey potion and swallowed it down. Mark and I followed suit, happy to wet our whistles on the Kool-Aid tasting drink with a kick. Needless to say, John listened to Aunt Maryann as if she was handing out a top-secret science formula. She was right. Kid stuff it was, but she gave the recipe to the wrong kid. He memorized every word of the recipe and then immediately got to work, buying all the ingredients at the grocery store. He learned that the grape juice was much more costly than he had planned for, so he simply bought less than the recipe required, figuring he could tweak the concoction to make it work. The total cost came to about $1.25 per gallon for the combined ingredients. Mark and I helped him gather up and wash six gallon-jugs. John mixed everything up in Dad's turkey roaster pan and then we funneled it into the bottles, secured the balloons on top and hid the whole project in a cupboard out in the garage.

We opened the cupboard to follow the development on a daily basis, and sure enough, after a few days, those limp balloons began to stand erect and slowly expand. A couple weeks later, Dad was out fidgeting in the garage and came across John's stash of swelling balloon-topped jugs.

"What the hell is this?" he asked.

John felt compelled to explain what he'd been doing, mentioning who gave him the recipe, and instead of reprisal, Dad just laughed, deciding to let him ride out the wave of his new experiment.

Once the month had passed, Mark and I helped John filter his nectar into four empty whisky bottles or 'fifths' that he sold for a dollar and a quarter per bottle to select 'clients', earning him a whopping $3.75 per gallon with a profit margin of $2.50. He couldn't sell the last fifth, because it was nothing but gooey purple sludge that remained stuck to the bottom of the jug. I know, I can do the math. John should have made $5.00, but one fifth out of each gallon was tithed to our mafia don Dad who paid the rent on the garage. John's new enterprise made him quite popular with Snorky and Rich and yes, the neighborhood gang quickly gathered to celebrate and gulp down too much way too fast of the new brew, barely living to tell the tale through the hangovers we all experienced after consuming that sweet swill until, green-faced, we puked up so much we could have probably refilled the bottles.

Sporty Roofs continued to flourish, and summer offered Mark another opportunity to work full-time with Dad and Lyle again. Business was so good, that Dad incorporated the company, naming himself as President, Lyle as Vice-President, and added a new partner named Vince who joined the company and became Secretary/Treasurer. We didn't know Vince like we knew Lyle, as he pretty much kept to himself in the office, taking care of the books, handling all the billing and payments, whereas Lyle always teased us whenever we saw him. John and I went to the shop a few times on weekends to help out and make a few extra bucks. Mark would be topping and tucking cars in assembly line formation along with Lyle's brother, who had also been hired for the summer rush.

I remember sweeping up the shop one Saturday when an older gentleman, a well-dressed guy we had all seen more than a few times, approached me. His 1959 tan Cadillac was his baby. He paid dearly for the best of everything to express total devotion to his four-wheeler and was completely addicted to the handiwork and services Sporty Roofs provided. His Caddie-baby had been completely re-looked by now, fins and all. Lyle had done the top and added siding and Gordy had done some fancy interior work, but the obsessed puppy came around every once in a while to find out what new amenities were available.

"Hi ya, kid. Is Lyle here today?" he asked me with worry in his voice.

"Yes sir, he's right over there," I answered, pointing to a far corner of the shop, where Lyle was fixing a glue gun. I guided him over and listened to the conversation. He told Lyle how he had, by accident, left his car outside in the rain one day and by the next, the rain had dried, leaving white water spots all over the vinyl top. The man thought he'd have to replace the entire top, and Lyle just smiled as he listened to the guy tell his story. Lyle walked out to the guys' car, and sure enough, white water spots covered the entire top, creating white lines where the raindrops gathered and created a ripple effect.

"Well, what do you think? Do we have to replace the whole thing?" the Man whined.

"No, it just needs to be cleaned up, that's all," Lyle answered.

"Really, you sure that's all it needs?" the man begged.

"Sure, the vinyl isn't damaged. When you wear a leather coat out in the rain, the same thing happens to the leather, you just gotta clean it up."

"Sweet Jesus, that's a relief. Can you do it today?"

the Man's begged.

"Me? You can do it yourself with any vinyl cleaner on the market."

"C'mon Lyle, you do it for me, would you?"

Lyle couldn't refuse the loyal client's request.

"Tell you what," Lyle cooed, "leave me the keys, come back tonight and I'll see what I can do."

The man went away happy as a kid at a carnaval. As soon as the guy left, Lyle told John and I to wipe the top down with the same solvent and rags we used to clean up all the cars, and then sent me to the grocery store to buy a bottle of cheap vinyl cleaner to restore his top with a new luster. Later that evening, the man returned and danced around his car, caressing the shiny renewed top of his baby and purring like a kitten. Lyle charged him thirty-five dollars for the job, which in reality only cost just under three dollars for the bottle of vinyl cleaner plus thirty minutes of cheap child labor, but hey, Lyle tried honestly to explain that he could easily have cleaned it up himself and the guy wouldn't listen, so, some lessons are fated to be learned at a cost. The owner was so happy, he all but peed his pants.

"This is wonderful, Lyle! Tell me, when can I bring it in again for another cleaning?"

Lyle couldn't refuse a client's request.

"Bring it in again next month!" Lyle offered.

Returning home early that afternoon from the shop, we drove into the driveway, passing right in front of Marguerite, who smiled and waved at us from the corner where she stood with her pal Anita and sister Barbie, behind a few folded TV trays piled high with toys and junk. I got out of the car and walked over to see what she was doing.

"Hi guys, whatcha doin'?"

"Hi Matt, I'm havin' a garage sale," Marguerite answered.

"Oh, so how's business?" I inquired, looking around at the stuff she had displayed.

"Okay," she answered.

Then I spotted a miniature drill set sitting amongst her dolls and toys.

"What's that doin' there? That's my drill," I said, shocked.

"Well you never use it!" She blared in her defense.

"So what, it's still mine and you ain't got the right to sell it!"

I saw something else that looked familiar.

"And that's John's!" I said in disbelief. That little miser had gone into our room and taken whatever she wanted to add to her sale, and by now, there was no way telling what she had already sold.

"John never uses it, either," she whined with purpose.

"So what! It's not yours and I'm tellin' him. Hey JOHN!" I screamed towards the house.

"Here, just take it back," she snapped disdainfully.

"I will! What else did you take from our room, huh?"

Anita tried to come to her rescue.

"She didn't sell anything, Matt, nobody wanted any of that junk."

"Junk? That's what you say!" I told her.

John came out of the house.

"Whaddya want?" he yelled.

"Marguerite's been sellin' your stuff, you better come see," I warned.

John ran over to join us. After arguing and threatening Marguerite to stay out of our room and away from our belongings, we grabbed what remained of our stuff as she boxed up the rest. Her friends went home and that ended her garage sale exploits. We went into the house and heard Dad laughing out loud.

"What's so funny, Dad?" John asked.

Dad held up the paper, shaking it as he tried to calm his laughter.

"Listen to this! Some silly sonofabitch put a want ad in the paper," he said, reading on with a grin.

WANT AD

Nice brown dog with a big red thing

Will be ten years old if he lives 'til spring

He has four white legs and a hole in his ass

He will piss on your carpet and shit on your grass

His eyes bulge out and his ass sucks wind

But he's a damn good dog for the shape he's in.

We all laughed and reread the poem out loud a few times.

"Damn, I wish I'd a wrote that!" Dad giggled.

"Dad, you haven't written any more poetry for a long time," I said.

"Yeah, I know. I been too busy with the shop n' all."

Dad may not have had time to write anymore, but he always had a soft spot in his heart for good poetry and verse. He retired to his bedroom to stretch out and read, telling us to not wander far as he'd be taking us to the drive-in movies that night. He handed the newspaper to Mark, leaving us to argue over which movie we wanted to see. A few hours later, when the time came for John to make our requisite two big brown grocery bags of popcorn to take with us, Mark went into our bedroom and found John lying on his bed, eyes glued to a book.

"John, it's almost time to go to the movies. Better make the popcorn."

"Mmm," John mumbled. Mark couldn't believe what he was seeing. Normally, when the popcorn hour came, John bolted upright, ready for action.

"John, c'mon."

"I'm readin', leave me alone," John mumbled, not moving.

"But you gotta make the popcorn, John," Mark continued.

"Get someone else. Stop buggin' me!"

Mark left our room in disbelief and knocked on Dad's bedroom door.

"C'mon in," Dad answered.

Mark entered and found Dad lying on his bed, deep in the pages of his book.

"Dad, something's wrong with John."

"Whaddya talkin' about?"

"He's been lyin' in bed ever since we came home and when I told him it's time to make the popcorn for the movies, he told me to get someone else to do it."

"What's wrong with that?"

"John always makes the popcorn for the movies."

"Is he sick?"

"Nope. He's just lyin' on his bed, reading."

"Reading? John? I'll be damned. What the hell's he reading?"

"Some book. He never reads except at school when he has to."

"Well, hell, Mark, leave him alone!" Dad instructed.

Mark left and ordered Marguerite and Monica to make two huge bags of popcorn, which they prepared along with a gallon of Kool-Aid lemonade. As soon as we all jumped into the car, John sat in the back, book in hand, his eyes glued to the pages with concentrated intention. Everyone glanced at him from time to time, even Dad peered at him through the rearview mirror, but John was mesmerized and ignored the rest of us. Dad made a stop at the grocery store to purchase our favorite candy bars, and John didn't budge from the parking lot, eyes scanning his paperback. When we arrived at the drive-in, John sat in the car reading away while I followed the girls to jump on the swing sets below the big screen. As dusk fell, we were all sitting in place with the loudspeaker hanging on the window, eager for the movie previews to begin. After what seemed like an eternity of silence, John smiled and let out a big sigh as he read the final 'happy ending' paragraph of what he chalked up as the first major literary classic he had actually read on his own (not counting books at school) cover to cover: *101 Dalmatians*.

In contrast to our lives in Portland, we no longer attended Mass. St. Vincent de Paul's Catholic Church was only six blocks further up 8th Avenue, but we never once participated in the services. Mass had simply fallen by the wayside on our agendas. Dad wasn't much for organized religion although he appreciated the higher-level education parochial school offered us in Portland, but we hadn't tasted a Communion host since the day we left Blessed Sacrament, more than two years ago.

Weekends for Dad usually consisted of playing nine holes of golf with his three boys or laying low around the house reading and napping, unless he had to work. One Sunday July morning after breakfast, John, Monica, Marguerite and I got into a game of croquet in the back yard. Mark watched TV while Dad tried to nap but was constantly awakened by the annoying sound of the telephone ringing. Mark did his best to run to the phone but nobody would respond on the other end of the line.

"Hello? Hello, can you hear me?" Mark asked politely.

No response. It was probably one of Marguerite or Monica's girlfriends who didn't want to speak to anyone but them directly. This routine went on for over an hour. Every ten minutes or so the phone rang again. Mark jumped up to answer but nobody would say a word back to him. Finally, once again, the phone rang again. This time, Dad came barreling out of his room in his underwear and t-shirt, all steamed up and pissed off for not being able to nap through the noise of one ring too many.

"Wait a minute, don't answer it, Mark, I'll get it!"

Mark stood frozen in his tracks. Dad shuffled into the dining room and just let the phone ring endlessly.

"You got any more o' them firecrackers left over from the fourth of July?" he asked Mark.

"Sure, in Mom's desk."

"Get 'em for me! He barked.

While the phone kept chiming, Mark ran over, opened the desk drawer, dug through the junk and pulled out a packet of firecrackers, handing them to Dad.

"I'm gonna teach that cocksucker a lesson they'll never forget!"

Dad grabbed a book of matches, ripped one out and snapped it onto the flint paper, ignited the firecracker and then picked up the receiver of the phone, holding the firecracker next to the microphone. The fuse burned down until the firecracker exploded, making the house shake. Satisfied, Dad slammed the receiver back onto the phone.

"That oughta fix the sonofabitch!"

He stomped off back to his room to nap in peace while the phone, surprisingly, didn't ring all throughout the rest of the afternoon. A couple hours later, book in hand, Dad hopped into his trousers, came out to say hello, sat on the throne and read for another hour, then came into the kitchen to cook up something to watch us all descend upon it like a cloud of locusts. On Sunday afternoons when Dad's cooking odors filled the house, somehow all five of us were right there, lined up, plate and fork in hand, ready for communion. But this Sunday, I had pulled out Mom's cookbook *The Joy Of Cooking* and found a recipe for stuffed green peppers. I followed the recipe with the hamburger meat, added chopped onions, rice, tomatoes and spices, and had them baking in the turkey roaster as a surprise for Dad. He got one whiff when he got up from his nap.

"Hey, what the hell's cooking in here?"

"Some stuffed green peppers. I got the recipe in Mom's cookbook."

Dad came in and opened the oven door, peering inside.

"Damn, that smells good. When'll they be ready?"

"In about another fifteen minutes or so, I guess."

He sat at the table and chatted with everyone, waiting out the time as if it were an eternity. As soon as the peppers were ready, every man grabbed a plate and I served up my new concoction. Dad devoured those peppers like Graham Kerr on the *Galloping Gourmet* TV show, relishing every mouthful as if it was the best thing he'd ever eaten in his life. As soon as the meal was over, the usual weekly trip to the laundromat completed our Sunday routine. The next day, Dad came home from work carrying two big bags of groceries, one bag filled with two-dozen green peppers for me to stuff again that night, and after that, my stuffed green peppers became a staple food at our house, like Dad's pork chops and gravy.

In August, during one of the few times he ever got a chance to use the phone, Dad had a conversation with his sister Marcella, who lived in Idaho with Uncle Keith. She invited Monica and Marguerite to spend a couple of weeks with her, and naturally, both sisters were thrilled to receive the invitation and I was thrilled at the thought of getting rid of them for a spell. At first, Dad refused, explaining that he could never afford to take time away from work to drive the girls to Idaho. Aunt Marcella proposed another plan that none of us would have even fathomed possible, and a few days later, Monica and Marguerite were climbing aboard an airplane. I was jealous of my sisters that day, as they were going to be the first among us to experience flight. Once the girls had taken off, Mark and Dad went back to their full-time work schedule at the shop, leaving John and me alone to fend for ourselves. We had no problem with that. We did whatever whenever we wanted and were free to watch only our favorite cartoons on Saturday mornings, beginning with my favorite, *The Bugs Bunny Show*, followed by *The Road Runner Show*, *The Harlem Globetrotters*, *Deputy Dawg*, *The New Pink Panther Show* and ending our morning marathon with reruns of *Jonny Quest* and *Lancelot Link, Secret Chimp*. Since the girls were gone, we didn't have to watch their boring cartoons: *Scooby-Doo, Where Are You?*, *Help!...It's the Hair Bear Bunch*, *The Pebbles and Bamm-Bamm Show*, *Archie's TV Funnies*, *Sabrina, the Teenage Witch* or God forbid *Josie and the Pussy Cats*.

We were happy bachelors, napping if and whenever

235

we felt sleepy. We cooked for ourselves, just like always, rode bikes and goofed off with our pals, Snorky and Rich, enjoying our freedom with no sisters around to sell our stuff in garage sales. Soon enough, however, word got out that we were home alone, and it seemed to bother others much more than it disturbed us, so invitations for dinner began popping up and neighbors brought cooked food over for us in Tupperware containers. John and I thought it was cool that everyone worried about us now when they never showed interest before. As a result, Snorky's mom invited us over for the best lasagne dinner with Snorky's whole family, and his Dad showed us the poster of Raquel Welch, Neanderthal fodder, wearing her *One Million Years B.C.* costume he had proudly hung behind the door of his bedroom. After dinner we watched TV in their family room while Snorky's Mom sat crocheting an afghan. Once the show was over, we thanked them for their hospitality and went home.

Another day, Mark, John, Rich and I were playing touch football on the lawn at Mirror Lake Elementary.

"Where's Snorky? I thought he was gonna hang out with us today."

"He's on a date with some girl," Rich answered.

"Really? Cool."

So we played amongst ourselves until about an hour later, Snorky meandered up to us and the game came abruptly to a halt. We rushed over to fire questions at him.

"So, how was it?"

"Nice."

"What did you guys do?"

"Ya know. We kissed a while in the woods."

"With your tongue?"

"Yeah."

"Oh God. French kissing, ha ha ha…and then?"

"I finger banged her."

"Ya what?"

"I put my finger in her…you know," he said, pointing down there.

"You're kiddin', what was it like?"

"Kinda like stickin' your finger in raw hamburger."

"Gross."

"And she liked it?"

"Yeah, a lot."

Then he changed the subject.

"You guys gonna play some more?"

"Naw, we gotta go home."

"Okay then, see ya tomorrow."

"Yeah, see ya."

We all went our separate ways, but I was fascinated by what I just heard. Snorky's experience haunted me. The next day I went down to the Safeway store, rushed over to the meat department and poked my finger right through the plastic-wrap of a pound of raw hamburger, deep into the moist, ground flesh. It felt cold and sticky. I got lost in the moment, poking my digit through the plastic film of a few other packages, twirling my finger deep in the gooey chopped beef and imagining a girl writhing in ecstasy, when all of a sudden the butcher saw what I was doing and rushed over, yelling at the top of his lungs, shaking me out of my fantasy.

"What the HELL do you think you're doing? Get outta there, ya stupid little SHIT!"

I jumped, yanking my meat-stained finger out of the package without a word in my defense, turned and ran out of the store.

On the way home, I saw garage sale signs stapled to the telephone poles. Intrigued and forever seeking a good deal, I walked by the house, which was only a block out of my way to see what the people had displayed for sale all over their front lawn. There, next to the piles of junk, clothes, appliances and old toys laid a homemade steel minibike frame with a seat and wheels. I asked the man of the house where the motor was, and he explained that the motor had died so he removed it, adding that all it needed was a lawnmower engine, a welding repair to a cracked bar and the bike would run once again like new. He was selling the frame for five bucks, a steal at that price, I thought. I paid the man and rolled the steel frame home, where I called Rich to share the news. He told me the man who lived in the house across the street from him did welding jobs on the side and would certainly be able to fix the frame, so I walked down to get Rich, and together we knocked on the door of the house across the street. A nice lady answered the door.

"Hi. I'm Matt n' I got a minibike with a broken handlebar n' my friend Rich here said you guys do welding?"

She smiled and looked at me in a strange uncomfortable way.

"Matt, huh? Are you one of the Gonders that live down on the corner?"

How does she know, I wondered, but I swallowed the lump in my throat and continued.

"Yeah, how do you know who I am?"

She smiled kindly and responded vaguely.

"Oh, I just like to know who my neighbors are. Your sister Monica comes over to babysit every once in a while."

"Oh, yeah," I answered, relieved.

"And yes, my husband does welding. Why don't you bring your minibike by next weekend? He welds almost every Saturday."

"He does?" I smiled.

"Yes, and I'll tell him to expect you."

"Okay, thanks! See ya next weekend, then." I smiled and waved.

"It was really nice to meet you, Matt, and you too, Rich."

She said that as if she already knew me, which was eerie. Rich and I walked away.

I had ample time to purchase an old lawnmower engine during the week, thanks to the want ads in the paper, and found just what I was looking for at the same five-dollar price. Mark, John and I bolted the engine in place, easy as pie, hooking the chain onto the sprocket wheel, gassed it up, pulled the cord and rode down the driveway towards the street on its first trial run. The handlebar was dangerously wobbly, still in need of welding repair, but we all took turns riding it, hanging on for dear life.

The following Saturday, I rode the bike down to the house across from Rich's, where the man was working in his garage with the door wide open. He heard me pull into his driveway and came out to greet me and laughed, telling me how funny-looking my contraption was, but I didn't care. It worked, which to me was all that mattered. He saw what needed welding and rolled the minibike into his garage. His weird wife was nowhere around, thank God. Ten minutes later I handed him two bucks for the welding job he did, thanked him and rode the bike back to our house. The whole thing was up and working for twelve dollars, plus gas. Naturally I let Mark, John, Snorky and Rich ride it alone, and we all took turns spinning the wheels down the street around and through the parking lot at Mirror Lake Elementary, riding that noisy minibike every day for the rest of the week.

Monica and Marguerite finally returned home from their Idaho vacation and I couldn't wait to hear their stories about flying, so I ran to them as soon as Dad drove the car up the driveway.

"Hey you guys! What was it like?"

Monica answered first.

"Fun. Aunt Marcella and Uncle Keith were really

nice and Kirk and Mike say hi."

"That's good but it's not what I meant. What was the airplane like? Flyin' up in the air?" I begged.

"Oh, okay." Monica offered without emotion.

By that time, Marguerite joined us.

"Just okay?" I couldn't believe my ears.

"It was like bein' in a big bus in the air instead of on the ground. You could get up and walk around and go to the bathroom and look out the window but you didn't feel nothin'."

"So what did you see out the window?" I whined for more.

"Just clouds," Monica added dryly, killing any hope of adventure for me. But then Marguerite became more animated.

"And we got lunch, too," Marguerite teased Monica, who woke up on that point, laughing.

"The lady," Monica began.

"Stewardess." Marguerite corrected.

"Yeah, the stewardess tried to give us a tray of food, but I told her we didn't want any, because we didn't have any money."

Marguerite couldn't help but join in.

"She was given' everybody a tray but nobody was payin', so then I asked her why and she told us that it was free so I told her to give us one, too."

Monica laughed at her embarrassment. I couldn't believe they thought flying was nothing special or worth remembering, so I changed the subject.

"Guess what, you guys, I got a minibike."

"A minibike? Really? I wanna see it." Marguerite squealed.

We went out to the garage and I presented my new baby to my sisters.

"Can we ride it?" Marguerite asked.

"Sure, tomorrow, if ya like," I answered, remembering something I wanted to ask Monica.

"Hey Monica, you know that lady who lives across the street from Rich and Nancy's? She said you babysit for her."

"Is her husband the man who works on cars n' stuff all the time?

"Yeah, yeah. He welded my handlebars back together."

"Yeah, I know her, why, does she want me to babysit again?"

"I don't know, she didn't say nothin', but she looked at me funny, like she knows me."

"She knows all of us. She was the judge when Dad went to court after Mom died."

"What?"

"Yeah, she knows the Andersons, too. She's the one who found 'em for us to live with."

Monica, the quietest of us five, rarely spoke out, and to hear her blurt out this news bulletin with such insight in a nonchalant way completely chopped me off at the knees. It took me a minute to regroup and collect myself. I stood there stunned as thoughts surged through my head. So that's why that lady looked at me so weird and knew who I was. We all had been told the story of how Dad battled the court system to gain custody of us in '62 and how he stood before the judge and yelled "I'll be GOD DAMNED if ANYBODY thinks they're gonna take MY kids away from ME! I'll take 'em off n' we'll hide out in the goddamn Canadian FOREST before I let any sonofabitchin' court split US up!" The judge, touched by Dad's courage and devotion, promised she'd find a solution within the law, which she did, and hence we all lived with the Andersons so that Monica and Marguerite, still in diapers at the time, could have a maternal presence in their infant lives. And now I learn

that the same judge lives down the street and her
husband just welded my minibike? This was too Twilight
Zone for me.

The next day Monica and Marguerite told all their
friends about my minibike, and all of a sudden every kid
in the neighborhood showed up for a free ride.
Marguerite and Monica had all their friends over and I
proudly gave rides to one kid after another, sitting
behind me on the seat. I rode past the judge's house a
few times, but nobody was home. Was she following us?
I wondered what I would say to her if I did run into her
but the opportunity never arose. I forgot the whole thing
as we enjoyed riding my minibike until Marguerite
complained, refusing to sit on the back of the seat like
the other kids.

"I don't want to ride on the back of it with you. I
wanna ride it all by myself like Snorky and you guys."

"You don't know how to ride it, you're gonna get
hurt."

"No I won't!" she defended.

She caused such an uproar that I finally gave in,
showing her how to accelerate and slow down, yelling
instructions over the loud noise of the motor. She hopped
on the minibike with confidence, smiling at Anita and
Barbie.

"Watch me, Anita. I can do it."

She cranked the accelerator full throttle and her hand froze, jerking the bike into forward motion, much faster than she had anticipated. She let out a scream louder than the engine noise and sped across the lawn. I tried to yell at her to release the throttle, but she couldn't hear me. I ran after her in an attempt to stop her but she was going too fast. She pulled the handlebars and headed straight for the bushes next to our house, going in with such force that she snapped a couple of big branches. The motor died and we pulled her and the bike out. Thank God nothing bad happened to the minibike. A few branches got caught in the motor and frame but once I yanked them out, it started right up again and I hopped on, riding it down to the school. When I came back, Marguerite was sitting on the lawn, putting pressure on her leg, surrounded by her friends.

"I'm bleedin', Matt, I'm BLEEDIN!" she moaned.

I killed the motor and went to her side.

"I'M BLEEDIN'," she cried.

"I think she might need stitches, Matt." Anita announced.

"Stitches? God, Marguerite, I said you couldn't ride the bike alone but you wouldn't listen, would ya?" I yelled at her.

"I'm bleedin'," she whimpered.

"Let me see it," I said.

She uncovered her leg, and sure enough, one of the branches that snapped had cut deep into her leg, and although I felt sorry for her, I was more afraid of losing my minibike forever.

"That's nothin', put a Band-aid on it. It's just a small cut, a scratch."

"It is not! I'm bleedin' lots," she cried dramatically.

She was telling the truth and had blood all over her hands, and I was angry with her and myself for letting her ride the minibike alone.

"God, Marguerite. Always gotta have it your way, don't ya?"

When Dad came home and caught wind of what had transpired, he fortunately didn't take my minibike away from me, but insisted I stop giving rides to the little kids and to keep them away from it. Dad took Marguerite to the hospital to have her leg stitched up, and afterwards, in typical Marguerite fashion, instead of moaning about her leg *bleedin'*, she sought sympathy if anyone touched her leg by crying "My stitches! My stitches!"

Dad was leaning over the stove making chicken and dumplings to calm the stitches storm with comfort food, and while scooping spoonfuls of dumpling batter into the hot gravy, he spoke out to all of us.

"Hey kids, I got a call from your Aunt Mary the other day."

"Really? How is she?" Mark asked.

"Where is she? I added.

"She's fine. She called from Portland. She asked me if she could come stay with us for a few months until she finds a place of her own in Tacoma. What do you all think about that?"

"Aunt Mary's comin' back?" Monica inquired, wide-eyed.

"If that's okay with you," Dad answered.

"Why does she want to go to Tacoma?" I cringed.

"Well, she knows a lot of people there. Her ol' pal Father Blaes is still at Bellarmine."

"Father Blaes!" Marguerite screamed joyfully.

"Well, Padre could help Aunt Mary find a job in nursing. How's that sound to you guys? Can Aunt Mary come stay with us for a while?"

Dad, always put major decisions before us to discuss and decide upon democratically. Of course, no one opposed the idea, so a week later, on the following

Saturday, Dad pulled his car into the driveway and hit the brakes. In a heartbeat, Aunt Mary hopped out of the passenger seat of the car, wearing a fancy linen dress and her usual big sunglasses, squealing in giddy delight. She looked better than ever, but didn't quite seem her old self. I wasn't used to seeing her in something other than a nurse's uniform or a floral print muumuu.

"Matt! What a lovely tan you have."

She scuttled over to kiss me on the cheek.

"Hi Aunt Mary!" We all bellowed.

"Hello!" she squeaked as she kissed and hugged each one of us as she ran through our names.

"Oh, my, look at you! You've all grown so fast! Moni, how long your hair is!"

Marguerite jumped in, showing her leg.

"Look! I got stitches, Aunt Mary."

"Oh, and that little scab is going to make a beautiful scar, Marguerite. Come inside and tell me how that happened."

We were all happy Aunt Mary was back with us again. After all, she had become an integral member of our family. She lived with us for over three years of our young lives where we'd seen every colorful facet, heard every joyful laugh and painful cry she was capable of mustering, nursed her through many of her depressing and long binges with John Barleycorn that took her to hell and back, so it seemed totally natural to have our beloved prodigal aunt return to the fold. She was as alive and as honest with her feelings as Dad was, so we loved her in spite of her flaws. And so, as if she'd returned from a long sabbatical, Aunt Mary had finally come home.

Over the next couple of days, Dad installed a bed and dresser for his favorite sister in the living room, where she lined up her enormous collection of 33 LP's against one wall and had everything else piled up or boxed against other walls. She then set up her stereo right outside the open door to her bedroom against the dining room wall, and the classical music began to fill our house, honoring every composer from Bach to Beethoven, just like she had when we lived together in Portland and before that in Chehalis. Finally, Dad placed her rocking chair in the family room, and everything had found its proper place. Marguerite was the first to ask if she had kept all the Christmas albums in her collection, so Aunt Mary pulled them out of the piles in confirmation, loaded the stereo with all our holiday favorites and we celebrated a musical Christmas in August, singing for days until our hearts were satiated with Christmas carols.

The following Sunday after she moved in, Father Blaes drove up from Bellarmine Prep School in Tacoma for a visit, carrying his faithful box of tools. Our favorite Jesuit carpenter, he installed a curtain rod in the open doorway to the living room to give Aunt Mary some privacy. That evening, Dad served Father Blaes' favorite meal. Father Blaes said grace, blessing the pork roast and each of us in Latin like always, and we were once again the same old crazy extended family reunited, exactly as we had been in Portland, just as fate had ordained it to be. I thought Father Blaes might give us some grief for never attending Mass, but he didn't even mention it. He just laughed with Dad and Aunt Mary as they caught up with each other's news. The topic of the "instrument" he made for Dad in Portland never came up either, thank God, however Father Blaes did bring up one memory during dinner that tickled him, recounting the day back in Chehalis when we all accompanied Aunt Mary to her Alcoholics Anonymous meeting. The meeting host called out to the room.

"Who here is an alcoholic? Raise your hands!"

Almost everyone in the room raised a hand in the air in admission. Marguerite looked around and blared out in full voice:

"I'm not an alcoholic, I'm a Catholic!"

We all laughed hard, and it felt good to hear Aunt Mary's familiar cackle rattling on with everyone else. We continued sharing memories all throughout the meal.

In no time at all, it was as if Aunt Mary had never

been separated from us for a minute. Our little Irish elf Aunt who drank cup after cup of black coffee and rocked in her chair for hours on end, was back just like always. I loved listening to all the classical music she played morning to night, and I brought her up to date on everything that had or was happening in my own musical world, from Mrs. Habedank and the all-city choir in Tacoma to Mr. Warner's Boy's Chorus, not forgetting to mention the superior rating I received at the solo contest.

"That's wonderful, Matt."

"Yeah, and I can read music, now, too."

"Can you, now? Where, may I ask, did you learn this marvelous skill?"

"At school in choir. Mr. Warner teaches everyone."

"Does he now. Well, may God bless him for that."

I couldn't help but inquire.

"Aunt Mary, did Grandma Gonder teach you how to play the piano?"

"No. She was too busy. We were a family of twelve children, you know."

"Well then, who taught you?"

"We had an old upright in the shed, and I taught

myself, when I didn't have to help with the chores. I was the eldest sister, too."

"But then you became a concert pianist, didn't you?"

"No. I had a scholarship at Gonzaga, but, well, let's just say it didn't work out."

"What happened?"

"Matt! Stop asking so many questions. Life happened. Then I went into nursing, and that, my dear Matt, is the end of me story."

She didn't want me to continue badgering. I got the clue.

"I wish I could play the piano like you did. Dad tried to get me one, but nobody would give him credit and he feels real bad about it, so don't tell him I told you."

"Oh, I see. Well, pianos are very expensive."

"Yeah, I know."

"Matt, I have an accordion in my room, if you might be interested in learning to play that."

"An accordion? You play the accordion, too?"

"I did, many moons ago," she sang out in her Irish

accent.

"Really? Can I see it?"

"It's somewhere behind all those boxes in my room."

"I'll help you get it, if ya want."

"I can do it myself. I'll bring it out for you, tomorrow, Matt."

The next day, there it was, sitting in the dining room waiting for me when I came home from school. Aunt Mary sat rocking away and pointed to an old suitcase covered in fake alligator skin. I snapped open the case and looked at the accordion.

"How do you play this thing?"

"Bring it over here, and I'll see what I can do to show you."

I lifted out the heavy instrument and carried it over to her. In rapid gestures, she had those straps wrapped over her shoulders and her right hand placed on the keys, while her left hand tickled the black buttons on the left side. She pulled the instrument apart to fill the chamber with air, and then began playing a simple waltz. I watched, amazed, until she stopped playing.

"I can't play like I used to. I've lost all dexterity in

my fingers. Here, it's yours, Matt."

"For keeps?"

"Yes," she said, pulling the instrument off her shoulders and handing it to me.

She helped me into the accordion, adjusting the leather straps to fit my body. I couldn't see the keyboard nor the black buttons and felt something was wrong.

"But I can't see the keys."

"You're not supposed to, Matt. With practice and in time, you'll *feel* the keys."

She was being generous and trying to offer a solution to quench my musical desire, but I felt no connection whatsoever to that heavy accordion attached to my body. I'd dreamed of playing a distinct Rachmaninov piano sound as opposed to the organ noise this thing emitted that reminded me of roller-skating at the shopping center, but I didn't want to hurt her feelings.

"Thanks, Aunt Mary."

"You're welcome, Matt."

I felt her watch me as I walked away, full of disappointment I couldn't conceal. I went into my room and freed myself from the contraption, placing it on my bed. I sat there and looked at it, poked a few of the buttons and admired the pearly white of the keys, wondering how I got myself into this mess, then got an idea. I sat in front of the keyboard, anchored the instrument between my feet on the bed and pumped air into the bellows using my legs and feet, playing only the keyboard side like a piano and ignoring the black bass buttons on the other side. The accordion keyboard was definitely lacking in the number of keys it had compared to the eighty-eight you found on a piano, but I had found a solution. Rudimentary, yes, but where there's a will there's a way. Eventually, the bedcovers got entangled in the folds of the bellows, so I placed the accordion on the wood floor against the wall. In this position, the bellows slid easily with my feet and legs pulling back and forth. I owned my first "piano", and would play for hours, plucking out the notes on the sheet music I brought home, and decided to make the accordion my 'rehearsal' piano, that I could, once the music mastered, show off on the real pianos, once I got back to school.

10. COLOR MY WORLD

As the new school year cycled around, my brothers, sisters and I jumped feet first into our own agendas of adventures, activities and interests. We still did things together, but the more we grew, the less time we spent with each other, choosing rather to run around in other circles of interest with new friends. It's odd that growing up often makes us grow away from our families. But we still saw each other at home, especially if Dad was cooking something, or whenever inclement weather kept us indoors which legend says happened on occasion in the Pacific Northwest. On such days, the Monopoly set, much to Dad and Aunt Mary's dismay, was always around in some handy place, ready for a good game of sibling warfare where absolutely no mercy was granted towards one another. No sir, kindness and fair play had ne'er a place at our game table. We played for blood and aimed directly at our opponent's jugular.

Mark had moved up to Federal Way High School to

begin his sophomore year, joining the football team as expected but also a Mechanics class. One of the requirements for every student of Mechanics was to furnish an engine to study and practice on. Mark begged me to 'lend' him my minibike engine that he would strip, clean and reassemble at school, promising it would run better than ever once he had finished. I categorically refused his request and there was no way I was going to trust him. I loved my minibike, but Mark hounded me constantly, promising the moon. Finally I gave in. What an idiot I was. Mark unbolted it from its frame, carried it to school, took it apart but never put it back together, and that, sadly, was the last I ever saw of my minibike.

John, a ninth grader at Sacajawea, was looking forward to his return to school, as Mr. Warner, not only the choir teacher but also the extra-curricular sailing teacher, had commissioned the Shop class this year to make laser-sized fiberglass sail boat hulls, which would actually be sold to fund school programs. John quickly learned to cope with the annoyance of itchy fiberglass on his skin and spent more time scratching his arms than actually building hulls. John signed up to play football again as well.

Monica had joined the throng of teenage girls in the seventh grade, and as we rode the bus to school on the first day, I was relieved to know she wouldn't suffer the humiliation of wearing a training bra to P.E. class like the poor girl Jerry Leavenworth told me about last year.

Marguerite was the only one of us remaining at Mirror Lake in her fifth grade year (she was held back a year before first grade due to her late birthday on September 24th) with her neighborhood girlfriends.

I was in nirvana, an eighth grader, now enrolled in two of Mr. Warner's choirs, the "Concert Choir" of eighty mixed voices, and a smaller choir class of elite voices that Mr. Warner called "Select Singers". I was a bit envious of Sue Warner (no relation to Mr. Warner), who played the piano for choir and could sight-read the accompaniments with ease. Mr. Warner passed out folders full of songs to rehearse including the classic arrangements of *Exultate Deo*, *Hosanna*, *How Excellent Is Thy Name*, added to the unaccompanied 'a capella' arrangement of *The Paper Reeds By The Brooks*, the modern arrangements of *Who Am I?*, *American Trilogy*, and finally a very difficult arrangement of *It Is Good To Be Merry*, which wasn't merry at all, because it changed time signatures in almost every darn measure. I loved drowning in the four-part sound that filled the room and could count out my part as well as anyone else, outside the time we spent on *It Is Good To Be Merry*, where everyone fumbled and toiled daily. Mr. Warner threw us a curve ball with that song and enjoyed making us sweat it out, making it very clear to everyone that the singers in Concert Choir would not have an easy ride but would be required to work hard.

I had never experienced singing four-part vocal music before and I felt like I had joined the Mormon

Tabernacle Choir that I heard many times on Aunt Mary's Firestone Christmas records. In Select Singers, we concentrated on jazzier version of popular songs we all knew, including: *Sunshine In My Soul, Unchained Melody, Like To Sing About Sunshine* and *Walk On By.* Both choirs were full of hormonally blossoming girls, and being one of the best tenors admired for my vocal prowess in last year's solo and ensemble contest, I had earned the reputation of being something of an eighth-grade singing stud. One of the female singers I quickly befriended was Esther Schmeichel, a bouncy blond who laughed constantly. I had a crush on this girl who was always smiling and full of positive fun energy. Whenever Esther spoke, her eyes danced and darted about the room as her thought process connected with her words, giving me the chance to steal free views of her perky and perfectly shaped boobs without being taken for a pervert. I would have bet money she totally skipped the training bra phase of her growth and was born directly into a C-cup. Yes, in my eyes, Esther was simply bursting with talent. Oh yeah, she could sing, too. Soprano or Alto or something, who cares?

That afternoon, I hopped onto the first bus home. Walking through the front door, I immediately knew something was wrong. I could hear Aunt Mary's rocking chair grinding the linoleum floor of the family room but there was no music coming from the stereo and filling the air as usual. I peered in from the dining room and saw Aunt Mary in her muumuu and slippers, caught in the early stages of one of her dark moods, rocking in a trance and staring out into space. I had lived through her binges and mood swings in Portland and Chehalis, and knew I was powerless in the situation. It's never easy to watch someone you love suffer, but sometimes, there really is nothing you can do but pray the storm will be gentle and pass swiftly.

"Hi Aunt Mary," I said softly.

She didn't respond. As it was my turn on dish duty, I went into the kitchen and tried to be as quiet as possible as I got to work. A few minutes later, I had forgotten my intention to remain quiet and was singing out loud to myself with my hands deep in the sudsy water when the doorbell rang.

"Can somebody get that please? I'm doin' the dishes," I yelled out, hoping Monica or Marguerite were around. Then I flinched, remembering I was trying to be quiet for Aunt Mary. Nobody responded. No one was home but Aunt Mary and I.

"Oh, I'll get it," Aunt Mary grumbled, annoyed at the interruption, but she dutifully got up to answer the door. She could pull herself out of her demon dance whenever she had to deal with something, as if the devil had held the macabre orchestra in paused suspension long enough for her to deal with the pending issue and wait for her return to her rocker. She opened the door and there stood one of Lori Moss's little brothers. I could easily hear the conversation from the kitchen.

"Yes?" she inquired.

"How much do ya want for that gold bike frame hanging in the garage?" asked the nine year-old boy.

"It's Mark's bike, Aunt Mary!" I yelled from the kitchen.

"And where, may I ask, is he?" She inquired.

"At football practice!" I bellowed back.

"Very well," she said, then turned to the Moss boy to offer a kind word.

"Well, I'm told the bicycle belongs to Mark."

The kid continued.

"How much you want for it?"

"You'll have to ask Mark. The bicycle belongs to him, I told you."

"He never uses it. It just hangs in the garage. I wanna buy it."

Aunt Mary's was being challenged, but she remained calm and firm.

"I understand, but Mark is not HERE right now to answer your request, so I'll put it to him when he comes home, yes?"

"You should sell it to me."

Aunt Mary was beginning to lose her patience but kept her anger at bay, trying to reason with the nine year-old.

"It's NOT mine to sell, and Mark may very well have other intentions for it. Now be a good boy and come back later to ask him yourself when he returns from football practice, yes?"

That seemed to settle the matter.

"Okay, thanks."

"Goodbye," she closed the door on that.

The boy went away. Aunt Mary returned to her rocker and trance, growling to herself. Not a half hour later, I was in my room pumping the accordion against the wall, playing out the musical parts of a song Mr. Warner assigned and didn't hear the doorbell. Again, Aunt Mary got up and answered the door. As soon as I heard voices, I stopped playing to listen.

"Is Mark back yet?" the Moss boy asked in his whiny distinct voice.

Oh God, I thought, Aunt Mary is going to blow a gasket, but she surprisingly kept her cool. Barely.

"NO, he hasn't returned from football practice just

yet, and by the way, it hasn't been thirty minutes since you asked me the LAST time," she answered back to the kid, hoping he'd get a clue that he was annoying her.

"Ya think he'll sell me the bike?"

He began pushing her buttons and didn't know what he was in for.

"I can't answer for HIM. He'll have to do that himself when he comes home. Now go away and come back later and ask HIM!"

"I'll give him five bucks for it. That's fair."

She began to steam up.

"FAIR or NOT, the decision is not MINE to MAKE!"

It was obvious that he didn't know my Aunt Mary. I wondered if I should run to her rescue but I decided to stay put, safely hidden behind my accordion-piano.

"Well, when's he gonna be here? I can't wait around my whole life, ya know," the kid complained.

Aunt Mary lost it.

"YES, WELL, NONE OF US ARE GOING TO GET OFF THIS PLANET ALIVE!!"

She slammed the door, growling between her teeth

as she hurried back to her rocker.

"AHHHH!"

And finally, not fifteen minutes or so later, the doorbell rang again. This time, I heard the ding-dong. It took me a minute to pull away from my accordion straps and run to the door, but Aunt Mary beat me to it and stood there steaming in front of a kid that was about to lose his life.

"LEAVE ME BE!" she barked.

The kid was undaunted.

"Here, why don'tcha' just take the five bucks and give it to Mark and I'll take the frame," he said, handing a five-dollar bill to her. She all but foamed at the mouth, delivering her clincher.

"SEE YOU IN THE SOUP, BUDDY!" she blared as she slammed the door shut, turning to me.

"GAD," she growled, adding, "YOU WONDER WHY I DRINK!"

Monica and Marguerite finally came home, followed by John and Mark from football practice. Aunt Mary, still worked up from the episodes with the Moss boy, gave Mark the message from the Moss kid, and as soon as Mark said he didn't want to sell the frame, she announced that she'd be taking us out to dinner that night. The thought excited everyone, as we couldn't afford to eat at restaurants too often, so we were all trying to decide which one to go to, not coming up with a solution everyone could agree upon.

"How about pizza? Johnny LOVES pizza," Aunt Mary offered.

She didn't get any resistance, so pizza it would be. We all hopped into her car and drove down to Fife, a small town between Tacoma and Federal Way, to an Italian restaurant with red and white checkerboard tablecloths and empty Chianti bottles filled with colored water lined along shelves against the wood-paneled room. We placed orders for our own pizza with our favorite toppings, while Aunt Mary poured down one Miller High Life beer after another, making it clear that pizza was not our reason for being there. That Moss kid was the straw that pulled her off the wagon.

As soon as dinner was over, Aunt Mary paid the bill but could hardly stand up straight. We guided her out and she managed to pour herself into the driver's seat of her car. Once the rest of us were in place, we drove off, heading for the I-5 freeway. She swerved a few times, scaring the hell out of us, but regained enough control to continue, until all of a sudden, in the middle of the freeway, she passed out at the wheel, heading towards the embankment. A car passed us and honked his horn.

"AUNT MARY WATCH OUT!" John screamed from the passenger seat next to her, as we sideswiped the car in the oncoming lane next to ours. The crunch snapped her back to reality, but she cranked the wheel hard in reaction, pounding the accelerator with her foot at the same time, so we veered quickly to the shoulder on the opposite side of the lanes. We all screamed, certain we were looking death in the face, but then, calmly, it was as if some divine hand mysteriously grabbed the car and placed it delicately in the right lane. We weren't wearing seat belts, as no one did in the early '70s, but miraculously, no one was hurt.

Our little episode was just enough to wake Aunt Mary out of her drunk, enabling her to drive us home in semi-sobered silence. I remember getting out of her car and crossing the threshold of our house, happy to be alive and relieved to learn that pizza in Fife was not to be our last meal. Afraid as we all were while it transpired, the freak accident was forgotten almost as quickly as it happened. It wasn't an event anyone felt the need to publicize, and thank heaven our multiple school activities took precedence over our dance with death, while poor Aunt Mary lost herself in the throes of a binge that lasted a couple of weeks. She didn't come out of her room except when absolutely necessary until finally her demons granted respite, allowing her to come up for air. Dad, empathetic and patient as ever, was right there, nursing his sister back into the arms of the living. The moment classical music embalmed the air of the house again, we knew she was on the road to recovery.

October rolled around and we were at the grocery

store one day. While standing in the check out lane, Dad saw a sign for big bags of bubble-gum near the cash register and couldn't contain himself, speaking to the sales clerk in his most charming manner.

"Well, look at that! Your sign up there reads: '60-cent value, yours for only 69 cents'. That's a hell of a bargain you got goin' on there, I'll take two!"

The sales clerk laughed nervously.

While other folks were shopping for their Halloween candy, they also purchased snow-covered pumpkins as two inches of heavenly dandruff fell on Oct. 27, heralding hope that the weather God would indulge us this year so we could enjoy our favorite winter sport, hooky bobbing. Sadly, the snow melted all too soon. November brought us to our first performance in Concert Choir. In the back of the choir room there was a closet in which Mr. Warner kept gold blazers he would hand out to dress everyone up, and we wore them as proudly as we sang. The holiday season began like every year with the annual television presentation of *The Wizard of Oz*, which we were able to watch for the first time at home, in color, and when the first day of December arrived, Aunt Mary's diamond chip needle began to grind through our holiday collection of vinyl 33's, filling our home and hearts once again with the music we all cherished, performed by our favorite artists. The concert at school gave us the opportunity to sing *The Little Drummer Boy* in four part harmony in addition to other holiday crowd pleasers, and then, once school let out for Christmas vacation, we were all together to celebrate the birth of our Lord following the traditional ways we reprised each year, complete with Dad's laundry basket full of nuts, fruits and goodies, and this year Dad surprised us by bringing home six boxes of chocolate-covered grapes in addition to the dreaded chocolate-covered cherries that always made us sick to our stomachs. Like vultures, we descended upon our stuffed turkey with all the trimmings swathed in gravy and cranberry sauce until the carcass was clean, and finished it all off with our favorite pineapple upside-down cake with maraschino cherries.

With the holidays behind us, heaven finally came through with another winter blessing that answered our prayers during the second week of January 1972, when a few inches of snow fell on the streets of Federal Way. The first clue we got was waking up and blowing smoke rings with our breath as we lay in bed. Dad called out to us from the kitchen.

"Up and at 'em, kids, c'mon in the kitchen where it's warm!"

We jumped out of bed and ran to huddle around the kitchen stove, just like we had done in Portland. Dad sometimes had trouble paying or forgot to pay the heat bill, but we didn't mind. We drank hot "Swiss piss" chocolate to warm us up and ate cinnamon toast while gazing at the snow out the kitchen window.

"Man, it's freezing," Monica shivered.

"Yeah, it got a little cool," Dad answered, sending us pealing with laughter.

We couldn't wait to get out there and play in the white fluff, so we hurried to get dressed and ready to leave, only to discover the front door had frozen shut. John yanked and pulled with all his strength, but the door wouldn't budge. Dad poured boiling water along the door seam, breaking the seal, and we ran out to the bus stop just as the bus pulled up to the stop. Naturally, we couldn't wait to initiate Snorky and Rich in the art of hooky bobbing, but thanks to the time we lost opening the frozen front door of the house, we had to wait until we got home from school later that afternoon, when we played our winter sport together throughout the neighborhood, teaching Snorky and Rich the finer techniques.

The next day, we put our skills to the test and grouped together to hooky bob on the back of a huge flatbed truck that came down the street. There was room enough for all five of us lined up on the bumper of the big monster. We squatted down, grabbed on and glided past a few houses, having the time of our lives. Unfortunately for Mark, the ride eventually positioned him right over a metal manhole cover that didn't freeze over under the snow, the metal grid scraped his feet and made him break his squat position, falling forward. Afraid of being called a "wuss", he hung on for dear life, rode it out on his belly and ended up with a very nasty freeze burn stinging his chest and stomach. Everyone else eventually let go of their grip and fell off, then stood up quickly to chase John, the reigning hooky bob champion, who rode the bus clear down the street and onto 312th avenue. On the way home from school that day, the gang jumped off our bus at the stop, and ran around the back and grabbed a hold of the school bus bumper. The bus pulled away from the stop and we hooky bobbed down 8th Avenue South, past our house and clear down the street to 320th, letting go just before the bus turned onto the busy street. The snow didn't last long, but it was better than not having any at all that winter.

Along with many other students approaching their 16th birthday, Mark was enrolled in Mr. Sandstrom's Driver's Ed class at Federal Way High School, where he was given the code pamphlets to study and was taking his driving classes religiously with Mr. Anderson, one of the football coaches. Mark came home one day and shared the story of one of his fellow students that afternoon. Apparently, Mr. Anderson told the student to "check the rearview mirror." The student fixed his eyes on the mirror for what seemed like an eternity until Mr. Anderson, exasperated, finally said: "Just look where the cars are, you don't need to check whether or not the guy shaved this morning or if he's wearing green socks!"

In a heartbeat, January turned into February. In Concert Choir and throughout every other choir, we were preparing for the solo and ensemble contest. I signed my name on the sheet right away and true to my personal promise to cooperate, Mr. Warner chose and gave me the song *Drink To Me Only With Thine Eyes*, written on a poem by Ben Jonson. I didn't put up any resistance whatsoever this time. I gratefully worked on the solo arduously, and when Mr. Warner asked me to sing tenor in a barbershop quartet in addition to my solo, I instantly accepted. He picked three other boys to sing *My Lord, What A Mornin'* in a TTBB (Tenor 1, Tenor 2, Baritone, Bass) arrangement with me, and we jumped at the challenge, working together like a team of athletes in harmony, singing out:

My lord what a morning,

My lord what a morning,

My lord what a morning,

When the stars begin to fall.

You'll hear the trumpet sound,

To wake the nations underground,

Look in my God's right hand,

When the stars begin to fall,

When the stars begin to fall.

When I announced the news to Aunt Mary, hoping

the news would excite her as much as it did me, she was caught in the throes of depression. She wasn't drinking this time, but she wasn't her normal bouncy self. I thought my news would pull her out of it.

"So will you come hear me sing at the contest, Aunt Mary, please?" I begged.

"We'll see, Matt, we'll see," she answered without conviction.

By then, well into my second year of choir under his direction, Mr. Warner was without doubt my musical champion and I no longer questioned his authority, or should I say choices of what I should sing. I didn't give anyone authority over me to be honest, excluding Dad, who held veto power but never exercised it. Written on my solo sheet music was a dedication "To Celia", a derivative of Mom's middle name, Cecilia, so once again I found a personal correlation between the solo I was to sing and my mother. I just took it for granted that Mr. Warner knew everything about my life by this time, but that it was okay for him to know. He never mentioned any details so I didn't feel threatened. I memorized the words and melody in a day and sang the song constantly at home or at school, making it mine:

Drink to me only with thine eyes and I will
pledge with mine

Or leave a kiss within the cup and I'll not
ask for wine

*The thirst that from this soul of mine doth
ask a drink divine*

*But might I of Jove's nectar sup' I would
not ask for wine*

*I sent thee late a rosy wreath not so much
hon'ring thee*

*As giving it a hope that there, it could not
withered be;*

*But thou thereon did'st only breathe, and
sent'st it back to me,*

*Since when it grows and smells, I swear,
not of itself, but thee!*

Mr. Warner organized long rehearsals, guiding each student through rough passages of their songs until the big contest day arrived, and again, we all bustled off to some school where pianos had been installed in many of the rooms. Like last year, there was a huge grade board set up in the cafeteria with everyone's name listed in columns. Throngs of noisy people milled about, looking for information or seeking a room on the map tacked up next to the grade board. I found my room and calmly went in a few minutes before my appointed hour. People were shuffling all over the place, some jumping up to leave and others arriving to watch my performance. The adjudicator was talking to the singer who had just done her solo but she didn't appear to be happy with what she was hearing. I panicked a little, figuring I was going to have a tough judge. Finally, the singer stood up and walked to the door fighting back tears. Just as I began to feel sorry for her, the adjudicator read the name off the form on his desk.

"Matt Gonder? Is he here?" He asked.

I raised my hand.

"I'm here."

I stood up and walked to the front of the room with my pianist. All of a sudden, I saw Dad and Aunt Mary scuttle in and take seats at a couple of empty desks near the front. I smiled at them and felt so happy as it was the first time anyone from my family had acknowledged my singing by attending one of my musical events, and there they both were, looking out of place and oversized, squished into two student desk chairs. Aunt Mary had left her flowery muumuu at home and was looking sharp in a navy blue suit, giving her a strong aura that commanded attention. Everyone's eyes went to her wondering who was that important and scary woman in dark sunglasses with Dad, who looked like he could be her bodyguard. I loved the attention they were given, which made me feel even more important as a result. The adjudicator nodded his head in my direction, my cue to begin. I felt butterflies in my stomach at first, but as soon as Debbie Reugsegger played the piano introduction, I had calmed down and sang out to Aunt Mary and Dad in the audience, not caring about anyone else. I arrived at the last note and everyone applauded as I joined the adjudicator at his desk. He stood up as I arrived, shaking my hand and inviting me to sit down. I peeked down at his desk, hoping to catch a glimpse of the contest form with my name on it, but he had nothing written on the paper. At first, I thought "Oh, no", but then he spoke.

"That was beautiful, Matt, very beautiful. It has been a privilege to listen to you, young man. You have quite an instrument. I have nothing else to say but to thank you for singing for me."

I couldn't tell him I sang it for Aunt Mary and Dad.

"You're welcome," I said.

I walked over to Aunt Mary and Dad, both standing near the door.

"Hi Aunt Mary. Hi Dad. You guys came!"

Aunt Mary kissed me on the cheek.

"Matt, that was wonderful!"

Dad had tears in his eyes and smiled silently, shaking his head.

"We better get outta here unless you wanna hear the next singer," I informed them.

We left the room and stood outside the cafeteria

where Dad and Aunt Mary could smoke and have a cup of coffee. I stayed with them, explaining how the whole shebang worked, with music and pianos in all the schoolrooms. I was so happy they were there for me, even though I could tell Aunt Mary was putting up a brave front. A little while later, one of the assistants entered and began to write up the grades of the past hour on the big board. My adjudicator gave me a "1+" grade for my solo and I was on top of the world, because Dad and Aunt Mary were both there to witness the near-impossible mark being written up. I had to remain a couple hours longer to sing my barbershop quartet number, but Aunt Mary was uninterested in hearing anything else so I said goodbye to them and Dad drove her home. I ran around to other rooms to give support to friends of mine as they performed, and my quartet performed on schedule later on and were given a "1" for our performance. At the end of the day, drained from the full day of music and emotion, everyone bid farewell to each other and went home, Mr. Warner more exhausted than anyone.

Right after the contest, while still on a high from friends congratulating me for my performance, sad news burst my happiness bubble when Aunt Mary announced that within a month she would be moving to Tacoma. She had undergone many medical examinations and tests; it was decided she needed surgery. Father Blaes, with his many connections in Tacoma, helped her set the medical wheels in motion. I didn't know what to think. I felt like our world was crumbling again. Aunt Mary had only been back with us since just before school began and now she was leaving again. I guess I should have become accustomed to the constant upheaval, moving and changes that happen in life. Lord knows we had moved so many times that our family alone probably kept U-Haul in business, but I just wished everything would stay as it was. I wanted my crazy family to remain together right there in that rambler on 8th Avenue South, but that wasn't to be. The only choice given me was clearly stated in Reinhold Niebuhr's Serenity Prayer that I had learned back at the Alcoholics Anonymous meeting I attended with Aunt Mary in Chehalis.

God, grant me the serenity

to accept the things I cannot change,

The courage to change the things I can,

And the wisdom to know the difference.

On March 20th, we celebrated Dad's forty-eighth birthday. Marguerite asked him what his favorite cake was, and when he answered "a burnt sugar cake like Grandma Gonder used to make", I found the recipe in Mom's 'Joy Of Cooking' and got to work. My cake, made from scratch, turned out chewy and tough once baked, but Dad was touched that I made the effort for him and choked down two pieces, rinsing it down with coffee to avoid suffocation and early death. Aunt Mary barely got through her first piece. Nine days later, on

Monday, March 29th, Monica and Marguerite baked and frosted a cake for Mark to celebrate his sixteenth birthday and join the ranks of young adults. Mark grabbed the phone first thing in the morning to schedule his appointment to take the driver's permit test at the Department of Motor Vehicles office in Auburn. The next day, Dad drove Mark down to Auburn to take the test, but Mark didn't pass, getting nervous and making six mistakes when the maximum number of errors allowed was five. One error in particular sent Dad into a tizzy.

"Dammit to hell, what was the sixth question you missed, Mark?"

"Is alcohol a stimulant or a depressant?"

"Hell, that's an EASY one! How could you get that question wrong?"

"I thought of how you always get excited when you drink, so I answered 'stimulant'."

"JE-SUS CHRIST!"

Mark reviewed his errors and studied throughout the week, relieved to pass the test on the second round a week later.

Days after Mark's driving test drama, Father Blaes drove up in a truck early one morning. I tried my best to think positive, but my heart was shattered. Silently, we

279

all carried out and piled Aunt Mary's bed, clothes and her huge and heavy collection of records into the back of the truck. We shared a last pork roast lunch that Father Blaes blessed, and afterwards, Aunt Mary bid us farewell and they drove off to Tacoma. I stood there at the end of the driveway, watching the truck until it turned way down on 320th Street, then I went back into the house. I looked around. Aunt Mary's stereo left no shadow on the dining room wall where it stood. The living room was once again cavernous and empty, except for two of Mom's paintings that remained like orphans hanging on the walls and a few dust bunnies hovering in the corners of the wood floor. It didn't feel the same way as when Lyle left, because he was just a friend. Aunt Mary leaving us was like losing a family member and I felt sad and lonely. I wondered what would become of this empty space next and I couldn't stand the echo of silence, so I pulled my accordion into the barren living room and pumped it against the wall where her bed stood, but didn't make much music. Dad heard me plucking the keys and came in.

"Hey Matt, you wanna take a drive with me?"

Sad as I felt, I was always game for a trip with Dad.

"Okay, where we goin'?"

"It's a surprise," he answered.

Dad rarely said that. I was intrigued. We hopped into the car and drove a short distance to the parking lot of a furniture warehouse.

"What are we doin' here, Dad?" I asked.

He looked at me with a smile.

"C'mon, let's go inside."

I followed orders, got out of the car and walked with Dad up to the glass doors, not certain at all what he was up to, but there wasn't any reason not to trust him and play along.

"Matt, I know you're sad that Aunt Mary left today, but she'll be okay. She has some health problems she's got to attend to, and soon as it's all over we'll see her again."

"We will?" I asked.

"Sure we will. Now, you're the 'artiste' of the family, so I brought you to this here store to choose some furniture for the living room. It's high time we got some use out of that damn room ourselves. What do you say 'bout that?"

I looked at him in disbelief.

"You kiddin' me?"

"No, I'm not. You choose it, and it's ours." He laughed.

"Wow! Okay."

I burst through the glass doors and ran around the whole warehouse floor, closely followed by a salesman who cringed as his young client shopped and jumped on every couch in the store, until I finally chose a long, gold "L-shaped" couch, a couple of arm chairs, a long coffee table, a carved side table and a lamp. Once I had made my choices, Dad looked at the salesman.

"Okay then, that's what he wants, so I guess it's time to fill out the paperwork and I'll start makin' the payments."

I had a question for the salesman.

"When are you gonna bring all this stuff to our house?"

I could tell he thought it strange to be taking orders from an eighth grader, but he complied. After all, a client is a client, no matter how young.

"We could deliver Wednesday or Thursday, if you like."

"Can't. I got school. Nobody's home then."

"How about next Saturday afternoon?"

"Wow. Okay, Saturday's good. I'll be home, waitin'."

The following Saturday, the furniture was delivered on schedule. We had swept and mopped the floor to welcome our new furnishings that once installed, made us feel like normal people who sat watching TV together just like they did at Snorky's house. Marguerite popped popcorn for everyone to munch on together, fistful after fistful until nothing remained but the uncooked kernels she tossed out the back door into the flowerbed next to the stairs.

A few days later, John brought home an incredible lamp of golden glass in a wooden frame that he designed and had made in Wood Shop. He screwed a couple of hooks into the ceiling and draped his work of art on a long golden chain. From that day forward, his lamp presided majestically in the corner over the couch that, when turned on, cast a warm golden hue throughout the entire, now furnished living room, which softened the blow of Aunt Mary's departure. Rapidly, we began to invite our friends over to the house rather than just meeting up in the street somewhere, especially since there was now a place for everyone to sit like normal people. The novelty of having furniture wore off quickly. We had felt inferior to others during the time we didn't have any furniture, and now that we had some, the whole thing seemed ridiculous and trivial. Dad began making the monthly payments as we began to take our furniture for granted, jumping or flopping onto it, as we would abuse our beds.

Something unexpected caught us off guard in the

middle of spring, when, on April 17th, right in the middle of a freezing cold morning at school, a little over an inch of snow fell on Federal Way. We daydreamed as we watched it float down delicately through the windows of our classrooms, but it melted almost as soon as it touched ground. However, once school let out for the day, while the school buses drove in and began lining up, the whole gang rallied together to goad John, our hooky bobbing king, into giving a demonstration in the school parking lot for the poor souls not initiated into our novel winter sport. John couldn't back down and immediately accepted the dare. The snow had almost completely melted on the pavement, but we all knew it would take more than that to deter John. While Snorky, Rich, the Hilderbrands and I scrambled to the back seat of the bus to watch out the rear windshield, John grabbed onto the bus bumper just as the driver accelerated, pulling him through the slush and water puddles down Sacajawea's driveway. Other students, waiting for their buses on the sidewalk, screamed support and team cheer. The school office windows overlooked the parking lot, and next thing we knew, Mr. Pocrnich, the principal himself, came running out.

"John Gonder, you LET GO of that bus right NOW!" He yelled.

John pretended not to hear and continued sliding a dozen feet more until he started burning the rubber of his shoes on a patch of dryer pavement. Mr. Pocrnich flagged the bus driver to stop, and as soon as she hit the brakes, John let go, standing up to receive his punishment. The other students listened silently as Mr. Pocrnich gave John both barrels.

"You could get yourself killed pulling stunts like that! I'm suspending you from school!"

John stood there taking it all in.

"Does that mean you're gonna give me a paper to have my Dad sign or somethin'?" John inquired.

"No paper. You have your Dad call me!"

That meant serious business. Quietly, John climbed onto our bus where we had a seat waiting for him. But as soon as we pulled out of the parking lot, we burst into laughter, slapping John on the back and congratulating our champion, all the while aware that John had to tell Dad.

"Too bad Pocrnich didn't just give you a piece of paper for Dad to sign that I could forge for ya." I said.

"Yeah, that would've made things easier," Rich piped in.

"Oh, well, can't change it now," John pointed out.

"Nope, what's done is done, as Dad would say," I added.

We continued to recount and laugh at the whole

incident along with the other kids on the bus. When we arrived at our stop, Snorky and Rich bid John "good luck" and went home. That night, John realized it wasn't his lucky day, when Dad, oiled up from his stop at King's, came in. John took a deep breath for courage and spilled the beans.

"You stupid sonofabitch, right in the school parking lot? What the hell got into you?" Dad howled.

"I was just havin' fun." John offered lamely.

"Fun? You call that fun? You think gettin' your ass suspended from school is fun? Shit! So now what the hell are we supposed to do?" Dad barked.

"You hafta call Mr. Pocrnich or he won't let me back in school."

"JE-SUS Christ! Okay, then, gimme the goddamn number!"

The next day, Dad called the principal and got a scolding on proper parenting that he knew was coming to him, but he just let Mr. Pocrnich empty his sack, affirming everything he said with a "Yes, you're right, I know," and afterwards, John's suspension was lifted.

Everything about school became routine and each day its own adventure, however common, until the year quickly came to an end. Final tests and report cards were being handed out, yearbooks were penned with promises of everlasting friendship, and Peni Englestad invited me to work on a project she was finishing for one of her classes in which she had to make a short movie on her super-8 camera. Along with pals Dawn Arend and Cindy Cummings, Peni's mom drove us all to Southcenter Mall in Seattle where we filmed all afternoon after first treating ourselves to an Orange Julius drink. Once edited, our masterpiece became a "GonEngAreCum" production. I don't know why she gave me top billing, after all, it was her project. Maybe I just convinced her it sounded better that way, who knows?

11. POPCORN

The day school let out for summer we were ready for the sunny play days ahead of us. Mark went to work right away with Dad in the shop, where Dad handed Mark the keys to his first car: a light blue 1964 Pontiac Catalina that one of Dad's buddies in the used car business sold to him for the outlandish price of $35.00. The vehicle had power but the engine was tired, and knowing Mark's limited experience behind a steering wheel, that was all Dad was willing to spend to get him a car that would not only give him more freedom, but also come in handy with the family shopping, errand runs and Sunday evening jaunts to the laundromat. As soon as Mark got his wheels, he willingly drove everyone around to pick up or do whatever required his chauffeur skills, but after a couple of weeks he grew sick and tired of the constant demands on his time; therefore he limited his driving chores to certain days for certain tasks. He was always available to drive if it meant having fun with the neighborhood gang, however.

Since Dad was in the car business, it was natural to see him drive around in an array of cars, and often times he showed up at the house in a different model that he'd return the next day. One night, he drove up in a 1970 Plymouth Road Runner, saying this one was his new baby for keeps. We all jumped in as Dad tossed the keys to Mark. That car had power and a kick that startled everyone at first, but gave a fast, exciting ride and was fun to flaunt around town at the time. After a week, just as Mark was getting used to driving the powerful motor and the rest of us to the status symbol, Dad drove home a sensible and much calmer 4-door Ford LTD.

"So what happened to the Road Runner, Dad?" Mark asked.

"Aw, that car is just too much car for me. I need something a little less powerful and a little more comfortable," Dad replied.

Boy, was Mark disappointed. The rest of us, however, were relieved, as Mark never did get a handle on that Road Runner and we thought each errand we ran might be our last with him behind the wheel.

A couple of weeks later on a late June Saturday morning, John, Monica and I were watching cartoons. Mark went outside to discover the passenger's right back quarter panel of the Ford LTD was all smashed in. He came in and told us. A little over an hour later, Dad was up, had shaved and was drinking the cup of instant coffee I made for him at the dining room table. He got up and went out to pick up the newspaper off the front porch and returned to the table in a sour mood, slapping the paper down hard, his face contorted in anguish.

"What did you do to your car last night, Dad?" Mark asked innocently.

"What the HELL do you mean what did I do to my car, what did YOU do to my car?" Dad snapped.

"Me? I didn't drive your car, Dad," Mark replied in defense.

"Ya didn't?" Dad said, stumped. He became silent for a moment, trying to remember what he had done the night before. Well, Dad had been to King's as usual, tied one on, left and got into his car without looking at the other side. We watched as his mind worked silently until, finally it came to him.

"Aw, SHIT! Someone must have tagged my car when they pulled out of King's parking lot. God Dammit! Well, let's get going," he said to Mark. From Road Runner beauty to smashed LTD within a matter of weeks, our status in town plummeted back down to the lows.

That evening after dinner, we were all watching TV when the phone rang. Monica ran to pick up the receiver.

"Hello?"

A short pause followed.

"Oh, hi Aunt Mary!" Monica said.

All heads turned to her as she continued talking.

"U-huh. Sure, just a minute," she said then turned in our direction.

"Dad, it's Aunt Mary. She wants to talk to you," she said, handing him the phone.

We all listened and watched Dad as he held a short conversation with his sister.

"That sounds real good, Mary. I'm glad to hear it," and then, after a long pause,

"Okey dokey, lemme ask the kids."

He pulled away from the phone to speak to us.

"Hey kids, you wanna go down and visit with Aunt Mary next Sunday?"

"YEAH!" we screeched in unison.

Once Dad hung up the phone, he announced that Aunt Mary's surgery had been a success, that she was released from the hospital, back on her feet and was doing better than ever, now living in an apartment of her own and working full time as a nurse. The following Sunday, we drove south on I-5 through the "Tacoma Aroma" and up to a house that had been divided into two apartments. Aunt Mary lived on one side. We knocked, and she quickly opened the door and welcomed us in like royalty in her muumuu and slippers. She had piles of freshly baked chocolate chip walnut cookies for us to snack on while she and Dad rocked and visited for a few hours. I was so happy to see her doing so well that I had to find out more about what she'd been through.

"So, did you have an operation, Aunt Mary?"

"Indeed I did, Matt. A very big operation, and I feel better than I have in twenty years!"

"I'm glad, but what did they do to you?"

She stopped rocking and looked deeply into my eyes.

"Matt, you remember how depressed I would get, don't you?"

"Sure, who doesn't?"

"I know, honey, and I'm sorry I put you all through my horrible moods…"

"And almost got us killed," John interrupted.

"Please! Don't remind me! I didn't know WHY I felt so bad, God, so horrible, until the doctors here in Tacoma found seven, SEVEN very large tumors in my uterus, the size of GRAPEFRUITS, that were messing up my hormone balance and killing me every time I had my period."

"Ooh, that sounds yucky."

"Yucky it was, Matt. VERY yucky as you say, indeed, but that's all ancient history now and I feel WONDERFUL!"

"Good."

She let it go at that and had us all set the table for a huge taco meal. When we opened the fridge to get the hot sauce, there sat a one-gallon jug of mayonnaise, right in the middle of the main shelf with nothing else. We teased Aunt Mary constantly about living alone but needing mayonnaise by the gallon. She cackled her familiar laugh and we had one of the best afternoons we ever spent with her. She no longer felt any need to drink and guzzled glass after glass of her new favorite drink: "cool, clear water".

On the return drive home from Aunt Mary's, Dad announced that Gordy, from Sporty Roofs, had passed away.

"What? Gordy died?" John asked.

"Yep," Mark answered.

"What did he die of, Dad?" I inquired.

"Well, let's just say he died right in the middle of enjoying the oldest profession on earth."

"You mean a hooker?" John asked.

"Yep," Dad said, grinning. "At least he went out with a smile on his face."

We all laughed and silently wished good ole' Gordy a safe trip to heaven, asking him to say hi to Mom, while on the radio, Chuck Berry sang a song that became a huge hit:

Now this here song it ain't so bad

Prettiest little song that you ever had

And those of you who will not sing

Must be playing with your own Ding-a-ling

All I can add to that is thank God we had two bathrooms at home to appease the three pubescent boys in our house with no traffic jams outside the bathroom door.

As soon as we arrived home, Marguerite went out into the back yard, but quickly screamed from the patio.

"You guys, hurry, come out here and LOOK!" she yelled.

John, Monica and I ran out the screen door to see what her problem was. She stood there, pointing at a green plant pushing out from the flowerbed and jumping up and down.

"It's my popcorn. It's GROWING."

Sure enough, a stalk of corn was pushing up towards the heavens. I poked the plant a little, which seemed strong and robust.

"Don't hurt it. I'm gonna water it and make it grow real big so we can have our own popcorn."

We couldn't challenge her. It was too cute. Besides, fantasies just need a little air to breathe and a little love to grow into realities.

"Go for it, Marguerite." John encouraged her.

She watered and cared for her plant daily and the darn thing grew so fast I thought it might be a manifestation of Marguerite's will in action. That stalk of corn kept on pushing towards the heavens more and more each day.

So, while Aunt Mary had quit drinking altogether, Dad, contrarily, rarely met a drink he could refuse, but luckily, he had a strong resilient metabolism that burned it out of his blood during the night, and he bounced up the next day, ready for work. He'd say "If you're gonna hoot with the owls at night, you gotta soar with the eagles during the day", in other words, if you party at night, that's fine, but you better get your ass out of bed in the morning. His bottle stories were fodder for legends. His reputation had been secured long before the day he returned home from the navy in late 1945 after World War II, when he went out to the Idaho State Line to enjoy the dance halls, bars and cheap vice that was sold everywhere. He and his brother Vince were out painting the town, drinking and cavorting until they got so drunk they poured themselves back into their Ford 1938 2-door sedan to drive home. Vince was so drunk that he passed out in the back, and Dad, true to his strong-willed seafarer's constitution, was behind the wheel. However, as he was really too drunk to drive, he literally crawled at a snail's pace on Highway 93, going so slow that a cop didn't even have to chase him in his car, he simply walked up to the slowly running sedan and spoke to Dad through the driver's window while strolling along next to the car.

"Sir, I think you should pull over."

Dad, still driving, turned to the cop and mumbled through his forty-proof breath.

"What's the maaatter, Officer, was I speeding?"

"No, you're going too slow! You're impeding traffic!" he answered.

Vince woke up in the back and slurred:

"I'll drive, I'm okay!"

Once parked on the side of the road, the cop asked them where they lived.

"Valleyford."

Life was more forgiving back then, especially for men just home from the service. The cop told them to drive carefully and get home safely.

There's a saying that goes: "The apple never falls far from the tree". Jim Gonder's offspring were definitely chips off the old block, and as such, shenanigans, not necessarily connected to a bottle, were our specialty, too. The gang decided to go to the drive-in movies one night, but no one had much money. No problem, we stuffed Snorky, Rich, John and me into the trunk, and Mark drove up in his Catalina with Rusty next to him in the passenger seat and paid for two tickets at the gate. As soon as he parked his car, he opened the trunk and we all jumped out, making too much noise in celebration of our prank. Well, soon enough, one of the security guards caught us and lead everyone into the office, where we had to give our phone numbers before they threw us out. Rich was scared shitless that his Dad would kill him, so he told the guard he was a Gonder, too. We drove home and told Dad what we had done that night, pleading with him to help us protect Rich. The next day, Dad got a call from the drive-in owner.

"Yes, this is Jim Gonder...yes, they're my boys, yeah, all *four* of 'em...uh huh...oh, they did, did they? ...Well, yeah, but I slid under the circus tent a few times in my day, too...uh huh...I'll make sure they pay the ticket price in full the next time...okay...goodbye." Dad wasn't mad and told us to watch more carefully to see who was keepin' an eye on us whenever we pulled a prank like that in the future!

Merely a few days after that episode, we were looking for another fun summer activity to engage in. Since Mark was the only licensed driver among us, we developed a burning desire to go camping without our parents for the first time in our lives. Snorky and Rich joined Mark, John and me in the organization of a long camping weekend that would begin on July 29th. We presented the idea to everyone's parents, running through the lists of things everyone was to bring, the menus of what we would eat for every meal and other details. They all laughed at us but agreed to let the crazy boys have their fun. We gathered everything we needed, including Rich's dingy we planned to tie on top of the vehicle, and on departure day, piled everything into Dad's LTD, as Mark's Catalina often had engine trouble and we didn't want to end up stranded anywhere. Heading east, we drove over the Snoqualmie pass in the Cascade Mountains, continuing on 114 miles until we arrived at the Ellensburg KOA campground, a flat camp site with very few trees. The site had good bathroom facilities and a pool table in the community recreation room, which we enjoyed, but we spent most of the night tying down the tent and fighting the strong winds that kept trying to make everything fly away.

The next day, we drove to Yakima State Park, where thank God the "answer wasn't blowing in the wind". We pitched our tent, goofed around and fished the Yakima River, cooked meals over an open fire and wasted time out in the wilderness. Returning to Federal Way, all we could think about was doing it again, so we organized an even bigger trip, borrowing a 6-foot dinghy from Rich's Mom. We left a week or so later, drove up to North Bend, about thirty miles away and floated down the river in the boat near Snoqualmie, then spent an hour skimming stones, until John, hurling rocks anywhere and everywhere, threw one that hit me in the back of the head. It knocked me down and out, but I came to, finding everyone admonishing John for his lack of control. Sporting a welt on my head for the rest of the trip, we soon found a bend in the river and decided to swim across against the strong current. Knowing the danger before us, Snorky, Rich, Mark and I float/swam across comfortably, letting the current carry us to the other side at an angle. John, however, with a mix of fear and adrenaline rushing through his veins, paddled like a madman, making a straight beeline for the other side. We watched him in amazement as he darted so fast he didn't seem to get wet. We lost track of time having fun, then drove home, arms stretched out the windows to keep a firm grip on the dinghy that kept wanting to slide off the roof of the car.

Soon after our camping trip, a prodigal visitor no one ever expected to see came back into our lives. Dolores Tan, the short, curly-haired woman Dad dated back in Tacoma came home with him one night, running through the door, squealing and howling like a banshee. She really overdid the welcome, as my brothers, sisters and I basically just stood there in shock and disbelief. We all knew Dad went out with her in Tacoma when we arrived from Portland but that had ended eons ago, and yet here she was again, standing in our dining room in Federal Way, hugging each one of us as if she had gone on a short trip and had missed us like you would family, but she wasn't part of our family. I was dumbfounded. Dad hadn't announced her visit, which was strange behavior on his part. He always let us know in advance when someone was coming, if, that is, he himself was aware there lurked a visitor on our doorstep. Maybe she caught Dad by surprise, I thought, but no, that couldn't be right because they came in the house together. Anyway, she asked lots of questions about our school activities and interests, told us how good we all looked and how much we'd grown while she and Dad smoked and drank lemonade. We learned that she had driven up to Dad's shop that day and they ended up at King's, which by then was easy to figure out since they were oiled up, their breath a surefire giveaway. The 'reunion' with Dolores continued through dinner and when I woke up the next morning, she was still there, coming out of Dad's room. I tried to pass by her.

"Hi Dolores. 'Scuse me, I gotta ask Dad

somethin'."

She held her hand up in defense.

"Your father is still sleeping, Matt. Can it wait until later?"

I wasn't used to anyone coming between my Dad and me under any circumstance, so I did not like her reaction, even though she was probably acting out of consideration for Dad's welfare. We had become too used to our open-door policy and she was putting up a wall where there never was one before. She could see I wasn't happy with her choice of words.

"Is there anything I can do?" she asked kindly.

"No, I'll tell him later," I said with a cold attitude, and walked away.

When, a little while later, Dad got up, he said a quick hello and went out to the bathroom off the laundry room to shave. I hoped I'd catch him once he came out, but Dolores was standing guard in the kitchen near the bathroom door making coffee and scrubbing the counter to prove her usefulness. I felt invaded. Okay, so we were slobs and the counter tiles were dirty. So what. Nobody asked her to clean. Why was she doing that? Finally, Dad came out of the bathroom and sat at the table to tie his shoes.

"How's about a quick cup 'o coffee?" He said. We

always took turns making Dad's coffee, so I jumped up, ready for duty, but this time, Dolores was too fast on the ball.

"Comin' right up!" She said, rushing in and placing his cup on the table. I sat back down and watched as he gulped it down, unable to say a word until they left together for the shop, bidding us all goodbye.

In a matter of days, Dolores drove her VW van up to the house, packed full of her belongings, and we knew that was the sign that something serious was beginning. She opened crates of oil paintings that she had collected, boxes of ornate knick-knacks and antiques that once displayed, really gave our home a soft feminine touch. The only paintings we owned were Mom's framed prints of Degas' *Ballerinas*, Renoir's *Dance at Le Moulin de la Galette*, and my favorite, Monet's *Poppies*. Dolores had enough sensitive tact to not move any of Mom's prints, but added hers on the walls here and there around them, creating a museum effect. Her things really set off our new living room furniture, creating a sense of abundance and wealth, but it wasn't our house anymore. She was intelligent, kind and smart enough to never make any rules for us to abide by, but at the same time, we walked around on eggshells, afraid to undo her many efforts to create a home of beauty for all of us to share. She donned an apron and rubber gloves and sterilized every room, except she didn't go into our rooms, thank God. She made sure the kitchen cupboards were stocked with all our favorite staples and comfort foods, and only proposed to prepare other dishes for us if we felt like trying her cooking. She made an effort to not interfere with our established ways, but to add something to them if we accepted.

Once she got the house in order, she started working full-time with Dad, doing secretarial and billing work with Vince. She got up with Dad, went to work with Dad, came home with Dad, slept with Dad, and this routine went on almost every day. Slowly, we all began to resent her, because we felt like we lost our Dad somewhere in the Dolores shuffle. She'd talk to us and tell us what Dad was doing or what he wanted us to do, creating a filter between us, and none of us liked that at all. She was only trying to be of service to Dad, and do what she thought was right for all of us. Dad seemed to be happy with the new living arrangement, so we all swallowed our frustration, focusing more on things to do away from the house.

One Friday night, Mark drove his Catalina with Snorky, Rich, John and I in tow, out on the town for some fun. We ran into a buddy of ours down by the High School who was walking slowly, had bloodshot eyes and spoke in long, stretched out phrases.

"What's with you, you drunk?"

"No, I'm not drunk. I don't drink."

"Well, somethin's wrong with you. Your eyes are all red, too."

"Ya wanna know what's wrong with me? This is what's wrong with me."

He pulled a plastic baggy out of his pocket.

"Is that...?" Snorky asked.

"That's what that is. This here's weed, boys," he answered, looking around and seeing someone familiar nearby. "I gotta go. See ya later," and he ran off to join some other friends, leaving us in wonder. We'd heard about marijuana before but had never seen it.

I turned to John.

"That's what weed looks like? Looks like the Italian seasoning Dad puts in spaghetti sauce."

"Maybe so, but I hear it don't have the same kick," Mark answered.

We laughed and hopped back into the car, turning on the radio. Gilbert O'Sullivan began to sing a song called *Alone Again, Naturally* that shot through my heart like an arrow.

"Hey turn that up, will ya?" I begged.

Mark cranked up the volume and I listened to every word of the number one hit for the first time. I couldn't believe my ears. Here was a sad song of a guy who wanted to kill himself because he got stood up at the altar, he doubted God, his Dad died and his Mom had a broken heart, all in the same song? How could he expose his life like that to music? I had to fight back tears myself as I felt such compassion for that poor guy singing his heart out, feeling alone again, naturally, the same way I had felt so many times in my life. I don't recall what else we did for fun that night, because I only wanted to hear that song again and again.

All throughout the summer, aside from the odd babysitting and yard work jobs that came my way, I worked as a volunteer at one of the local convalescent centers, spending every Thursday in the Arts and Crafts room, receiving group after group of elderly folks who wanted to exercise their motor skills in creative ways. We cut colored paper and made collages, finger-painted, wove macramé plant holders, did all sorts of artsy-crafty activities and I had a great time chatting with and getting to know the lives of some of the inmates while making cool stuff at the same time. Family members would join the old folks on occasion and join in on whatever project their seniors were working on. I was happy to see other people arrive on occasion, if only to learn that the old folks weren't totally abandoned and forgotten. One elderly woman in particular, Anne, had a sweet manner and all her marbles. She'd make dry comments about this and that and always smiled at everyone, but never once did a family member visit her when I was there. One day I learned that it was her birthday, and thought surely a daughter or son would come by to honor such a kind old woman, but nobody showed up. Time ticked away, Anne smiled and worked on her yarn project all by herself, and it began to bother me. I went out into the hall and called home, hoping Mark would be there with his car, but Dolores answered the phone.

"Hello?" she said.

"Dolores, it's Matt."

"Hi Matt" she said, full of affection.

"Is Mark home?"

"I'm sorry, he's not. I'm the only one here."

"Oh."

"Anything I can do?" she offered again. I didn't want to ask her of all people to do me a favor because I didn't want to owe her anything in return, but my desire to make Anne happy was more powerful than anything else, so I caved in and sold out.

"There's an old lady I like here that's all alone and it's her birthday. Would you do me a favor and drive down to the bakery and buy a cupcake and bring it here so I can sing "Happy Birthday" so she won't feel forgotten?"

"I'd LOVE to," she blew into the phone. She'd been waiting for me to throw her a baited hook and I knew the price I'd have to pay her back, which meant being nice to her. It was obvious that what she wanted was for me to accept and befriend her, but I was holding back in my snotty, ice-cold manner, a character trait that Dad had long ago said I got from my mother. Apparently Mom was that way, too. According to Dad, Mom "could make the sun shine if she was happy, but if she was mad, the best thing to do was to run in the opposite direction as fast as you could." He would tease me whenever I manifested this facet of my personality by saying "whenever Matt's happy, EVERYONE'S happy, but whenever Matt's unhappy, EVERYONE'S unhappy." Dad made light of it, but I wasn't proud to own that character trait, because whenever I exercised it, I always ended up building a wall between me and my opponent, which made me hate myself, and poor Dolores was now bearing the brunt of my "gift" for no other reason than for being present. I felt guilty and ashamed as I waited for her behind a bay window to show up. Not twenty minutes later, her Volkswagen van pulled up into the driveway. As I hurried outside, Dolores jumped out of the driver's side and handed me a cake box, grinning as if she was giving me an award.

"Hi Matt! I got you four cupcakes, different flavors, so you can share with the others, too. And I bought some candles and put a book of matches in there too, for ya."

I took the box, looked up at her and smiled, full of contrition. She'd gone way beyond the call of duty and looked so hopeful, wanting to please and be my friend.

"Thanks, Dolores," I mumbled. "I better get these in, so I'll see ya later, ok?" I said, apologetically. She understood my message, nodded her head with a victorious grin and hopped back into her van. She waved and blew me a kiss as she drove away and I sighed, actually feeling lighter for releasing my anger towards her. I went inside, displayed the cupcakes on a paper plate and put a candle in each. I lit the wicks with a match and got everyone to sing *Happy Birthday* to Anne. She was very touched and even shed a few tears. Her happiness became my compensation for finally giving in to Dolores. I went home that afternoon, and Dolores was disinfecting the refrigerator. I thanked her again for the cupcakes and she smiled, relieved to know I had changed my attitude. Looking around, I saw that the last few drawers in the kitchen had received a thorough scrubbing by the curly-haired woman in rubber gloves, and I admit it was nice of her to put herself out for our comfort. Before she came, we straightened up, swept and wiped things down from time to time but rarely used any elbow grease unless Aunt Fran was in town, but Dolores scrubbed as if she was on a mission to dethrone Mr. Clean.

So, Dolores became a new member of our family shortly before the new school year began. John joined Mark at Federal Way High School, Monica and I were at Sacajawea, while Marguerite was now a big shot in her sixth and last year of elementary school at Mirror Lake, singing Michael Jackson's *Ben* non-stop with her girlfriends. The daily agenda of the first day at school each year was usually an easy ride of reuniting friends sharing tales of summer vacations, but Mr. Warner had a very serious tone as he welcomed us back, announcing the good news that Sacajawea's Concert Choir had been selected to perform at the All-Northwest M.E.N.C. (Music Educators National Conference) General Session on Monday, February 19, 1973 in Ballroom A at the Hilton Hotel in Portland, Oregon. This was truly an honor that excited us all, and naturally, Mr. Warner had already selected the list of songs we would perform, many of which were beyond normal junior-high school level. He set the tone, making sure we knew we'd have to work harder than ever to make the cut as he passed out *The Last Words Of David*, a song with an incredible virtuoso piano accompaniment of octave arpeggios that ran on forever. It was so complicated in fact that a man named Ron Williamson came in to play the accompaniment that far exceeded our student pianist's capabilities. Mr. Warner also gave us: *Sure On This Shining Night*, a tender arrangement of the traditional prayer *Old Irish Blessing* that Lori Lundberg would accompany on her classical harp, *Carousel* with a four-hand piano arrangement, *Let The People Praise Thee*, and last but not least, Mr. Warner's a capella and personal favorite *The Eyes Of All Wait Upon Thee*. It became quite clear that there was going to be no time for fun or rounds of "Musical Chairs" in choir this year. Our sight-reading skills were immediately put to test.

Each day, we worked so hard on those songs, rehearsing the nuances Mr. Warner directed until our shirts were dripping in sweat and our eyes were bloodshot. He rode us hard, his arms slicing through the air dynamically, pushing us to memorize our parts much more rapidly than ever and he chided us if we needed to look at the music once we passed his deadline. There were moments of intense stress, but we all knew our reputation was at stake, so we bit the bullet and sang on, expending as much energy as the entire football and track teams combined, and as a result we made more beautiful musical sounds than ever. Yet, just when we thought we had given him what he wanted from us, Mr. Warner would flip back through his music, wipe his sweaty brow, raise his arms in preparation and ask for more.

"Let's take it again from letter C, measure 5! Ready? And... 1, 2, 3, and..."

Aunt Fran called Dad while we were in school that day, announcing that she was coming through town on her way to Tacoma to see Uncle Joe. When Dad shared the news that night, we were as always, excited to have her visit, but I also wondered if she wasn't coming to meet Dolores and check up on us. Dad orchestrated a huge picnic for everyone, and that following sunny weekend, Aunt Fran showed up on schedule at our house with her daughter Diane and her friend Eve. In preparation for the day, I had purchased two packs of film for my Swinger camera and took photos of everyone in front of the house with Aunt Fran, and snapped a photo of Diane and Eve before they continued driving on to other destinations.

Our house was buzzing with activity. Inside, Mark, John and Marguerite were busy gathering and bagging up picnic items for the day. Dad was in the kitchen whipping up his special potato salad when Aunt Fran came in. He handed her a beer, which instantly put her in a silly mood, and we piled everything into the huge blue and white GMC bus that Dad parked in the driveway. Dad had purchased the bus earlier that summer to use on business trips, so he and Mark could carry materials to other cities on jobs, but today the mammoth vehicle had been emptied of vinyl tops and tools to drive everyone on an inaugural family fun trip.

In the back yard, Monica modeled her new bikini for Aunt Fran, so I took my sister's photograph that forever captured her in bathing beauty glory. Dolores, busy putting on her make-up when Aunt Fran arrived, came out, introduced herself and shook Aunt Fran's hand in greeting, saying she had an appointment to run off to before joining us later at the lake. Camera happy that day, I then took a picture of Marguerite on the patio. Afterwards, I called Dad out to let me take his photo, and he meandered onto the patio with Dolores and posed for me happily, but when I tried to take one of him with Dolores, she ran back into the house, refusing to have her photograph taken. Not wanting to take her "No" as an answer, I had Monica stand on the patio with my camera as I went in and tricked Dolores, telling her I put my camera away, and then I pushed her out the back

311

door. Monica snapped the camera and got a photo of Dolores in mid-air, right next to Marguerite's popcorn plant that by now had grown over four feet tall. Dolores drove off to her appointment and the rest of us piled into the GMC bus and drove off. During the ride, Aunt Fran asked a few questions.

"Dolores seems like a very nice lady," she said, obviously wanting information.

"She's okay," I answered.

"Well, your Dad seems happy and it's nice to have a woman around the house, isn't it?" she asked.

"She's not here that much, she works with Dad at his shop." Monica added.

But Aunt Fran was forever looking on the bright side.

"I can see she's done a lot and I think it's good for you all," she said, and left it alone.

Dad saw a couple of hitchhikers thumbing for a ride. He pulled the bus over to the side and opened the door, asking where they were going.

"High Dive," the young Man answered.

"Well so are we, so hop in!" Dad said. They climbed in and sat down. There was more than enough room in the bus for them and a few more. Dad asked if they were hungry and offered them something to eat, but they declined, saying they were meeting friends for a picnic. As soon as we arrived and parked the bus in the lot, the hitchhikers thanked Dad and went their way. Uncle Joe and Aunt Lorraine were standing there waiting and helped us carry our food to the picnic spot they reserved with tables for everyone. Our hitchhikers went their way, and we basked in the sun and sat around the picnic table stuffing our faces.

There was a huge wooden platform built over the lake, where divers could climb ladders to jump off decks at ten, twenty, thirty, forty or fifty feet. We swam and splashed around under the sunny sky and took our turns climbing the ladders behind other swimmers to the platforms. Ten feet was easy for all five of us. Twenty feet was a slight challenge for Monica and Marguerite, but as soon as all three boys jumped from the twenty-foot deck, the girls forced themselves against their fear to follow suit. Dad watched from the shore and laughed at all of us, commending our courage. But then, both Mark and John climbed to the thirty-foot deck and jumped off. I was afraid to follow them up any higher, until Dad offered me fifty cents if I jumped off the thirty-foot deck. Fifty cents? I couldn't refuse that deal. I climbed up to the thirty-foot deck and looked out at the horizon. Fear overcame me and it felt like my balls were caught in my throat. I held onto the wooden pole and hesitated, trembling. I could hear Dad yelling at me from the shore.

"Jump, Matt, JUMP!"

I was slowing down the jumper traffic with each moment I waited. My heart pounded hard as I held on for dear life. Then the swimmer behind me said just what I needed to hear.

"If you're not gonna jump, ya baby, then move over and give the rest of us a chance!"

That was it. I jumped off the platform and swam to meet Dad and collect my fifty cents, proud to witness me overcome my fear. We swam all afternoon and I jumped off the thirty-foot deck a few more times after that. Dolores drove up as planned, and as soon as she arrived, Dad threw her in the lake, fully clothed. As she fell into the water, she banged her hip on a rock that bruised her, but she didn't complain, laughing all afternoon with everyone else. At the end of the day, Aunt Fran kissed every one of us before she left with Uncle Joe and Aunt Lorraine to drive to Tacoma, and we all piled back into the bus, heading for the brown rambler we lovingly called home.

12. COUNTRY ROADS

Our joyful picnic at High Dive Park was to be the calm before the storm. The following week, Dolores had us all sit down in the living room after school as dark storm clouds gathered and hovered overhead. She began speaking in a very serious tone.

"There was an important meeting today at Sporty Roofs. Your father and his partners think it's time to expand the business. They decided that Lyle will be moving to Yakima to open a shop there, Vince will stay and run the Seattle shop and your father will move to Wenatchee to open a shop there to handle jobs in the eastern part of the state."

We sat there in silent shock and dismay. How do you swing at that kind of curve ball? Wenatchee? We loved visiting Dad's sister, our Aunt Peggy, her husband Uncle Jim and our cousins Joanna and Michelle who lived in Rock Island, only seven miles south of

Wenatchee, but now to move there and leave Federal Way? My heart ached as my world shattered. All the resentment I felt for Dolores when she moved in came back to me a hundred fold and I hated her for being the one to announce the news, because this was a major upheaval and I was also mad at Dad for not telling us himself.

"Why do WE gotta move to Wenatchee? Why can't Vince go there and let us stay here?" I asked.

"Your father feels that Vince can run things better from here, especially since Vince doesn't have the technical know-how to install vinyl tops like your father and Lyle do," Dolores answered calmly.

"I wanna talk to Dad," John said, standing up and walking out.

"Me, too," Mark added, standing up in turn.

Marguerite tried to find the silver lining.

"Monica, if we move to Wenatchee, we're gonna get to play with Joanna and Michelle all the time."

"Yeah, and remember all the free fruit we got to eat there?" Monica pointed out.

I stood up and made my exit. Dolores watched me walk out and I knew she felt terrible, but I couldn't stand hearing her say 'your father this and your father that' because each time she said it I got the feeling she was adding one more brick in the wall between Dad and us. I didn't want to say something hurtful but I was so mad that my tongue would have lashed out easily, so I kept my mouth shut, joining my brothers to mope around the front yard. Dad came home later and we all gathered around, milling about with long faces. He confirmed the news, saying we'd be moving sometime in October, hoping we'd jump at the news, but when Marguerite was the only one who showed any elation, he changed his tune. He tried to lighten the air by mentioning positive things we already knew about Wenatchee but I couldn't adhere to the points he made.

"Yeah, but what about the All-Northwest Choir concert I'm supposed to sing at in Portland, Dad? I been workin' real hard for this."

For once, Dad didn't have an answer. I turned and went into my room. We all went to bed early that night, and on the bus ride to school the next morning, we shared the news with Snorky, Rich and our other pals. The news hit everyone like an anvil had fallen on top of his head, as nobody wanted to see us move away. I told Mr. Warner the news, and he looked at me sadly, saying he understood but that he would sorely miss his star tenor. Peni Englestad, not wanting to see me go away, offered a solution.

"Why don't you stay with one of our families, Matt, then you could sing in the concert."

And that began a rally that swept through the school like wildfire. Mrs. Paige got wind of the dilemma and stopped me in the office.

"Hi Matt. I heard your family is moving to Wenatchee?"

"Yeah."

"Are you excited?"

"No, I'm not. I'm sick of moving."

"Wenatchee is a real nice town. I'm told they have over three hundred days of sunshine every year."

"Yeah maybe, but I don't wanna miss the concert in Portland next February."

"Well, you can come stay at our house if you like."

"Really? Cuz' if you mean it, I'll ask my Dad."

"Yes, I mean it, Matt. We'd be proud to have you stay with us. You ask your Dad and have him call me here at school and we'll talk about it, okay?"

"Okay, gee thanks, Mrs. Paige."

"My pleasure, Matt," she smiled.

So that night, I told Dad my news, offering Mrs. Paige's solution so I could stay and participate in the

February concert. His eyes welled up with tears.

"Well, I'm sure gonna miss my Matt-sue, but if that's what you want to do, then that's what you should do, Matt, and I'll support your decision."

Throughout the following weeks, we packed up our belongings into boxes, tossing out the broken junk we didn't want to carry to Wenatchee. Dolores crated up her oil paintings and boxed up her antiques and stacked everything against the wall in the family room, and then we carried it all out to her VW van. I no longer felt sad, because I knew I was staying in Federal Way, so I helped everyone pack up and organize all the stuff we had with a smile, labeling the boxes by the rooms the stuff belonged in. Then, a couple of days before the move, I was stuffing something into a box when Dolores came in and put her arms around me, holding me tight against her and kissing me hard on the cheek without uttering a word. When she pulled away, I watched her tearfully repeat the same thing with Monica and then Marguerite. It was so strange. She then walked out to her van and drove off. I went into Dad's room. He was lying on his bed.

"Dad, is something wrong with Dolores? She's actin' really weird."

He sat up and invited me to sit next to him by patting the mattress.

"Dolores won't be coming with us to Wenatchee,"

he said, sadly.

"She won't? Why not?"

"She doesn't want to leave Seattle to live in a smaller town."

"Oh. Is that okay with you?"

He sighed.

"It is what it is, Matt. You can't make anyone do something they don't want to do."

A few days after that was said, the big moving day arrived in early October. I was scheduled to go to Mrs. Paige's house that afternoon once I helped with the move. Dad pulled a big U-Haul truck into the driveway and we started carrying out our furniture, bunk beds and all our stuff, piling it onto the lawn.

"Okay kids, let's get this show on the road!" Dad said, adding,

"And whatever don't fit in the truck, ain't goin' with us!"

We carried out box after box, handing it to Mark and Dad who stood in the truck on the receiving end organizing, piling and cramming until everything was stacked inside. Snorky and Rich rode their bikes over to say goodbye, then left quickly to hide their sadness. The

Moss kids along with Anita and Barbie also came by to give Marguerite and Monica a last hug.

"Matt's the only one stayin' here, right?" Anita asked.

"Yeah, Mrs. Paige is gonna pick me up later on today." I confirmed.

But then, after our friends had all said their farewells, I watched Marguerite and Monica climb into Mark's Catalina and sit next to Katie, chirping away in her cage, and the thought of everyone leaving without me became too much for me to digest. Dad was busy locking the back door of the truck, and called me over to him. He had tears in his eyes and I knew he wanted to say goodbye.

"Matt?"

I wasn't strong enough to listen to Dad utter goodbye to me. Without a second thought, I climbed into the cabin and sat next to his driver's seat, then John hopped in next to me, pulling the door shut. Dad came around to his door and looked up at me, bewildered.

"Matt, what are you doin' there?"

"Let's go," I said.

"But, you're supposed to wait here for Mrs...?" he added.

"Let's GO," I ordered.

He looked at me again, but climbed in and took his seat, turned the key in the ignition and put the truck into gear, pulling out of the driveway slowly. I glanced one last time out the window at 31408 – 8th Avenue South, silently bid farewell to the brown rambler full of memories, and then sat back, ready for the next chapter of our move out west, even though we were now heading east. As soon as we were on the freeway, Dad wiped a tear from his eye.

"I'm glad you're goin' with us, Matt."

"Me, too."

"You sure about this?"

"Yeah."

"Okay then, and we'll find a way to get you to Portland in February so you can at least see the concert, how's that sound?"

"Fine with me."

I had no mixed emotions whatsoever about leaving Federal Way, because I was sitting right where I was supposed to be, next to my Dad. I didn't have a thought for Mrs. Paige, who was expecting me, or Mr. Warner, who had taught me so much or for anyone else because when push came to shove, there was no room for doubt;

I had to go wherever my family went. That was my fate, no matter what. Mark's Catalina drove faster than the truck, so he guided the whole circus as we drove east over Snoqualmie and Blewett passes in the Cascade Mountain Range. Dad wanted to share the beauty of our state with us, so we made a short diversion when we hit Highway 2 and headed a couple of miles west to go over to Leavenworth, the famous Bavarian Village built to resemble the Swiss Alps, before once again heading east to Wenatchee. Then, as we descended along the Wenatchee River past Cashmere, the water glistened in the sunlight, and Dad mentioned how much fun five kids could have with a bunch of inner tubes floating down the rapids. John and I looked at each other, planting the idea firmly in our heads. We drove past the Tree Top apple cider plant and whizzed by the small town of Monitor. Whenever Dad drove, we rarely made any stops unless we needed to gas up or go to the bathroom, so in less than three hours from the moment we left Federal Way, we veered to the right, and just before crossing over the bridge where the Wenatchee river joined the Columbia river, the famous Red Delicious Apple sign beckoned:

Welcome to Wenatchee

Apple Capital of the World

Population 17,500

The city was named after the nearby Wenatchi Indian tribe, a name that meant "river which comes from canyons" or "robe of the rainbow", and also referred to as the "Power Belt of the Great Northwest" thanks to the hydroelectric dams built along the Columbia River. As soon as we entered the city, we rolled down the windows of the truck, as the air in North Central Washington was much warmer compared to the mild coastal peninsula breeze we had grown accustomed to in Federal Way. The surrounding mountains had all browned from too much sun and we arrived at the end of the hot season on the tail of an Indian summer.

Dad had been here and scouted around to make all the new living arrangements prior to our move and even signed up for milk delivery every morning, but since we couldn't pick up the house keys until the next day, we stayed overnight at the Town and Country Motel (today called the Moonlight Motor Lodge) at the top of the hill near the entrance to the city. Marguerite noticed the swimming pool before anyone else and dug through sacks of clothes until she yanked out her swimsuit, Monica's new bikini and our trunks. Dad couldn't have made a better choice of motel, as room #11, near ours, was set up as the free beer keg room for occupants. We didn't unpack much except for the few necessary items to get us through until the next day. Not ten minutes after Dad checked us into the motel, we were jack-knifing and doing belly flops in the pool, splashing water everywhere like a herd of retarded sea lions. Dad, who had never learned to swim as a kid, came out of the room in a pair of trunks and joined us, stretching out in an inner tube to cool off. Seeing him in the pool for the first time in our lives, I remembered the story of how he forcibly held the heads of his little brothers Porky and Butch in buckets until they opened their eyes under water in what Dad called his "open your eyes or drown" swimming method. Although Uncle Porky never learned how to swim, as an adult whenever his head got wet, he'd open his eyes wide by reflex after being well "trained" by Dad. Ironically, it was Porky's wife Aunt Val, who calmly taught me how to swim on a family camping trip without the help of Dad's torture training and with no bucket in sight.

We dried off in our motel room and Dad took us to dinner at the Chuckwagon, an all-you-can-eat restaurant that stood in the parking lot of the Valley North Mall, where I'm sure the owner didn't make much money that night after having six hungry Gonders attack his buffet like a sea of locusts.

The next day, Mark guided our circus down Wenatchee Avenue past Denny's, Sambo's, and then pulled in to the parking lot of an old-fashioned diner named Rooney's, "the place with the tree in the roof". We had a great breakfast of home-made pancakes and sausages at a table right next to the famous tree that the whole restaurant was built around, then jumped back into our vehicles to continue our drive down the avenue past more shops and the Cascadian Hotel. We had been here many times before on visits to Aunt Peggy's, so things looked somewhat familiar, although it had been a few years. Then Dad turned right after we passed the Bonanza 88 store and drove up Orondo Avenue past

Memorial Park where the Library and the Court House stood. We continued driving further up Orondo, passing the Plaza Superjet grocery store on our left and other homes on both sides of the street, until a few more blocks later he turned right onto Idaho Street and down one block to Douglas where he parked the truck. There, across the street from the Eye, Ear, Nose and Throat Clinic on the corner, stood an old white Craftsman house at 535, unassuming among the other homes on the street. We all jumped out and stood before the dwelling that was to be ours and looked around.

"Well, this is it, kids, what do you think?" Dad asked.

"It kinda reminds me of the one we had in Portland," I commented.

"But the porch is smaller," John blurted out.

"Let's go look it over!" Dad said.

We climbed the wooden stairs to a small porch. Dad retrieved the key from the mailbox and unlocked the door, inviting us to cross the threshold into an entry room with a carved wooden staircase on the left leading to the rooms upstairs. Under the staircase was a tiny room only big enough for a toilet behind the door, next to a swinging door to the kitchen. On the right of the entry were big wooden sliding French doors that opened into the living room with windows on every wall and built-in cabinets that created a separation into the dining room. The dining room had a huge window seat below a full-sized window that covered the entire wall and bathed the room in light. Off the dining room was an office den with built-in bookshelves, and every room boasted hardwood floors, crown moldings, leaded windows and typical Craftsman high ceilings, just like the one on Emerson Street in Portland. There was a second door in the dining room that swung into a huge kitchen with a peninsula shaped counter extending out into the center and lots of cabinets everywhere. A back door from the kitchen opened onto a screened back porch, which led to nowhere but a small space between our house and the one behind it, with no back yard to call our own. Another door on the opposite side of the kitchen led to the full basement below. Upstairs, three bedrooms, each with enormous walk-in closets and a full bathroom with a claw-foot bathtub filled the upper level. Dad had it all figured out; Mark, being the oldest, would take the bedroom in the back that had a door to its own small terrace above the back porch below, John an I would share the big bedroom in the middle, with Monica and Marguerite in the front bedroom, saying that he would make the den off the dining room his bedroom.

After exploring the house from top to bottom, Dad called us out to the front and opened the back of the truck. I took Katie out of Mark's car and placed her cage on the window seat in the dining room, thinking she'd enjoy the sunshine and the view, then I ran outside and joined the assembly line formation as everyone pulled out and carried in the boxes and furniture, setting everything up in a jiffy to create our new home with the same belongings that gave us comfort in Federal Way, and before that, in Portland. Once again, Marguerite, Monica and I were left to distribute the boxes to the rooms while Dad, Mark and John went to the Safeway store to buy groceries, and once they returned, we spent the first evening together in our new house, putting things away and settling in to our first meal with Dad at the helm. The following morning, Sunday, Marguerite came down for breakfast and let out a scream that shook the walls. Everyone ran to her to see what the matter was, certain she'd been attacked or something.

"OH, NO! I forgot to bring my popcorn plant!" she whined.

Dad reassured her that she could grow another one on the side of the house. Once that drama was behind us, we drove downtown and returned the truck to the U-Haul lot. Afterwards, we rode together in Mark's car down to Aunt Peggy's house in Rock Island to spend the day with our cousins Joanna and Michelle. Joanna had become quite the guitar player and singer, and Michelle laughed at everyone just like Aunt Peggy, known for possessing the most infectious laughter next to Uncle Leo's daughter Jeannie. Uncle Jim, an avid rock collector, had his noisy saw humming in the garage, slicing through some pretty crystal he had found. We hung out in the huge back yard under the same trees we had climbed during visits back when we lived with Uncle Porky and Aunt Val in Spokane. Aunt Peg made pot roast with potatoes and gravy and we all pigged out as usual, thanking her when it was time to go home and rest up for school the next day. However, we barely made it home in Mark's Catalina. The car made weird noises and grunts and then died when Mark parked it on the side of the house, refusing to start up again. We pushed it behind the house where it was blessed and given its last rites.

The next morning dawned. Dad stood at the bottom of the staircase, yelling.

"Up and at 'em, kids, time to get up!"

We grabbed some toast and milk, got ready and hopped into the LTD, that Dad had driven to Wenatchee one week prior to our arrival. Dad signed Marguerite up at Columbia Elementary School, only two blocks from our house, and then drove Monica and me up to Pioneer Junior High School, four blocks further up Orondo Avenue. During registration, I asked to be put in both Choir and Art. I was given the two classes I wanted most, mixed in with the other prerequisite subjects. Finding my way through the halls, I was, once again, a stranger in a strange place with new faces surrounding me everywhere. I made my way to my homeroom, Mrs. Eakin's English class. She was a tiny woman of mature age, but as sweet as a grandmother, and she welcomed me to her class with tenderness beyond measure. She introduced me to the other students and showed me to my desk and got on with her lesson of sentence structure the class had been working on for the past few weeks. Very quickly she discovered that English was a breeze for me. I dissected adverbs, nouns, verbs and adjectives faster than she had expected, and proved I was no dummy. At the end of class, Mrs. Eakin told me she was happy to have me in her class and wished me good luck as I went out into the hall, seeking the music department.

Full of positive expectations, I silently prayed that choir at Pioneer would resemble the one Mr. Warner had weaned me on in Federal Way, but boy, was I in for a nasty surprise. I went into Mr. Wilder Jones' Ninth Grade Chorus class, took a seat and was handed a folder of music. We began to 'sing'. I couldn't believe my ears. The singers were lame, mediocre and undisciplined; the music they worked on was bland, simplistic and two of the songs were easy ones we had performed last year at Sacajawea. At one point, Mr. Jones didn't like what he was hearing from an unruly student, so he simply stormed out of class, leaving us to our own defenses with no direction, wasting time. I instantly hated him and despised choir, wondering what I was going to do to fill the gaping musical hole in my life. All I could think about was the Concert Choir at Sacajawea Junior High school in Federal Way, blissfully perfecting crescendos, decrescendos, phrasing and fermatas, following the dynamic direction of Mr. Warner, while the only nuance this choir had mastered was off-key triple forte.

As soon as the bell rang, I left the music room, disappointed yet relieved the torture was over for the day and went to my History class with Mr. Hedges. I sat at a desk next to a shy brunette named Pam Rogers, a quiet girl who didn't speak much at all, but when she said 'hi' to me, she gave me a smile as pretty as the long thick locks of hair that cascaded down her back to caress the seat below. History class was no problem for me, and afterwards, out in the halls, I hurried to the other side of the school to find my Art class. My nose filled with heavenly odors of paint and art supplies as I entered paradise. Mrs. Blumhagen was a nice, free-spirited woman who wore macramé necklaces and turtlenecks and gave me the chance to awaken and express something I had repressed for over two years. The class was presently drawing abstract art in pencil to learn about shadings and dimensions. I delved into the task with joy, forgetting everything else as I drew non-stop, until the bell rang, pulling me from my nirvana, and I left to seek out my Algebra class.

I had taken Math at Sacajawea with Mrs. Scott, but didn't have a clue what Algebra was about. However, Mr. McPhee had room in his class and Algebra worked better into my new class schedule, fulfilling my Math requirement, so that's where they sent me. He welcomed me kindly, but when I looked up at the chalkboard, I knew I had passed through the gates of Mathematical hell.

Matthew Gonder

$$
\begin{array}{r}
2x^2-3x-4 \\
5x-3\,|\overline{10x^3-21x^2-11x+12}} \\
(-)\,\underline{10x^3-6^2} \\
-15x^2-11x+12 \\
(-)\underline{-15x^2+9x} \\
-20x+12 \\
(-)\underline{-20x+12} \\
0
\end{array}
$$

The number written at the bottom indicated precisely how much I understood of that equation, and it only got worse as class progressed. Polynomial long division was something that I had never done before and it could have been Chinese or Greek to me for all I comprehended. I didn't know an integer from an "outeger". A horrible mistake had definitely taken place. I did not belong in Algebra. My head ached as my school day slowly came to an end.

Kitty corner from Pioneer Junior High stood the brand new Wenatchee High School. Built in 1972 for a student population of 1200, the sprawling complex erected on the corner of Millerdale Avenue and South Miller Street was an incredibly vast, pristine architectural expression of how local government and the community believed in their school system. Equipped with the best that taxes could buy, the edifice possessed everything from a 900+ seat auditorium with a Broadway-sized proscenium theater to an indoor pool and gymnasium facilities that would have made other schools weep. An austere structure of brown concrete, there were almost no windows on the outside walls, probably a design choice made to encourage student concentration. Some of the building construction had yet to be completed, so many gym classes still took place on the warped floors of the old High School that stood like an abandoned ghost on Idaho Street, not one block from our house.

The High School colors Purple and Gold were prominently displayed everywhere, and Mark felt like he had found the motherload. Wenatchee, he quickly learned, had a moderately closed society when it came to High School sports. Not having any professional or major collegiate games locally, sports were organized around and for the students who had participated in the system for many years, especially in Junior High, which was sort of a minor league or formation league for the High School. There were no other ways from which to recruit as in larger cities, where a student might attend a different school outside his own district in order to participate in better sports programs. However, in Wenatchee, "transfer athletes" generally found it very difficult to advance, as the community usually supported their own before they would encourage newcomers. The football program was much more evolved to say the least, than what Mark had known in Federal Way. In comparison, it was like leaving a sandlot football program and joining the NFL. The coaching staffs also taught other scholastic subjects like Math or Spanish and were not solely hired for sports.

Mark eagerly joined Head Coach Lee Bofto's football team and worked his butt off through a tough regime of agility drills that he never knew existed before. Fortunately, 'challenge mechanisms' were put in place for athletes to compete with each other for placement on a sport-by-sport basis, left entirely to the coaches to decide. Football had such a system during the weekly practice days, where any player could challenge his rival for a position by simply writing his name, position and the challenged player's name on the blackboard. If a player won the challenge that week, he would start that weeks' game and wear the purple jersey until he lost the position through another challenge or if one of the coaches decided otherwise. It was solely the coaches' decision as to how much practice and playing time each player received, which created very competitive and sometimes contentious situations between coaches and athletes. So, one day during practice, Mark challenged the 4th string player and beat him. The following week, feeling confident, he challenged the 3rd string guard but was beaten by the player he challenged. Mark got a depressing wake-up call in Wenatchee, in that he came from starting on the first string team in Federal Way, playing both offense and defense every Friday night to being relegated to the Sophomore team that only played on Saturdays in Wenatchee. But Mark was never one to shrink at a challenge, and vowed to work hard to improve.

John didn't want to play football that first year in Wenatchee. He spent his time getting acclimated to the workings of our new city and was more interested in obtaining his Driver's Permit and License than anything else. Dad was reticent as we had only one car running at the time. But hey, it wasn't John's fault that Mark's Catalina laid dead, rusting away behind the house with only one worthy and redeeming reason for keeping it, which was to provide a trunk for John to hide his stash of beer. It just didn't seem fair that John be grounded for Mark's dead car. Soon enough, John passed his driver's test the first time around and earned Dad's blessing to drive the car.

Monica, the quiet one, pretty much kept to herself but said she liked her classes at Pioneer, while Marguerite held her own at Columbia Elementary, made friends quickly and seemed to be jumping into her sixth grade class with both feet. She dutifully prepared and bagged up everyone's peanut butter and jelly sandwiches for school lunch each morning. It was really sweet of her to make our lunch, but we all had a hunch her kindness only masked a desire to make sure the lumps in the Empress strawberry jam (or "bees" as she called them) didn't end up in her sandwich. We didn't say anything to her in any case, because we were content to have a slave who relieved us from the job.

Meanwhile, Dad located an old garage down on Wenatchee Avenue and the corner of Kittitas Street that he rented to start up his Sporty Roofs shop. He brought a glue gun and all the tools he needed from Federal Way, along with a selection of vinyl tops that had been cut, assembled and sewn. He began fulfilling orders he took from the car lots in town, slowly building his business from square one, confident that he had made the right decision to move to Wenatchee. He didn't have a lot of work at first, but the coffers were full in Seattle to give him time to ground himself with no financial stress, and lo and behold, just around the corner from the garage on Kittitas Street stood the Peppy Service Tavern, a small bar that became his new watering hole. Surprise, surprise.

Mark, John and I would help Dad out from time to time on weekends whenever asked. His little shop in Wenatchee offered Dad the opportunity to service clients in other eastern Washington cities who wouldn't drive all the way to Seattle for vinyl tops, and Dad accepted any job that came through to build relationships and develop his roster, even if it meant getting up and driving to Omak, a small town about a hundred miles from Wenatchee, which he did with John one morning.

Dad brought a huge wad of cash with him from Federal Way to help us get over the hump of the initial move, but once the cash flow thinned out in Dad's wallet, he took me down to the bank with him to open a new bank account. He deposited a big check from Sporty Roofs Seattle shop and added my name to the new checking account so I could continue handling the shopping whenever he couldn't, just like I had done in Federal Way. After school, I would walk a few blocks down to the Plaza Super Jet and write out a check to pick up a few things, yet the prices were higher there than at the Safeway or the Albertson's down at the Valley North Mall. Since I needed a ride to go that far so Dad handled the major part of the shopping himself, showing up with bags of groceries at night like always.

Within a couple of months, our lives had morphed into new routines and schedules all their own. One thing for sure, we had certainly learned how to adapt to change in our lives. I finished my pencil drawing in Art class, and Mrs. Blumhagen selected it out of many student pieces to place in the window outside the room where it remained on display, instead of handing it back to me to take home. When the Art class moved on to macramé, I designed and made a light blue belt that also ended up in the student display case. Art class became my mission at Pioneer, and I couldn't wait each day to attend. Although I went to choir and sang along half-heartedly, I was a good student in all my other classes except for one, where I never advanced beyond the back row. Mr. McPhee, truly a kind soul, became painfully well aware that I did not have a brain for Algebra when one day he drew more equations on the board for the class and then turned around to address the students.

$$ax^2 + bx + c = 0 \text{ ; find } x$$

"And now for Matt: Don't think of the A's, B's and C's as Chinese symbols you can't understand, Matt. Think of them as apples, cherries and peaches. Work the equation and x will be what you get."

"Fruit salad?" I asked.

He cracked up. I did fine with addition, subtraction, multiplication, division, ratios and simple geometry, but Algebra was where my nonmathematical brain threw in the towel. Meanwhile, Monica and Marguerite had become friends with Melanie Bush, a girl their age who lived down the street. Mark came home every night drained but thrilled with what his new mentor, line and defense coach Gene Baker (nicknamed simply "Coach") was inspiring him to give of himself on the football team.

Each in our own way took to Wenatchee as quickly as we had in Federal Way, making new friends as we began to settle into our new city. Peni Englestad and I wrote often to each other, sharing news of our lives. I did hear from a few other Federal Way friends as well, but Peni kept me in the know of the daily goings on in Federal Way, the choir, and dear friends at Sacajawea. I loved her letters, but they also made it hard for me to let go of the nostalgia I felt for what I had left behind.

One day, shortly thereafter, Dad got a call from the bank informing him that the check from Seattle hadn't cleared. Dad calmly told them to present it again, figuring there was a problem between banks with the transfer of funds and the new address change. Another week passed where he and I both had written a number of checks, putting us in the red, and the bank called the house, telling Dad that the Sporty Roofs check still hadn't cleared. Dad called Vince in Seattle and gave him hell over the phone. Vince said he didn't understand what the problem was, but reassured Dad, promising to take care of the matter.

That weekend, John was busy moving his bed into Mark's room. We couldn't stand rooming together, because he was a slob and I liked things orderly. We tried drawing a line through the bedroom so he could keep his junk pile on one side and my stuff on the other, but his crap grew over to my side, causing friction. Tired of my complaints, he simply moved in with Mark, leaving me the biggest bedroom all to myself, which worked fine for me. On Sunday, Aunt Peg called out of the blue, inviting us down for dinner. We all dropped what we were doing and hopped into the car to drive to Rock Island. As soon as we got to the bridge that crosses over the Columbia River into East Wenatchee, Dad jumped in his driver's seat.

"Shit....I put a roast in the oven!"

He turned the car around, stomped on the accelerator and sped back to the house. A Wenatchee City cop saw us, flashed his lights and Dad swore as he pulled the car over to the side of the road. The cop walked up to the car all too slowly, getting Dad even more excited than ever.

"Sir, you were going way too fast there and I'm going to have to write you a ticket."

Dad exploded.

"WRITE the sonofabitch, WRITE the sonofabitch! I left a roast in the oven and my goddamn HOUSE is gonna burn down!"

I don't think the cop believed Dad's story. He wrote out the ticket and handed it to Dad, who threw it onto the dashboard and drove home as fast as he could within the law, in time to stop the roast from baking our house to ash.

The following week, the shit really hit the fan. An envelope full of bounced checks arrived in the mail along with a bank notification that they were blocking our account. Another day, the milkman knocked on the door, telling me the check I wrote him was no good. Dad tried to call Vince, but the phone at the Seattle shop had been cut off. Dad couldn't find Vince's trace anywhere and sensed that something was very wrong. He tried many times, calling every number he had, but couldn't get a hold of Lyle, either. Dad didn't know what to do.

Financially, we were up shits creek with no paddle, stranded in Wenatchee without a dime to our name, and already deep in the arms of debt. There was nothing Dad could do about the situation but come to the sad realization that he had been swindled out of the company he gave his heart and soul to build. He called car lots and stores near his shop in Seattle who confirmed that Sporty Roofs had been closed down, and when he called his bank in Seattle that had plenty of money on deposit before we left Federal Way, he was informed the accounts had been completely emptied. Who else but Lyle or Vince could have signed those transactions?! It was all done in a perfectly legal manner with no questions asked, and now that neither of them could be reached, Dad could only surmise that one or both of them must have skipped town with a pocket full of cash.

In a frenzy, Dad drove all over Wenatchee, and being a survivor, took the first job that came through at Columbia Products, scraping apples to be freeze-dried off trays on a conveyor belt for salary of $3.10 per hour. Parallel to that, he would fill an order for a vinyl top whenever one came through, but demand wasn't high enough for him to make a living there, and he sensed that in a short amount of time, the vinyl top trend was waning down from its glory. We went on Food Stamps to feed ourselves. Dad became very depressed and we all felt terrible. Everything he had worked so hard for had been stolen from him. He lost his belief structure and began drinking more than ever, pouring down bottles and bottles of cheap white table wine every night instead of pitchers of beer at Peppy's, which were too expensive on his budget. I went into his bedroom to talk with him one morning.

"Dad, why don't we just go back to Federal Way and you can start all over again?"

He sat up and invited me to sit next to him by patting the mattress.

"No, Matt, we're not gonna move again. No more running. You kids have been bounced around enough. We're settled now, Mark's got his football, you have your Art classes and you all have made friends and I'm too old to start all over again."

"But, Dad?"

"No buts, Matt. I know I'm drinking more than I should, but I'm going through a mental breakdown. Part of me wants to go find Lyle and Vince and kill the sonsobitches, and another part of me knows that's not going to change the way things are. No, we're here in Wenatchee, we ain't got nothin' left, but we've been through this before, and I say we just stay put and make do the best we can, okay?"

"Okay, Dad, but you hate your new job."

"Well, I had worse and I had better. I feel like the Greek king Sisyphus, who was condemned for all eternity to push a big boulder up to the top of a mountain, then watch it roll back down to the bottom so he could push it back up again."

"That stinks."

"Well, sometimes shit happens on the move out west.

"Sure does."

"I'll find another job somewhere, Matt. Don't worry."

"If you say so, Dad."

So we stayed in Wenatchee and made do. The milkman was forgiving, once he got wind of what had happened to us, and continued to leave milk on the front porch without ever asking for a penny. He just let the bill add up, convinced we'd eventually get back on our feet. Whenever we paid something on our bill, he'd give us gallons of free ice cream and never complained about the balance remaining. But sometimes, when you think you've reached rock bottom, you will descend even lower before you catch your breath and begin a brand new upward climb. Soon enough, a moving truck showed up in front of the house. Two men jumped out and knocked at the door, having driven from Seattle to repossess the furniture Dad had bought earlier that spring in Federal Way. Those payment checks apparently had bounced as well. So we watched silently as the two men carried out our gold couch, the armchairs, side table and coffee table, then drove away.

"Well, kids, looks like we're back to an empty living room," Dad said.

"Yeah, but think how much easier it'll be to clean the room with nothin' in it." I answered.

"Well, okay, that's sure as hell one way of lookin' at it," Dad laughed.

That night, we pulled the faithful black and red floral vinyl dining room chairs we owned to the living room to watch the TV that sat on Mom's hope chest in the living room bearing nothing more than Mom's framed prints and John's gold lamp hanging on the walls. Well, we had lived through this before, so here we were again. Big deal. When you have nothing, everything is possible. A couple of weeks later, I came home from school and walked into the living room where Marguerite was sitting on a 1960s second-hand brown couch watching *The Flintstones* on TV.

"Where'd that couch come from, Marguerite?" I asked.

"Uncle Gene," she answered, turning her attention back to Fred and Wilma.

"Uncle Gene? When did he get here?"

"He was here when I came home from school. He bought us this at the Salvation Army and told me to say hi to everybody."

"Well where is he?"

"He went back to Spokane."

That night she told everyone the story of how that Uncle Gene, Mom's brother, drove through Wenatchee while we were all at school and Dad was working. The house was never locked, so he let himself in and either thought thieves had beaten him there, or that we were on the skids. Like a silent Samaritan, he bought a second hand couch with a fold out bed and had it installed just as Marguerite came in from school.

Through the people he had met, Dad found a better-paying job driving a forklift at Wenoka Sales, packing crates of locally grown apples, cherries and peaches onto the railroad cars. He had driven a forklift years ago and here he was, full circle around, doing it again. Courageously, he swallowed his pride, laid Sporty Roofs to rest and got on with the task at hand to support his family in whatever way possible, never missing a day's work. At least now he could afford to return to Peppy Service Tavern, which he did, but then, one night Dad brought home a bum he met at Peppy's, made him a meal and let him sleep on the fold-out couch, hoping the man would feel better about himself and life in general the next morning. The bum had left the house long before anyone woke up, emptying Dad's wallet and taking John's radio with him. We were furious when we discovered what had happened and wanted to comb the streets to find the guy.

"No, let's just forget it and put it to rest," he said calmly.

"But Dad!" We protested, "he took everything we got!"

"Yes he did, but it ain't the first time that's happened and we're still standin', and you can't judge all men based upon one bum's bad choices."

There stood my Dad, who had lost everything a second time and could still forgive the man who took every last dollar we had.

"Desperate times sometimes breed desperate actions," he said, and we left it at that.

Every so often, Mr. Jones would silently pass quickly through the music room where I sat taking turns playing the piano along with Karen Bensing or Sue Chapman, who could read any music put before them and play effortlessly. At home, I pumped my accordion against a wall of the basement to practice pieces I tried to master as well as I could. In Art class, Mrs. Blumhagen was teaching us to tie-dye and I made a whole collection of t-shirts that I wore everywhere. In Algebra, I failed most of the tests Mr. McPhee gave us, yet he would congratulate me with a big grin if I got a "D". What can I say? I came into Algebra 'a day late and a dollar short' as Dad would have said, and never caught up. When report cards came out, Mr. McPhee saw I was a straight A student in all my other classes, so he gave me a "B". When I asked him why, knowing I didn't deserve the grade, he told me.

"Matt, all in all you're a very good student. You just don't have a mathematical brain. I can't hold that against you. You're here everyday and you try. God knows you put in the effort and that's why I think you deserve a "B", but you'll never get Algebra. Don't worry about it.

It won't ruin your life."

Thanks to the "B" grade he gave me, I made the honor roll and was given a certificate signed by Max Taylor, the principal.

Fall turned into icy winter, and although we survived by the skin of our teeth, we somehow made do. Dad couldn't afford the oil to heat the house, so liked trained seals, we gathered around the stove in the kitchen in huddled formation. Unlike Federal Way, weather conditions were much more extreme in North Central Washington, where a foot of snow completely covered the streets of Wenatchee, but none of us wanted to hooky bob. Dad didn't have funds to buy us presents that year for Christmas, but he did recreate our traditional cornucopia laundry basket of goodies to chomp on throughout the holidays and gave us each spending money to buy gifts for one another so there would be something under our tree. Marguerite, cash in hand, ran down to the Bonanza 88 store on Wenatchee Avenue and had all her shopping done in a flash, whereas the rest of us took our time throughout the month. On Christmas day, sitting under the hues of colorful lights on a tree that filled our almost empty living room, we opened our gifts from one another and gave Marguerite grief for the cheap ten-cent piece of crap she bought each of us. Finally Dad said something.

"So where's the rest of the money I gave you to buy presents, Marguerite?"

"Upstairs in my piggy bank."

"Well, honey, you're gonna have to give it back."

"But, Dad!" she complained.

"I gave you that money to SPEND on your brothers and sister to put something under the tree, not to fill your damn piggy bank."

"Okay," she said, begrudgingly.

She was obviously under the wrong impression that Dad was going to let her keep the unspent remainder of her money, but Dad took it back, needing it for household necessities. Poor as we were, thanks to the Grinches (Lyle and Vince), Christmas, however meager, came to us just like it had come to the Who's down in Whoville, and we sat down to a beautifully stuffed roast beast (turkey) with all traditional trimmings and pineapple upside-down cake, too. Sadly, the collection of Christmas records were in Tacoma with Aunt Mary, but our TV had holiday shows on every channel to enjoy.

On the first day of school after Christmas break, Mark confirmed his questionable driving reputation when he offered Monica and me a ride home from Pioneer in Dad's Ford LTD. Coming down Orondo Avenue, he glanced in the side mirror and was almost blinded by the sun and glare off the snow. As soon as he parked the car in front of the house, he opened the door to get out and a car suddenly whizzed by, smashing and ripping off the door. Mark's arm would have been pulled out of the socket if he hadn't let go. Dad had to have a replacement door installed that didn't match the color, so from that day onward, we drove around Wenatchee in a J.P. Patches car.

In History class, I noticed that Pam Rogers' desk was empty and continued to remain so every day. I figured she had moved away like I had done so many times, and thought how sad it was to not have gotten to know her better. Sometime in January, I figured I might as well participate in the solo and ensemble contest in February. At least I would be singing by myself and not with this lousy choir. Mr. Jones chose a solo for me and handed me the sheet music. I looked down at the title, which I felt appropriately reflected my thoughts about ninth grade Chorus.

I'll Not Complain

Translated from German into English, I read the lyrics, which confirmed my thoughts.

I'll not complain although my heart should break.

Though thou art lost to me

Though thou art lost to me

I'll not complain, I'll not complain...

I thought of how much I missed Mr. Warner and

Concert Choir in Federal Way. Yep, that's what the song was about as far as I was concerned. Sue Chapman accompanied me and I got a "1" at the contest, but I didn't care, nor did I complain. I received congratulations from many classmates, but I just went through the musical motions and was content to return to the Art class that fed my soul at Pioneer.

Days after the contest, Dad kept his promise even though we had so little money, and bought me a round trip Greyhound bus ticket to go to Federal Way, so I could attend the Concert Choir performance at the Hilton Hotel in Portland on February 19th. I couldn't wait to see my mentor, Mr. Warner and all my friends. I packed a small suitcase and walked down Douglas Street and up North Chelan Avenue one block to the bus station. I climbed onto the bus and found a seat next to a lady, who was nice, but she chain-smoked the entire trip, as did many other patrons. I don't know how I was able to breathe, but back then in 1972, everyone smoked in public places and on buses and you just accepted it as an adult privilege. Peni Englestad met me in Federal Way and we went over to her house. Her mom didn't invite me to stay, because after all the letters sent between us, we had developed a pen pal crush on each other and her Mom wondered what music might have been heard if I slept overnight, so I crashed at Nancy Thorstad's house in their guest room.

Filled with nostalgia, I went to the choir room at Sacajawea the next day to watch the rehearsal. Mr.

Warner welcomed me with a smile and a kind word, but then applied himself to the task at hand, as he had lots on his plate to deal with. I was happy to see my neighbor pal, Rich Williams singing out in the Tenor section, and at first it was torture to stand back and watch all my friends in the risers. I recognized each face, every voice, Esther's boobs, all the nuances of the music and I wanted to dive into the lake of glorious blending sound surrounding me. My heart ached to sing out in that choir of familiar classmates that Mr. Warner harnessed and trained to become sensitive young musicians, as he had me, but it wasn't to be. During breaks, I told Rich and the others all about Wenatchee and what we were up to. Rich told me about Snorky, saying they didn't see as much of each other since we moved, and oddly, I began to feel as if my life, in only four months, had traveled light years away from Federal Way.

Finally the big day arrived. Everyone met up in the parking lot of the school very early in the morning. Mr. Warner made announcements, and we all hopped into busses and rode together down to Portland to the Hilton Hotel for the concert, scheduled for 10:15 a.m. Lori Lundberg's harp was set up and everyone took their places in the risers for a sound check, rehearsing a couple of select moments in each song in order to get a feel of the room. I sat as close as I could, about ten rows back, and felt as nervous as the rest of the singers. Eventually, Mr. Warner called a break for everyone while the room filled up with people.

The concert took place without a hitch. All my friends in Sacajawea's Concert Choir performed beautifully and I sang along with them in my heart. Mr. Warner conducted every measure of music with his heart and soul and I knew the tenor part well enough to feel as if I was standing up there with the others taking his direction, but as soon as they finished their last song of the program, the strangest thing happened. My emotional ties to Federal Way immediately and completely vanished in the applause. In an instant, I realized that the only thing holding me back was that concert, and as soon as it was over, the clouds had parted and I was ready to go back to Wenatchee. That sparsely furnished and unheated old Craftsman had become my home. I missed Dad, my brothers, sisters and Katie, and now I surprised myself as I thought of my new friends and teachers at Pioneer. We all funneled out of the Hilton Hotel Ballroom and met up outside. I congratulated my pals but quickly ran out of things to say. I enjoyed a last lunch with a few at Lloyd's Center and then rode the bus back to Federal Way with my Sacajawea choir classmates and Mr. Warner, and then Peni and her mom drove me to the Greyhound bus station and we bid our farewells.

The bus seemed to take forever to cross the mountain passes. We drove at a normal speed but it just didn't seem fast enough for me. The moment I jumped out of the Greyhound bus on Chelan Avenue in Wenatchee, I grabbed my suitcase and ran up to Douglas Street, passing 'my' library and 'my' courthouse. I told

Dad all about the concert and thanked him for keeping his promise and making the financial sacrifice that allowed me to attend the concert, and I was so glad I did, because I knew I was back where I belonged, right here in our cold Craftsman on Douglas Street in Wenatchee, be it ever so humble... Katie chirped loudly when I arrived home, but honestly I couldn't say if she was happy to see me or just happy to get fed by the staff that cleaned her cage.

I went back to Pioneer the next day with resolve to have fun in choir without comparing it to any other, ready to enjoy each moment as it presented itself with hearts that responded to mine. Sure, we didn't sing as well as Mr. Warner's Concert Choir in Federal Way, but I had grown accustomed to everyone and was now glad to see them all again. As soon as I made the decision to be happy, laughter came back into my life and I began to enjoy everyone and everything. Mark welcomed spring with a new, muscle-building contraption he purchased to help get him in shape, called a "Bullworker", consisting of two metal bars that slid into each other as you pulled on rubber-coated springs to create isometric resistance. Mark worked out daily, sweating through an exercise routine in his room while we teased and called him Arnold Schwarzenegger.

One day thereafter, I was watching T.V on the couch with Marguerite and John, the doorbell rang. Monica opened the door and greeted a saleslady who presented herself and the cosmetic company she worked for.

"Is your mother home?" the lady asked.

"No, my Mom's dead," Monica answered.

A true saleslady, she composed herself and changed angles.

"I'm sorry to hear that. How old are you? You have such pretty blue eyes."

"Thirteen."

"Well, I'd love to give you a free presentation of our cosmetics and revolutionary new face creams and tonics, if you're interested of course, no purchase necessary."

Hearing those magic words, Marguerite jumped up from the couch and ran to Monica's side.

"Hi," Marguerite said to the saleslady.

"This is my sister," Monica said.

"Nice to meet you. You know what, I could give you both a free presentation. You girls have such lovely skin."

"When?" Marguerite never lost any time when freebies were offered.

"How about this afternoon or tomorrow?" the lady offered.

"How 'bout now?" Marguerite spewed.

"I'd love to. Let me run to my car and get some supplies and I'll be right back."

Marguerite told us what they were up to, and not wanting to be a part of it, John and I went down to Columbia schoolyard to play tennis while the girls did their thing. An hour or so later we came in to see our sister's faces covered in make-up and playing with their free sample palette that the saleslady left for each of them.

"God, you guys look like clowns," I laughed.

"Look what she gave us, Matt," Monica said.

She held up the palette of eye shadows and lipsticks.

"We didn't buy nothin'. She tried to sell us stuff but I told her we didn't have no money so she went away and let us keep these for free," Marguerite announced. No saleslady alive could ever put one over on Marguerite, who definitely had a knack for getting something for nothing.

Back at school, I didn't think Mr. Jones cast a thought in my direction, but again, I was wrong. As spring came around, Gene Huber, the band teacher from the High School came to the school and nabbed me one day in the hallway.

"Are you Matt Gonder?"

"Yeah."

"I know you're on your way to your next class. I'll only take a minute of your time. I'm Mr. Huber, the band teacher up at the high school. Mr. Jones tells me you're a piano player and I just wanted to meet you and give this to you in the hopes that you might be interested in playing with us next year in the Stage Band."

"I, uh…wow!"

He handed me a pile of music. There were chord charts that I had no clue how to play, and others containing musical notation like I was accustomed to, but very rhythmic and jazzy. I loved the fact that people thought of me as a piano player but I had to let him know the truth.

"Mr. Huber, I'm not really a very good piano player."

He smiled and I could tell he thought I was just selling myself short.

"Well, why don't you look these over, and if you're interested, come see me before the end of the school year and we'll talk about it, okay?"

"Okay, thanks."

I took those charts home and pumped that accordion against the wall like a madman down in the basement, trying like the devil to figure out what Bbm7b5 and D∆7 and all the other weird looking chords meant. Music wasn't supposed to look like Algebraic equations, for God's sake, and there I sat on the concrete floor sweating it out, all the while wishing I had a real piano to play on. I don't honestly know if playing the music was the guiding factor for me at this point or maybe it was simply that I just wanted to rise to the challenge.

I took the sheet music to Aunt Peg's one night, knowing my cousin Joanna, who sang and played the guitar beautifully, could teach me a few things and answer my questions about 7th's, 9th's, 13th's, diminished and augmented chords. She was very helpful, being also a clarinet player at Eastmont High School and gave me pointers that I adapted to my daily accordion practice in the basement.

Meanwhile, Mrs. Eakin hosted her annual spelling contest in English class. I knew I could spell pretty well but had no idea what was to transpire. She gave us a long list of words to study for a couple of weeks, and then began her contest on a Saturday morning, offering twenty-five dollars to the winner and ten dollars to second place. Very quickly the room began weed itself out as students misspelled words. Hours passed by, and towards the end of the day, I was still in the running, spelling every word she gave me correctly . The room heated up as the clock ticked on, and finally there were only two contestants remaining; Terri Taylor and I. She spelled a word, I spelled a word, then she spelled a word, I spelled a word. This continued for over an hour. The heat finally got to me. Then, Mrs. Eakin gave me the word "Siege". My brain dried up. Hot and tired, I wanted to be sure of my call but I couldn't think anymore. I remembered the rule:

"I before E except after C or when sounded like A as in neighbor and weigh".

I flinched. That didn't sound right. I thought again, then looked up, wearily and said:

"Siege. S E I G E, Siege."

Mrs. Eakin's face crumbled. Terri won first place. When Mrs. Eakin handed me the ten dollars, she said:

"I thought for sure you would win, Matt. You knew how to spell that word."

"Yeah, I know, but I froze up. Oh well, it was fun. Ten bucks is better than none."

Monica, like many of her girlfriends, obtained self-esteem from her long blond hair that drew compliments from everyone. She foolishly listened to her girlfriends' advice and went down to a hairdresser they suggested she go to for a trim. She came back home, crying in hysterics over the bad cut she had received and how short her bangs were.

"Oh my God, look at my hair!" Monica whined.

"It looks good, Monica," Mark said.

"It's horrible! My bangs are too short. How could she do that to me?" she cried.

Poor thing, try as we did to convince her that she still looked good, she hated her hair and didn't want to return to school. Marguerite however, was sick of Monica's constant moaning about her haircut, so she moved out of the bedroom and into the large walk-in closet, to have more privacy. She decorated the walls and set up her dolls and toys to create her very own little nest, away from her sister. In an effort to calm Monica's tears, Dad used reverse psychology, telling her she could stay home until it grew out. She stopped crying immediately and did stay home from school one day, but she got bored and decided to bite the bullet, returning to school the next day, hoping nobody would notice.

John joined the baseball team in the spring and played the outfield, which seemed appropriate for someone known for always being "out in left field". Dad, who in his younger days played shortstop, was tickled that John wanted to follow in his baseball footsteps. Had the war not broken out, we were told, Dad played so well he could have gone professional.

The whole city began to sizzle as the end of April 1973 brought us to the biggest event of the year in Wenatchee: the annual Washington State Apple Blossom Festival, an eleven-day festival that takes place during the last weekend in April and first weekend in May. It was incredible. The city buzzed with events going on everywhere. After a long selection contest as important to Wenatchee as the Miss America pageant, Deloma Ensley, a sweet girl and wonderful singer, had been crowned queen that year, and everyone bustled around talking of nothing else but all the events lined up including visits to Rocky Reach Dam, the Tacoma Daffodil parade, the Memorial Park Food Fair, 'The Music Man', presented by Music Theater of Wenatchee at the Liberty Theater, the Spokane Lilac parade, the Youth Parade, luncheons, golf tournaments, a Grand Parade in Wenatchee and many more activities to celebrate the apple, a hallmark to a better life in the northern hemisphere that proudly gave Wenatchee its well deserved title of "Apple Capital of the World".

The day before the Grand Parade, people began setting up lawn chairs and squatting spaces along Orondo Avenue. Strange people appeared out of nowhere and camped out on our lawn that night to make sure they would secure prime seating to watch the parade the next day. Dad was a little worried that some vagrant might just waltz into our house unannounced so we began a mad scramble, digging through all the drawers in the kitchen to locate our house key, something we had never used before, as we never found any reason or need to lock the damn door. Dad and all of us watched the parade from the balcony off Mark's bedroom, giving us a coveted VIP bird's eye view of the whole parade without having to fight the crowds, not to mention comfortable access to a constant flow of snacks and lemonade from the fridge. Marguerite made sacks of popcorn and we had a ball watching the classic cars, marching bands and floats as they went down Orondo Avenue.

A few days after the Grand Parade, the city pace returned to normal, and all of us back to school. I went to my History class and Pam Rogers, the shy brunette, was sitting right there at her desk, now engulfed in a scary-looking body brace with a chin piece that held her head up in a locked position.

"Hi Pam." I said as I passed by her, walking to my desk nearby.

"Hi Matt," she smiled above the chin piece.

"Welcome back."

"Thanks," she answered sweetly.

I'd forgotten about her completely. Pam had been gone for months and I didn't dare ask what had happened to her. At first I thought she'd moved away, but now I figured she'd been in a horrible car accident or something and I didn't want to make her feel worse than she already had to in the contraption she was wearing.

Her long hair was braided and separated to the sides of her head, covered in part by the cast. I felt so sorry for her. She was such a pretty girl aside from the weird apparatus she had clamped to her body that made her look like a Cherokee trapped in a rotisserie. Mr. Hedges started our lesson and when it came time to take notes, Pam had to get up from her desk and kneel on the floor to be able to see and write on the paper sitting on her desk. She didn't complain, she just did what she had to do with positive determination, but at one point her pencil rolled off the desk. She tried to reach down to pick it up, but her cast prohibited her from bending or twisting, so I flew to her rescue and reached down, grabbing the pencil and handing it to her.

"Oh, thanks," she whispered. "I didn't know how I was gonna pick it up,' she said, laughing at her own predicament.

"Just ask me. I'll get it for ya, anytime, Pam," I offered.

Those were the most words we had exchanged since I met her. She never talked much, or at least not to me. She probably thought I was weird or something so I just stole glimpses of her during class and waited like a sentinel for her to drop another pencil. Besides, she had a crush on a guy named Paul Watson and everyone knew it so I didn't have a chance.

The last couple of months rolled by. I spent hours in the basement pounding on that accordion, trying to master the music Mr. Huber gave me. Thanks to Joanna's instruction, I did improve somewhat, but there just wasn't enough time to make me swing at the level of the Stage Band, so I gave up the idea to go see him at the high school. I figured my failure to show up would give him the idea I really wasn't up to par.

As school wound down to the end of the year, Mrs. Blumhagen gave me the pieces of art I had made months ago that were on display outside the art room. I was finally able to wear the light blue macramé belt I made and bring home my work to show Dad. On another day, award certificates were being handed out to students who had excelled and others who had made major improvements throughout the year. My Algebra teacher, Mr. McPhee, was also a master of Calligraphy, and as such became enlisted by many teachers to draw the student's names on certificates for posterity. Once again, thanks to the "B" grade he gave me in Algebra, which I didn't deserve, I made the Honor Roll for the fourth time that year and had fulfilled the High School Math requirement, which meant I wouldn't have to take Math at all throughout my future High School years, thank God. That was a relief, but I don't honestly know if Mr. McPhee was doing me a favor, or if he was trying to avoid witnessing one of his Math colleagues dealing with me in class and suffering a nervous breakdown. Let's just say it was a win-win situation for all concerned.

A hot blazing sun began to toast the Wenatchee

mountains a light shade of brown, and the day after school let out, Dad came into the living room and interrupted our cartoon watching to pour on even more heat with an ultimatum.

"Nobody owes any of you sonsobitches a living around here! Ya know I can't afford to pay for all the things you want and you're almost grown up now, so you can't just lay around all summer suckin' up the heat! I'm doin' all I can do to keep a roof over our heads and food on the table, but if you want new clothes and shoes and anything else next year for school, it's high time you get your asses off that goddamn couch and go find jobs!"

Dad wasn't angry with us; he just wanted to make a point in his own inimitable way. So, Mark got a job working for Gary Cusick as a Grounds Keeper at the Wenatchee Swim and Tennis Club, mowing the lawns and weeding flowerbeds, taking home eighty dollars each week. Dad dropped him off in the morning before heading to work at 7:45am, and Mark worked his eight hour shift five times per week, then ran home 2 miles each day and faithfully sweat through his daily Bullworker workout, having made a vow to himself to play first-string football during his senior year. At home, while he was working out, he'd grunt and repeat his mantra while pumping his muscles on the Bullworker.

"Second string is first loser, second string is first loser."

John earned his summer money by 'thinning' apple

trees (picking an apple or two from a cluster to leave enough room for the others to grow full size) in East Wenatchee, while I stayed down at Aunt Peg's in Rock Island and got a job with Joanna picking cherries in an orchard under the hot sun along with all the migrant workers that everyone called "Arkies". Joanna and I had to maneuver giant, heavy fourteen-foot ladders all day long between the trees, rocking the ladder to and fro on its legs to walk it around and we laughed at ourselves, commenting on how we looked like tall extraterrestrial creatures from some strange planet. We spent the day climbing up and down to pick a few branches, then maneuvering the ladder once again to pick clean one tree after the other. We made each other laugh to pass the time, and figured we would get great suntans that everyone would envy, so we promised to tell them we'd gone to Hawaii on vacation as we worked like slaves, filling crate after crate of the delicious sweet sun-ripened fruit. We crammed cherries constantly into our mouths that first day while we worked, enjoying the juicy nectar of each cherry, however the next day we both got the 'runs' and took turns rushing to the outhouse, thus curbing our binge.

Meanwhile, Monica babysat at various homes throughout the neighborhood and Marguerite, too young to get a job, played all summer with her friends and joined the Youth Theatre of Wenatchee, where Joan Fadden was preparing to direct "Dummling and the Golden Goose", starring Debbie and Bill Lapo. I called home to say hi to Dad one night from Aunt Peg's and

Marguerite answered the phone, almost bursting as she told me stories of the fun she was having with fellow actors Maria Diaz, Jeff Anderson, Karen Soland, Karen Ross and Carolyn Kingsbury.

On summer nights, if you wanted to find Dad after work, he'd usually be holding court and cooling off in a pitcher at Peppy's. That was a given we all knew. So, by the time July came around, I had made enough money to help Monica buy the Singer sewing machine she wanted, to allow her to make her own clothes and get the most out of her upcoming Home Economics class in the fall, and Mark and I split the cost to buy Dad a huge window fan to cool him off during the hot nights. My job was finished and the big cherry orchard completely stripped of its fruit. Dad drove down to Rock Island one weekend to spend the day at Aunt Peg's and pick me up. On the drive back from Aunt Peg's that night, Mark was behind the wheel. We drove across the bridge into the city and were heading up Mission Street until we got to Kittitas Street, where Mark pretended the car had a mind of its own.

"Dad, what's goin' on? I'm tryin' to drive straight and the car wants to turn right."

He would slide his hands across the wheel, fighting the car's 'desire' to turn into Peppy's.

"It's pullin' Dad! I can't fight it!" Mark acted.

"Shut up and drive," Dad would say, making

everyone laugh.

When August 1973 rolled around, Mark signed up to attend the Cascadian Football Camp at Wenatchee Valley College, to get his mind away from summer vacation and focused on the upcoming football season. As soon as that was over, the football season officially began and John joined the team. The young athletes suited up to run through the grueling drills to get their bodies in shape. Mark and John came home laughing after one of the first practices.

"So, how'd it go today?" Dad asked.

"Listen to this Dad, you're not gonna believe it. First thing they tell us we gotta do is run a mile. They split us up into big groups and John was in one of the first groups with Mike Allen, ya know, our all state sprinter and wide receiver? Yeah, so John ends up in a group with him and other guys who knew how to pace themselves to make the four laps around the track and do the mile. First lap, John sprints, no kiddin'. He's way ahead of the pack, including Mike Allen. Burnin' adrenaline, John keeps on runnin' at full speed. So a couple of guys come up to me and ask: 'What's your brother doing?' I say, I don't know, let's watch him! Well, John leads the pack for the entire first lap and halfway during the second one. Then his lungs start to burn, his legs start to go, and he slowly moves further and further to the back of the pack. Then, one by one, EVERYBODY passes in front of John! At the end of the mile run, John almost comes in last place, exhausted and coughing, cuz' half his lungs are hanging out his throat."

Dad couldn't stop laughing, but when he finally did, he had words for John.

"Je-sus Christ, John. What the hell were you thinkin'?"

"I dunno."

John eventually learned to pace himself better. During the latter part of August they started out in "two a day" team practices to be ready before the school year began.

13. THE WAY WE WERE

On the first day of my sophomore year, I walked through the cavernous halls of Wenatchee High School, overwhelmed by the size and dimensions of the building. Mark wasn't kidding. This school promised everything and more. The first memory I have is of the Art Department, where a group of classrooms opened onto a huge common area with silk-screen equipment and all kinds of supplies in the center. There, displayed on an easel stood an incredible abstract painting I admired every day I passed by. I met the painter, a senior class member named Barbara Ferguson, and we became friends, talking art and techniques. Mrs. Kirkpatrick, my teacher, gave us an assignment to create a cube and represent the same image on all six sides using different textures and techniques. I used the overhead projector and copied a girl's face. Using paint on one side, I gave her green lips, then used mixed macaroni for her lip shading on another side, then made a collage on another in newspaper to create the shading effects of the same face. I sat next to my buddy John Gormley in Mr. Beeler's Spanish class, loved the clatter of the typing class with Mrs. Vickie Lesmeister and found Mr. Eric Jensen to be one of the most dynamic teachers in his Psychology class. I never set foot in the Math department, much to everyone's joy, but did have Biology, where we had to gather wild flowers from all over the city to make a botanical diary, and also P.E., where I enjoyed the workout that gymnastics provided.

The music department, on the other side of the humongous school next to the theater, was bigger and more incredible than I could ever have dreamed possible, with soundproof practice rooms galore for the students to reserve. Mr. Huber "Sarge" as the students called him, had everything from beginning bands, Golden Apple marching band, a Stage Band (the one I wasn't apt enough to play in) that sounded like Doc Severinsen's jazz band on the Johnny Carson Show. Mr. Wilder Jones (the chorus teacher at Pioneer) directed the Orchestra class at the high school, and there were also many choirs, directed by Mr. Ron Jones. Placement in the High School choirs was granted by audition only. The best sophomore singers could only hope to sing in the Choral Society choir, reserving Bel Canto, the best choir of the school for the cream of the junior or senior class singers. I made it into Choral Society, and once we began to sing, the musical level surpassed my expectations with a blend of the best voices from both Orchard and Pioneer junior high schools. Leslee Reich, a pretty blond from Orchard

Junior High, was the indisputable star of the Choral Society. Her crystalline soprano voice and perfect pitch gave her a well-deserved reputation and musicality that raised the bar for us all. Every solo for soprano was given, justifiably to Leslee. Mr. Jones also handed out a spiritual called *Amen* in which there was a tenor solo. I was surprised and so happy that he gave the solo to me, and I had a blast singing for the first time in my life with a huge choir backing me up.

Mark, a senior, and I, his sophomore brother, both signed up for Theater class with Mr. Tom Oldoski. The High School auditorium had amazing acoustics, but sadly, during construction, the hardwood floor onstage was installed before the roof, and when rains fell in and warped the floor, slabs of cheap plywood quickly replaced it in time for school to open on schedule. As a result, the acoustics picked up every step made on the soft floorboards that echoed loudly throughout the house while we prayed the school board would cough up the funds to restore the floor back to its hardwood glory. Mr. Oldoski explained all the workings of the stage, showing us the Fresnels, Ellipsoidal reflector spotlights, the wings and fly systems. He shared an ancient Greek relaxation exercise, where all the students spread out on the floor, eyes closed, imagining the blood traveling through the veins beginning with the big toe and moving up to the heart. I fell asleep before the blood reached my knees.

The next day, Mr. Oldoski announced that Sherry

Shreck would be directing the tragedy of *John Brown's Body*, Vincent Benet's epic and tragic poem for Reader's Theater, and was looking for chorus members. Itching for a chance to experience being in an actual play in that theater, Mark and I both signed up as chorus members, not knowing at all what we were getting ourselves in for. Rehearsals began after school, and the stars: Gloria Brown, Marie Hill, Allen Bixby, Steve Lutz and Rick Mulligan rehearsed privately with Mrs. Schreck onstage, while Scott Hosfeld directed the musical rehearsals and the Chorus members: Kay-Lani Holland, Leslie Taylor, Kris Singleton, Leilani Johnson, Patti Allyn, Mark Gonder, myself, Linda Couey, LaDonna Brunz, Cyndy Corrick and Debbie Lapo in room 101, a large annex across the hall from the theater. The Chorus had a blast working together after school for a few weeks, learning the musical selections and practicing a spoken line of dialogue here and there until the big day, when we joined the rehearsals with the stars on the incredible stage to connect their speeches to our chorus bits.

Excited as fleas to feel the show onstage under the lights, we sat on our risers and quickly learned we were trapped in a hellhole bomb of long, dull, overacted monologues that went on forever, telling the story of how, in 1859, John Brown and his band of men conducted an attack on the arsenal at Harper's Ferry, Virginia. BORING. The stars talked and talked and talked and then talked some more, moving like snails about the stage if they moved at all. When given the cue, we sang out "John Brown's body lies a-mouldering in the grave" to the tune of which later became the *Battle Hymn of the Republic*. John Brown wasn't the only body mouldering in the grave as the whole Chorus felt like we were rotting along with him, but we'd given our word, so Mark and I honored our commitment with everyone else and stuck with it. It took monumental efforts on behalf of the Chorus to stay awake through the long speeches, and thank God there were only a couple performances scheduled.

Opening night finally arrived. Joyce Oldolski put make-up on us and stage fright finally claimed our nerves. The Stage Manager gave the call for "Places". The curtain went up revealing maybe two dozen people in the house of over 900 seats, but there in the center sat Dad proudly next to Marguerite to lend support to Mark and me. Then the torture began. Speech after monologue droned on and on until mercifully, the curtain fell at the end of the first act and we all filed offstage to room 101, where Gloria, one of the stars, screamed furiously:

"Who's that SNORING in the FIFTH ROW?"

Mark and I looked at each other and admitted in unison:

"Our Dad."

True, there he was out there in fifth row center, sawing logs louder than the speeches, and although we were embarrassed, we completely empathized. The poor guy was drained from working all day driving a forklift, but still made it to watch his sons do their thing onstage in a tedious show that was so awful it would have made John Brown want to hang himself. As soon as the curtain came down on the last performance, Mark was especially relieved to put that show behind him and get back to football practice, where each week he and John would dance with "Big Bertha", a four hundred pound hanging bag they'd each take a turn at tackling while she was swinging, and try their best to avoid getting hit or Bertha would knock their socks off. In an effort to 'show 'em how it was done', "Coach" Baker, who had been drafted by the San Francisco 49ers before a bad knee shortened his career, took out his partial two front teeth, borrowed a helmet and took his turn wearing no pads. He rocked Big Bertha like no one had ever seen before, the whole team standing around with their mouths wide open in awe.

Soon after John Brown was hung, dead and buried, Mrs. Pauline Peterson, one of the English and Drama teachers, held auditions to direct the Pulitzer Prize winning comedy *You Can't Take It With You!* by Moss Hart and George S. Kaufman. I auditioned and got cast in the role of Martin Vanderhoff, the patriarch who lived his life against the system and enticed his entire family to live their dreams, however crazy some of them were. How fitting was that? Our colorful cast included: Leilani Johnson (Penelope Sycamore), Lynne Buchanan (Essie Carmichael), Sherrie Bartlett (Rheba), Rick Mulligan (Paul Sycamore), Pat Shepherd (Mr. De Pinna), Roger Buckland (Ed Carmichael), Kelly Harrington (Donald),

Beth Hamilton (Alice Sycamore), Randy Mulligan (Henderson), Bruce Bartram (Tony Kirby), Eric Kuntz (Boris Kolenkov), Cathy Hall (Gay Wellington), Randy Mulligan (Mr. Kirby), Cory Moran (Mrs. Kirby), Alan Fife (Jim), and finally George Lauve (Mac). Mark, very busy in his football season, made the time to accept a small role as the stern G-Man who came in at the end of Act II with only a few lines to memorize; that way he could have fun in another play but didn't need to attend many rehearsals.

We worked hard, memorized our lines and put together the show on a set designed by Mr. Oldoski, while Mrs. Peterson fed us her theatrical passion, giving lots of helpful stage directions, teaching us that with comedy you have to pick up the tempo or explaining with examples how there were different ways to express happiness, anger, sadness and a wide range of human emotions. She challenged me, thus becoming my new favorite teacher, and never settled for mediocre performances, always coming at her actors with notes to fine-tune a performance. She never pandered to her student's egos, but tirelessly gave of her time, energy and devotion to her Thespians way beyond school hours to bring out the best in everyone and expected full commitments in return. She would often sit way at the back of the theater during rehearsals.

"I CAN'T HEAR YOU!" she'd cry out.

"YOU'VE GOT TO PLAY TO THE BACK OF

THE HOUSE! THEY PAY GOOD MONEY FOR THEIR TICKETS, TOO, AND THEY WANT TO HEAR YOU!"

"SLOW THE SPEECH DOWN AND PRO-JECT YOUR VOI-CES!"

"E-NUN-CI-ATE!"

Unhappy with our vocal execution, she made us each hold a pencil between our teeth and recite our lines until she could understand every word clearly from her seat in the back row of the theater. I felt like a Special-Ed student at first but I learned how to project my voice, thanks to Mrs. Peterson.

The day of dress rehearsal, things ran as smoothly as could be expected for High School students. Some of Vickie Kiser's lighting cues were missed, costumes still needed attention and some of the sets were still wet with fresh paint. Mark made his onstage entrance as the G-man at the appropriate moment, flipped open his wallet and flashed his "badge", a piece of aluminum foil he had attached to the leather that caught the light very effectively. The scene went well until the end, when Donald, played by Kelly Harrington, forgot to reassure Sherrie Bartlett by saying "It's okay, Rheba, it's okay." Mark had the culminating line before the curtain was to fall on Act II, but he just stood there saying nothing. I looked at him. He stared at me with a frozen G-man smile. Finally I said his line for him, thinking he got stage fright.

"I suppose you want us to line up or something?" I asked him, in my Martin Vanderhoff old man voice.

"Hey, that's my line!" he said, dropping character.

"Well then, why didn't you say it?" I answered like Matt Gonder.

"I can't say my line until Kelly says HIS line!" Mark defended.

Well, I had to admit he had a point. Kinda.

"Mark, ya gotta keep the play going...if Kelly or anyone else forgets their line, just go ON!" I scolded.

"Okay, okay, why didn't you just say so to begin with?" He whined back.

"DON'T BREAK CHARACTER!" Mrs. Peterson bellowed from the back of the theater.

"Everybody line up!" Mark reacted in his G-man character voice.

The actors got into position and froze.

"CURTAIN!" Mrs. Petersen yelled from the back of the theater.

On opening night, Cheryl Duvall, Cathy Hodde and Sheryl Skelton opened the house. There were plenty of empty seats, but more people showed up for this show than for John Brown's (decomposing) Body. Unfortunately, Thespian productions rarely received community support like the Music department's big budget musicals, but truthfully, the Theater department was a much better training ground for learning solid theatrical craft. For instance, the Thespians knew what an entrance from the USL or "Upstage Left" meant, as opposed to many singers in the Music department who would make their entrances from "over there". On opening night, Dad was out there in center seats with Marguerite and Monica, but didn't fall asleep this time, as Mrs. Peterson had directed the prize comedy to amuse her public that laughed in all the right places. Mark made his entrance from USC (Upstage Center) and was ready to bowl Kelly over or anyone else if necessary, to keep the scene moving.

The Music department, a completely separate unit from the Theater department, where rarely did the twain meet, selected and produced a musical each year, enlisting support from the community. The annual musical was the highlight of the choir program, and fall 1973 announced the production of The Sound of Music on the Wenatchee High School stage for three performances, starring Nyla Henderson as Maria and Toby Capps as Captain Von Trapp. Normally, only juniors and seniors were allowed to participate in the musical, but somehow I slipped through a loophole and was cast in the Chorus, probably due to my constant theater experience and the *Amen* solo I did with the Choral Society, I don't really know how. Anyway there I was having a blast with everyone during the rehearsals. At one rehearsal, the four main nuns Karen Sele, Connie Corrick, Marile Sexson and Martha Bean were in a silly mood. Standing stage center, they positioned themselves to sing about Maria's bad sisterly behavioral antics. Imagine four nuns looking out front, dry-faced and singing in the most serious manner "How do you solve a problem like diarrhea?" I didn't have anything special to do in the show, a few bits here and there, but I thought of Sister Raphael and had a grand time singing with everyone else to an orchestral accompaniment onstage for the first time in my life. Music and theater mediums mixed together gave me a buzz beyond words. The show received much support from the community and the performances sold out and gave everyone a good time.

John was making a name for himself in his first junior varsity football season, while Mark made his dream come true and started every game on first string as the pulling guard in what was to be a record year for football. After all nine games of the regular "Big Nine" took place in the season, the Offense record was 383 points to 0 allowed on Defense. After that, during the playoffs, the Panthers, with Steve Dils as their quarterback, continued to amaze when they beat Fort Vancouver 10-7 and then beat Evergreen High School 20-0 against Jack Thompson, who also went on to play in the pros. However, the Panthers' purple dream turned into a nightmare when they lost the State Championship for the 3A league to Kentridge 26-24, awarding Wenatchee the second place state trophy, which sent the whole school and city into mourning.

I ran into Pam every so often in the halls, while I was running from the cafeteria to the music or theater department. I was happy to see that she was no longer wearing the hideous cast with the neckpiece she wore at Pioneer, yet now she wore a hard plastic body brace that she hid as well as she could under maternity clothes, the only type of garments that fit over the brace. We always said hello to one another, but by that time, we were running in different groups and had no established common interests or classes in which to connect.

I had become so involved in the plays we were doing with Mrs. Peterson, the Choral Society music repertoire, my art projects and many new friends, so I had completely forgotten about Federal Way. There's an expression that claims: "today's news wraps tomorrow's fish", meaning that whatever happens today will be forgotten tomorrow. I don't totally agree with that because not only do I not want to forget everything, but I also find comfort in recalling the faces of so many good people who crossed my path and gave me so much.

Dad derived pleasure in seeing that all five of his children had become fully integrated citizens of Wenatchee, Washington. We climbed to the top of Saddle Rock or enjoying a visit to Ohme Gardens when we weren't engaged in some extracurricular activity. Aunt Fran, loyal and true to form, paid us a long visit in the fall and orchestrated the usual Sunday trip down to the laundromat she called the "washateria" near Stan's Merry Mart. Afterwards, she made us scrub all the corners of the kitchen floor until they passed her German inspection, then insisted Dad take us all to Mass at St. Joseph's Catholic church and dance with her like always to Lawrence Welk on TV.

The house remained unheated as we slowly headed into our second snowy Wenatchee winter, but we survived under layers of clothes and swallowed down cups of hot "Swiss piss" chocolate to warm us up. As the holidays drew near, Mrs. Peterson encouraged her actors to gain as much exposure to the finer arts, believing that the more you see and experience, the more you will have to bring to your acting performances. She announced that Joan Shelton, Wenatchee's ballet mistress, was going to present the annual holiday performance of the Marius Petipa Nutcracker Ballet at the Liberty Theater, and that we should all attend.

When the day came around, I bought a ticket and took my seat alone in the theater, not knowing really what to expect. Aunt Fran had previously told us stories of Mom's experiences as a young ballerina, taking classes and forcing all her siblings to attend her performances, and I grew up with Mom's Degas Ballerina prints on the walls, but I had never dreamed it could be like this. I had heard Tchaikovsky's famous music many times before, as Aunt Mary played it on her stereo back in Portland, but I had never fathomed it could also be an accompaniment for this incredible pageant of ethereal splendor. My eyes fixed onstage, I recognized Karen Smith, another classmate, smiling broadly as she floated with ease in a beatified state of grace, waltzing with the flowers. When the performance was over, I remained in a dreamy state all evening, feeling like Mom had been sitting right there watching the ballet with me. I felt for certain she was, because from that moment on, Mom's Degas ballerina prints seemed to dance to life on the walls in our house.

The next day, I was running through the hall on my way to thank and share my classical ballet experience with Mrs. Peterson in room 101, and passed the choir room. Mr. Jones had left the door open and I could hear the Men's Chorus rehearsing *The Water Is Wide*, one of the songs I sang in Boy's Chorus at Sacajawea. I stopped in my tracks and listened. My heart overflowed with emotion as I stood there, visualizing Mr. Warner on his conductor's pedestal, teaching me how to read music and count out the measures. Mr. Jones saw me lurking by the door and asked me if I needed something.

"Do you have anybody to play the piano for that song? Cuz' if you don't, I wanna do it."

Mr. Jones was caught off-guard, but smiled.

"As a matter of fact, Matt, no, I don't have an accompanist."

I stood there begging with my eyes.

"Okay, then, we'll give you a shot at it," he smiled.

We worked out a schedule and I came in to rehearse with the Men's Chorus once they had memorized their parts. Whenever possible, I nabbed one of the soundproof practice rooms to rehearse the accompaniment or pumped the accordion against the wall down in the basement at home for weeks to make sure I would feel comfortable and well-rehearsed when D-day came along.

At home, we celebrated another traditional Christmas with all the references we had grown to expect and take for granted. Dad's laundry basket cornucopia slowly got eaten up while Marguerite and Monica baked and decorated piles of sugar cookies that we descended upon like vultures.

When spring daffodils popped out of the frozen ground, the concert night finally arrived and the Wenatchee High School auditorium filled up with families and friends. Bel Canto was the best thing I'd ever heard in my life. They sang complicated pieces in musical perfection and I wanted to be a part of that group. We sang our numbers with The Choral Society without a hitch, and when Mr. Jones raised his arm to present me as the tenor soloist for *Amen*, I made sure to project to the back of the house like Mrs. Peterson taught me. I wasn't nervous at all to sing in front of everyone by now. However, my whole body trembled like it did the night I sang my first public solo at the Anderson's

New Year's party in 1970, when the Men's Chorus took their turn on the risers and I came in, sat at the grand piano standing below the risers and took the tempo from Mr. Jones. I swallowed my pounding heart in a deep breath and began playing the simple accompaniment to *The Water Is Wide*, which wasn't by far the best performance of a choir that evening, but it was a musical milestone for me. Luckily, I was able to calm myself enough to play through the piece that I had finally mastered with no mistakes. Okay, so it took me three years. Patience and tenacity are virtues, you know. The lame have as much chance of reaching their goal as anyone.

After the concert everyone crowded around, congratulating me on my *Amen* solo. Scott Hosfeld, the Bel Canto senior singer and musical director for John Brown's Body (now reduced to a pile of dust), told me how surprised he was. Then I ran into Dad, Marguerite and Monica outside the main doors to the theater. Dad, who never held back his emotions, smiled at me.

"Matt, that was wonderful."

"Good job, Matt, you sang good," Monica said.

"Thanks."

"And you didn't look scared at all," Marguerite pointed out.

Then Dad tried to utter words that would change me

forever.

"Yes, your solo was real good, Matt, that's no surprise to me, but when you..."

I was too excited so I cut him of in mid-speech.

"Did you see me play the piano?" I asked.

His eyes welled up with tears that he wiped away as he spoke.

"Yes, I did, Matt. That's what I'm tryin' to say if you'll give me the goddamn floor!"

"Sorry, Dad," I said, finally shutting my mouth to let him continue.

"Where'd you learn to play the piano?" He asked.

"I kinda taught myself, I guess."

"How?"

"Well, Mr. Warner taught me how to read music back at Sacajawea, and there are practice rooms here at school when you're lucky enough to grab one before someone else gets it, but mostly I played on Aunt Mary's accordion down in the basement." I confessed.

"You taught yourself how to play the piano on Mary's old accordion?

"Yeah" I confessed.

"I'll be damned. I always felt bad that I couldn't get you a piano back when you asked for one, and that damn guilt has been stuck in my craw for a long time eatin' away at me, until tonight. Now it's all gone. Watching you play the piano with that choir…I wanna thank you. I mean that. I sure as hell don't ever have to worry about you, Matt, because you do what you have to do to get the job done."

"No biggie, Dad."

"Matt-sue, my 'artiste'," he said in his comical French accent, the name he called me ever since he folded hats out of newspaper for Mark, John and me, way back when Mom was still alive, when Monica and Marguerite were babies. Mark and John always wanted fireman hats, but I had to have one like Merlin the magician.

"Thanks, Dad."

"Now, how's about some chicken curry?" He said.

Marguerite, Monica and I sang out in unison.

"YEAH!"

Dad drove us all home and put the long grain rice on the stove to cook and heated up the food he had prepared in our loyal turkey roaster pan earlier that afternoon. As soon as it was ready, the house was embalmed with odors of Madras curry, my favorite of all the meals Dad cooked. Mark and John were out back checking something in the trunk of Mark's Catalina, but came into the kitchen to join in on the feast just as Monica, Marguerite and I were piling up our plates.

The world kept on turning and we all lived on to create many more unforgettable memories as we grew into young adulthood, some with each other and others on our own or with new friends in Wenatchee. But from the moment Dad said he'd never have to worry about me, I felt like I'd been awarded the Cowardly Lion's medal of courage that granted me enough strength to face anything life would present. Again, nothing essential had changed in our lives. We were still broke, but Jeff Allen was right; we got the better deal. We may not have had lots of stuff, but we had our Dad, an honest man who fought a lonely and often times losing battle, always right there beside us, one hundred percent in the moment, laughing at our discoveries and successes, crying with us through our defeats or cooking up a comfort meal to soften the growing pains. That's how the cards played out for this family on the move out west; that was the way we were, and thanks to James Joseph Gonder, who we are.

ABOUT THE AUTHOR

Matthew Gonder is an actor, singer, dancer, author, composer and playwright, willing to take on any job that pays the bills. He lives in the heart of Paris, France with his lovely wife, Pamela.

More information: matthewgonder.com

Join and "Like" us on **facebook**

Christmas On The Move Out West

Music On The Move Out West

CPSIA information can be obtained at www.ICGtesting.com
Printed in the USA
BVOW08s1512141013

333702BV00001B/1/P